W9-AOY-904

A Faith for You

Books by Brooke Peters Church

THE GOLDEN YEARS

A FAITH FOR YOU

A Faith for You

BROOKE PETERS CHURCH

Rinehart & Company, Incorporated

New York *1948* *Toronto*

Printed in the United States of America

By J. J. Little and Ives Company, New York

Acknowledgments

IN WRITING this book I have encroached largely on the time and patience of many people. Some have been self-sacrificing enough to read the whole manuscript and comment upon it; others have sought out material; still others, and this the largest number, have educated me in the ways of doctrine and organization, and have finally revised the several sections dealing with the denominations in which they are leaders.

Far from finding it an arduous labor I have enjoyed the work, largely because of the response which I have had from all who have helped me with it, and from the eager questioning of all who have heard about it. If the book is helpful to anyone and in any way fills a need, the public with me owes thanks to the army of silent contributors who have made it possible.

I wish to thank my rector, Dr. Charles W. Lowry, Jr., of All Saints Church, Washington, D. C., for his unending patience in reading and correcting these pages, and incidentally in teaching me some of the basic doctrines of my own church. Rabbi Norman Gerstenfeld of Washington and Rabbi Hugo Schiff of Alexandria, Virginia, have toiled through a mass of manuscript and given me an insight into Judaism for which I am very grateful. Mrs. T. A. Polyzoides has been my coadjutor in research and inquiries, and Miss Marguerite J. Reese has given me invaluable help in my section on the Lutheran Churches.

For special work in correcting the individual manuscripts on denominations, and for graciously lending me books on the subject, I wish to thank Chancellor James E. Cowhig, of the Archdiocese of Washington of the Roman Catholic Church; the Very Reverend Joseph Stephanko, of the Russian Orthodox Church; Dr. J. M. Dawson, of the Baptist Church; the Reverend H. J. Kuiper, of the Christian Reformed Church; Dr. Warren D. Bowman, of the Church of the Brethren; Dr. Arthur J. Todd and Mr. James Watt, of the Church of Christ, Scientist; the Reverend John A. Morrison, of the Church of God (Anderson, Indiana); Mr. George W. Bailey, of the Church of Jesus Christ of Latter-day Saints; Dr. H. V. Miller, of the Church of the Nazarene; the Reverend Fred S. Buschmeyer, of the Congregational Christian Church; Mr. William J. Linebeck, of the Disciples of Christ; Dr. William E. Lampe, of the Evangelical and Reformed Church; the Reverend J. S. Stamm, of the Evangelical United Brethren; Dr. Oscar F. Blackwelder, Dr. Gerhard Lenski, the Reverend Carl E. Lund-Quist, Dr. Clarence D. Nelson and Dr. G. F. Wenchell, of the Lutheran Church; Dr. John C. Wenger, of the Mennonite Church; the Right Reverend Charles Wesley Flint, of the Methodist Church; the Reverend F. P. Stocker, of the Moravian Church in America; Mr. F. Roswell Flower, General Secretary, the Assemblies of God; the Reverend John C. Jernigan and the Reverend J. Andrew Rafferty, of the Church of God; the Right Reverend John Misiaszek and the Reverend Thaddeus F. Zielinski, of the Polish National Catholic Church; the Reverend J. S. Albertson, Dr. Charles A. Anderson, the Reverend Franklin B. Gillespie and Dr. C. E. Hawthorne, of the Presbyterian Church; the Reverend W. H. S. Demarest, of the Dutch Reformed Church; Dr. Elbert Russell and Dr. Douglas V. Steere, of the Religious Society of Friends; President Israel A. Smith, of the Reorganized Church of Jesus Christ of Latter-day Saints; Mr. J. R. Ferren and Mr.

Francis D. Nichol, of the Seventh-day Adventists; and Dr. A. Powell Davies, of the Unitarian Church.

I have had one critic from the scientific field without whose additions and criticisms I might have finished the book sooner, but only at the sacrifice of what seem to me some of its best passages. To Dr. C. K. Leith I wish, therefore, to render a special meed of thanks for his comments, suggestions, and unfailing interest. Without the collaboration of my husband, John A. Church, and my daughter Jessica, who have given me unstintingly of their time and encouragement, my task would have been far greater.

Brooke Peters Church

Contents

A Faith for You

CHAPTER ONE

The Purpose of the Book

THIS BOOK is written to serve two purposes, both of them arising out of the needs of an unsure and deeply troubled world. The economic and social structure which, whatever its defects, had existed for so long as to have become fixed in the minds of most of us seems to be crumbling, and what the future holds is still uncertain. Moved by a desire for some stable anchorage in this sea of change, many are turning to religion, which seems the one continuing link with the past, and which has survived so many periods of upheaval. This book, then, is meant, first, to offer to those (and there are many hundreds of thousands of them) who have no church affiliation, no early training in religious matters and no impartial source of information, a short and comprehensive history of religion and a guide to the leading religious groups of today, in the hope that out of these thirty or more sects there may be one that will answer their needs; and second, to serve as a reference book in which are listed, in simple and easily available form, the salient facts about the various denominations, their feasts and fasts, their origin and organization and their articles of belief.

It has been said that man is a political animal, but long before he began to organize himself in political groups he began to speculate about religion. For man's first instinct is to survive, and when survival depends on natural forces outside one's control, such as storms, cold, heat, floods and droughts, earthquakes and volcanoes, the natural response is to propitiate the unseen powers who cause these phenomena, and this propitiation is religion. To be sure, these early expressions of religion are crude, caused by fear and savoring far more of magic than of faith, but they are none the less expressions of man's first consciousness of an unseen and greater world than that in which he lives, and of a power greater than his own. It follows that the individual who "makes the best magic," who best propitiates the unseen powers, becomes the leader of the clan or tribe, and so, from the dawn of humanity, religion and politics are inextricably mixed. An echo of this comes down almost to this very day, in the conception of the "divine right of kings," which was prevalent in Western Europe certainly up to the seventeenth century, and in some countries later still.

Again and again during the millennia of man's sojourn on earth, there have been periods of widespread skepticism. In historical times these periods seem to recur with a certain rhythm, coming roughly speaking about once in each seven hundred to a thousand years, generally as the result of some world upheaval which brings with it great movements of peoples, social readjustments and epoch-making discoveries. We seem now to be passing through such a period, and the immediate cause is not, as one might suppose, the two great wars. They were only part of a far deeper movement which reaches back into the past.

The scientific discoveries and new inventions which led to the rise of industrialism and the consequent shifting of populations and uprooting of great masses of people from their homes and traditions was the real cause of the unrest, part of whose expression has been a loss of faith in things unseen. Materialism—the desire for possessions and an easy life—

has pervaded all classes, and more especially those who had broken with the past. The little man, the layman, became puffed up with his knowledge and decided that he knew, or would presently know, all that there was to know. Already he could control what he saw and felt in the world about him, and beyond that he could at least understand and explain natural phenomena, such as weather, volcanoes, earthquakes, movements of the stars. He flattered himself that having learned so much, in time he could travel through space and learn to harness the forces of nature. In all that he saw, he found no room for God, no sign of a power beyond and outside, yet including nature, nor did he feel the need of anything greater and stronger than himself. He threw religion aside as a superstition from an ignorant past, and set out to live without faith in anything but Science and himself.

Yet it is doubtful that the discovery of electricity marks as great a stride forward for mankind as did the discovery of fire, hundreds of thousands of years earlier; or that the invention of the alphabet was as important as the first use of speech. The train and the automobile on which we so pride ourselves could not have materialized were it not for some remote ancestor who worked out the theory of the wheel. Is it not true that the modern scientific and industrial era depends for its life on a past in which not science, but religion, was the moving force in man's development?

All this is true especially of the Western world, and one of the proofs of my argument lies in the fact that in the Orient, where science and industrialism have not gained supremacy, religion is still a vital force, a real power. A strange feature of the situation is that the West does not believe this of the Orient. To Western minds it seems impossible that men anywhere will still fight and die for their faith, and it is this same Western attitude that makes any real understanding of the situation in India or in Palestine today so difficult.

For at least six thousand years the guiding principle of

the world has been religion; for about half this time monotheism, as represented by the highest reaches of man's spiritual growth, has led in the development of the Western world. Is it probable that the fraction of man's conscious life on earth which is represented by the last hundred years has all at once, in the wink of an eye, changed human nature so completely that it can henceforth depend on its own efforts? True, apart from religion there exist systems of morals and ethics to live by, systems which have produced whole ways of life and thought, such as communism, socialism and enlightened capitalism. But these morals and ethics originated and grew out of man's religious aspirations. How long can they continue without a renewal of the spark which gave them life? Out of our worship of Science and materialism have already grown two disastrous wars, and in these modern systems of ethics the individual has been forgotten in the state, with utter disregard of the logic that the state was made for the individual.

Shining through the base metal of crass materialism, however, there is a vein of gold which seems to increase the farther we go. The search for God and the knowledge of God take many forms, not always recognized because they do not necessarily conform to any denominational religion. The scientists whose speculations have reached out into the infinities of space and time are awed at the inconceivable vastness of the universe and the regulated order of its workings. One by one they bow to the mystery of some guiding force, unknown and to finite man perhaps forever unknowable, but predicated by the laws of nature. To these men the minor triumphs of the gadget age—flying, splitting the atom—are less important than the unplumbed depths behind and beyond, and the still more remote guiding principle which, after all, is what the world is seeking under the name of God.

In the first chapter of Genesis it is written that "God made man in His own image." But from the earliest times man has actually made God in his image and worshiped or feared Him according to his own mental and spiritual development. He was a god of nature, a god of flocks and herds, a god of fields and harvests, a god of battles, a god of a tribe or of a nation. As man's knowledge and his mental concepts have enlarged, God's scope and powers have increased. He has become the God of the world, omniscient, omnipotent, all-wise, all-good. And now our greatest thinkers have widened His scope still farther, and pushed His powers out to embrace the illimitable vista of the past, the farthest stars and the unknown space beyond them.

The personal concept of God still persists also—the idea of a God of love, who, though infinite, demands righteousness and charity of each individual. The most human of our industrialists acknowledge this in the measures they take for the welfare of their employees, and the disinterested union leaders, in their struggle to better working conditions. It is evident in our social services, our public welfare organizations, our indignation over cruelty and persecution.

Morality and ethics alone, unaccompanied by the concept of a living and personal Force, offer a dry and comfortless rule of life, and a thin and perilous defense against the primeval instincts of fear and desire. Chinese civilization was built on such a foundation, and after its first impulse was lost, ceased to progress because there was no binding force of a common religion to hold the masses together. The exceptional person can live by such a creed, but he stands alone and can do little against a mass of ignorant and self-seeking groups. So deeply implanted in man is the need of faith of some kind that where traditional religion has been stamped out a new faith arises to take its place. In Russia the state became God, and the icons were merely replaced by pictures of Marx, Lenin and Stalin. State worship makes for narrow nationalism and recurring wars, unless all mankind is to be reduced to one way of living, under one rule. There is a unifying force in a religion which, above and outside of man and his creatures, recognizes some power greater than anything human, and which makes for good, however incomprehensible its methods.

Today we have two or three generations who have to a greater or less extent grown up without religious training, and the results are not altogether satisfactory. The current cry for security means that a profound sense of insecurity is abroad. The stuff of which our Puritan settlers and all the pioneers of the past were made seems to have run thin. They asked, not for security, but for opportunity, not for less responsibility, but for more. The Puritans certainly had faith, and so, I suspect, do most pioneers. There is no security in a world where death is the inevitable end, and where no wealth nor effort can save even the young from dying before their time. As for that, a passing star might at any time wreck the world, and we would be powerless to prevent the cataclysm. But still we and our children cry for security, and turn to psychiatrists and psychoanalysts as though they were all-knowing priests or seers to explain the past and foretell the future. Psychology has an important role to play in helping us to see ourselves, and in many instances the church has invited its co-operation with very beneficial results. But in spite of it, the psychiatric wards are overcrowded, and emotional instability is increasing. A noted psychiatrist once said that the people who came to him for help were seldom if ever those who had made a satisfactory equation with religion. Perhaps, did they but know it, some of the unfortunate inmates of our asylums merely needed the religion of their ancestors to heal them.

It is useless to say that the church is at fault. The church is composed of individuals and is a response to a need, felt and expressed in the meeting of these individuals in a group to praise and pray and worship the Unseen God. If the outstanding and intelligent members of the community keep out of the church, where is the world to find spiritual leaders and thinkers who might inspire the organization to grow and advance? It is not the church but the public who must make the effort, for there is no church where there are no members.

As a result of the neglect of religion and the consequent lack of training in religious matters, there are many who have no knowledge of the beliefs of the Western world today. There may be earnest people who are seeking guidance for themselves and for their children, and do not know where to find it. To them first this book is offered.

Its second purpose is to give information to the uninformed who are found even in the memberships of the various denominations, and to those who have forgotten or who never understood the teachings of their youth. Many of these had some religious training and were once members of a church, but broke from their background and traditions, and either forgot or never knew the creed in which they were reared. I have met Episcopalians who did not know how many sacraments the church recognizes, although in youth they learned the catechism and many times repeated "Two only." There is also ignorance about denominations other than one's own. So an Episcopalian, asked whether she was marrying a Christian, replied, "No, he is a Presbyterian." A more widespread knowledge of dogma and creeds, and some idea of how and why they came into being, might help to bring about a broader tolerance and a greater unity of faith. Religion is a very personal matter, and that people should vary in creed, church organization and forms of worship is but natural. Perhaps if they realized how superficial the differences, and how uniform and basic the common purpose, the striving for brotherly love and spiritual grace, there would be less intolerance and more charity in the world.

CHAPTER TWO

The Historical Background

IT SEEMS UNNECESSARY in this discussion to take up man's earliest religious development—animism, totemism, moon worship, sun worship, and the early fertility cults. All these are subjects for archaeologists and anthropologists, and have no direct bearing on religions of today, except in so far as they may recur in certain phases of our children's early development. For the individual is apt to reflect in his growth the various phases of the growth of the race.

The general tendency of the more advanced of the early religions was toward monotheism, the worship of one God. Frequently monotheism was preceded by belief in one tribal god, but an acknowledgement of other gods for other tribes. In Mesopotamia, Egypt and Syria there was already a strong monotheistic trend at the time of the rise of Judaism, the beginnings of which may be tentatively placed at about 1280 B.C. with the Exodus from Egypt under the leadership of Moses.

The development of a faith still living is a vivid example of the workings of the religious impulse, and fortunately we have such a faith among us and can trace its development almost step by step from its own records. It was not long after David's reign that the Hebrews began to collect their religious writings and organize them into a consecutive story for the edification of the people. These writings were added to and modified for hundreds of years to come, and therefore give a vivid account of the development of the Hebrew faith. Judaism became henceforth a religion of a "book" and the education of the people, which became more and more widely spread among all classes, was based on the ever-increasing mass of history and prophecy which this book came to comprise.

Origin and Development of Judaism to the Dispersion

Who the group of Hebrews were who left Egypt in the reign of Ramses II (*c.* 1280 B.C.), how they had come to be in Egypt, and why they left it, is told in the Old Testament books, Genesis and Exodus. Whether we accept the Bible record as fact or as tradition and folklore based on history, the broad outline of events is about the same. There were many migrations of pastoral tribes into the land of Canaan (modern Palestine) at an early date, and one of these, coming from the south and southeast, and traveling at the leisurely rate of people with flocks and herds and women and children, was led by a man named Moses. To him had come the revelation of a great and powerful God, Yahweh, who had chosen these tribes, the Israelites, or Hebrews, as they were later called, to be his own people, on condition that they obeyed his laws as given through his servant Moses. Moses seems to have been a man of force and vision, far ahead of his followers, and indeed of his times. His conception of God was so broad and spiritual as to be capable of indefinite development as new needs and situations, and a more advanced culture, arose. We find Yahweh at first as a pastoral god, perhaps also a storm god worshiped with sacrifices from the flocks and herds; with the need for combat on entering Palestine, he becomes also the god of war; and as the amalgamation of the Hebrews with the agricultural Canaanites takes place, the duties and powers of a god of the harvests are added to him. By about 1000 B.C. when Palestine has become a kingdom under David we find Yahweh, his powers and scope greatly widened, a national god, the one god of all Palestine, and a god who demands, not only worship and sacrifice, but also righteousness. One has but to read the biography of David, written by a contemporary of David's and contained in II Samuel 9-20, I Kings 1-2, to realize how far the Hebrew thinkers of the tenth century B.C. had gone in morals and ideals. Of course, it was long before the great mass of the people reached a high spiritual level. The Hebrews were not all descendants of the pastoral tribes that Moses led, but a mixture of several Semitic strains, in many of which Yahweh was not known or accepted for generations after the conquest of Canaan. The strength of the people as a whole lay in their leaders, who kept urging and inspiring the nation to greater and higher reaches of spirituality and moral regeneration. Again and again the people backslid, yielding to the temptations of ease and luxury, or adopting the cults of their neighbors. Each time they were called back into the strait and narrow path by a prophet, and each one of these prophets seemed to lift higher still the ideals for Israel to live by.

Before David's successor and son, Solomon, had died, the worship of Yahweh had become elaborated and corrupted to such an extent that the northern section of the land, raising the cry of "Back to the worship of our fathers," broke away from the south and set up an independent kingdom. It is strange and arresting to consider how often in the history of religion this cry of "Back to the past" recurs. The northern kingdom, henceforth known as Israel, was the agricultural section of the country, and on the highway between Egypt and Mesopotamia. The little kingdom grew rich and luxury-loving on trade and exchange, her reforms were forgotten, and Baal worship crept in to rival the simple cult of Yahweh.

It was at this moment (*c.* 850 B.C.) that another of the great line of Hebrew leaders appeared. Out of the desert came Elijah, rude and uncompromising, to preach Yahweh, not as the narrow tribal god of the past, but as a god more powerful than Baal, a god who could work miracles even outside of his own land, and a god who desired righteousness. There is little in any religious literature more exalted than the story of Elijah's mission, which was written down about fifty years after it took place, and which ends on a note of high spirituality, when God appears, not in the wind, nor in the earthquake, nor in the fire, but as the "still small voice." He has ceased to be the nature god as were all the gods round about, and become a spiritual guide.

Apparently any reforms that Elijah made were not lasting, for about a hundred years after his time there arose the first of the writing prophets—so called because personally or through their disciples they left written records of their prophecies. Amos (*c.* 750 B.C.), in a series of extraordinary discourses, arraigned not only Israel, but also her neighbors, for their indifference and inhumanity to others, whether nations or classes. By this time the gap between rich and poor in Israel was appallingly wide, and the utmost luxury and most abject poverty were in stark contrast on every side. Amos fearlessly attacked the rich and even the king in the name of Yahweh, demanding justice—again a new note in the development of God. After Amos, Hosea, who used his own life's tragedy with a beloved but erring wife as a text and preached Yahweh's love for his people if they would but repent and return to worship him and keep his commandments. Already by 700 B.C. some of the highest reaches of religious thought had been attained by these men—at a time when Greece was still just becoming an entity, a hundred years before Confucius was born, a hundred and fifty before the time of Buddha.

No preaching, however inspired, could save Israel, and in 723 the northern kingdom fell to the Assyrian invader, her inhabitants were scattered, and Judah, the southern kingdom, was left to carry on the religion of Yahweh. Judah was a poor, mountainous country and had never had much contact with the world outside. The Temple of Solomon in Jerusalem had long been the central shrine of the land, and there Yahweh seems to have been worshiped pretty constantly without too much contamination by other gods. From now on, with the northern shrines destroyed, Jerusalem became the shrine of all devout Hebrews, the hope of the future and the object of prayer and pilgrimage. Here too, however, there was deterioration and into the worship there seeped a dry formalism, which emphasized law and ritual, but neglected the spirit behind them.

Isaiah was the first of the great prophets to preach to Judah. In about 700 B.C. he taught holiness and righteousness in sermons of literary and poetical beauty which have seldom been surpassed. But the little kingdom was doomed and a hundred years later (*c.* 600 B.C.) Jeremiah, the last great prophet of the kingdom of Judah, was preaching and exhorting in a desperate effort to prepare his people for the inevitable end. His vision was of a personal god, a god to whom each man was answerable—again a new conception to the ancient world, whose gods were tribal or national and not concerned with the individual. It was Yahweh still, but a Yahweh developed from the god of storms, war, fields and flocks, to a god of spirit. It may be that the law against the making of idols helped this development, since the very image of God was never seen, but had to be imagined.

The Dispersion

The southern kingdom fell, the Temple was destroyed, the leaders and probably the better-educated of the people were carried into captivity—the dream of empire was shattered. In fact it was questionable whether, the kingdom gone and the Temple ruined, Yahweh worship could survive at all. For to the great mass of people of those days a god was severely localized and had no power in other lands than his own. How could Israel worship Yahweh in Babylon and Egypt, and all the other lands where she was now scattered? While the Temple had remained, pilgrimages were possible, but now even the Temple was gone. At this juncture Ezekiel began to preach from his exile in Babylon. He taught Yahweh as a god no longer confined to any one land or temple, nor even a ruler of only one people—his god was omnipotent, omnipresent, omniscient, a spirit who could be worshiped everywhere, and who demanded obedience and righteousness of all mankind.

It was not the Babylonian captivity alone that had scattered the Jews so widely. Long before, they had been migrating from Palestine, which was at best small and poor, and settling in other countries. There were, for example, large groups of Jews in Elephantine and Assuan, in Egypt, but most of the dispersion was toward the East, Babylon and Persia, until the time of Alexander. So long as the Temple at Jerusalem had stood, there was a center for their religion, however far the worshiper might be. It was therefore essential for this new conception of Yahweh to reach and hold not only the exiles in Babylon, but also the dispersed Jews of the world. To this end there must be teachers and texts which could be scattered everywhere and teach the faith in its authoritative and prescribed form.

Driven by these needs and perhaps guided by Ezekiel, the priests in exile began to codify, amplify and annotate their ancient religious books, which were still rather crude and unfinished, and quite unsuited to present conditions. This work went on for several generations and from it resulted the Old Testament Law and Prophets much as we have them today, i.e., Genesis, Exodus, Leviticus, Numbers, Deuteronomy, Joshua, Judges, Samuel, Kings, and the Prophets. At the same time synagogues were set up wherever there were enough Jews to warrant it, and devoted men gave up their lives to train and teach the people. Besides the Old Testament, the oral tradition, consisting of commentaries on the Law and illustrative stories, was also gathered in writing, and centuries later these grew into the Talmud. Perhaps without the fall of Jerusalem and the Babylonian captivity, Judaism would never have been driven to such a concerted effort of her greatest thinkers, nor to such definition of her faith, but, like most of the early religions of the Mediterranean basin, would in time have faded into the past. But out of her dispersal grew the conception of God and of righteousness which were to be the inspiration of Christianity—which, with Judaism, is still the predominant faith of the Western world; and as a result of the synagogues and the efforts of the priests and rabbis to instruct the people, the Jews became, and, for a thousand years and more to come, remained, the most widely and generally educated people in the Western world.

When Babylon was overcome by the Persians and Hither Asia become a part of the great Persian Empire, Cyrus, the Persian king, in 537 B.C., permitted the Jews to return to Palestine and rebuild the Temple. Only a small portion of them took advantage of the offer. Most preferred to stay where they were, for they had become accustomed to their new homes and in many cases were prosperous and esteemed citizens of the land they were in.

The refugees who did return found that in the fifty years of exile there had been sad changes in Palestine. The Jews who had been left behind were hostile to the newcomers, and did not even have the same form of Judaism. Jew and Gentile had intermarried, separateness—which had by now come to be of the essence of Judaism—was no longer observed. The returning exiles were bitter and intolerant and there was constant trouble between the groups, for with the codification of the faith had also come a crystallization, a stereotyping of form and belief which made change and growth difficult, and tended to increase the exclusiveness of the orthodox faith. Some Jews, more broad-minded than the rest, preached tolerance and the Books of Ruth and Jonah were written as a protest against narrow sectarianism. Indeed from this time on there seem to be two distinct lines of thought in Judaism—the priestly, which was dogmatic and formal, and the prophetic, which was spiritual and looked beyond the national bounds.

To this latter group belonged Second, or Deutero, Isaiah, the author of much of the last twenty-six chapters of the Book of Isaiah. He seems to have been one of a small group of thinkers who probably lived in Palestine about 400 B.C. He was a poet, a scholar, and a seer. His poems concern an Israel chosen of God, not for special favors, but to teach and lead mankind. The Jews in their tribulations had long looked for a Messiah, a king who would re-establish their kingdom and give them power and wealth. This prophet offered them only more suffering, more persecution, to the end that they might save the world. In his teaching Second Isaiah foreshadowed Jesus. But his teaching is national rather than personal, and therefore, lacking in direct appeal. It is Second Isaiah who is most frequently quoted in the Gospels, as the prophet whose words Jesus came to fulfill. The other great writer of the period was the unknown genius who compiled and completed the Book of Job, in which is discussed at length and in several aspects the problem of good and evil, reward and punishment, the nature of God, the purpose of life. These poems were taking final shape at about the time that Plato was writing in Greece.

In spite of their hopes and prayers the Jews were never again able to build a lasting independent kingdom. A small number continued to live in Palestine and pilgrims from all over the world sent gifts or made visits to the Temple; and under the Seleucid, or Syrian, rule, about a hundred and fifty years before the Christian era, a Jewish kingdom was set up under the Maccabees, which lasted for about a hundred years. When that fell, the history of the Jews ceased to be the history of a country and became instead the history of a people scattered far and wide over the face of the earth, with no homeland, no common background or past save what was contained in their sacred books, with nothing to hold them together but a faith which to a large extent separated them from others, and made them exclusive and excluded.

Empire followed empire, after Persia Greece, after Greece Rome, new religions sprang up only to give way to still newer and better ones. Through all the changes from the time of Ramses to the Christian era, the constant faith of Judaism ran like a continuous thread, developing from a tribal belief in a tribal god to belief in a creator and ruler of the universe, omniscient, and yet personal enough for any man to approach. In the latter half of the first century B.C., Hillel, a great Jewish thinker, but not included among the Old Testament prophets, was preaching the very essence of humanitarianism in words which are only the reverse side of the Golden Rule, "Do not unto others what is hateful to thyself; this is the whole of the Law, all the rest is commentary."

Probably the greatest danger to Judaism was the Greek influence. During the last two centuries B.C., Hellenism spread far and wide and its culture and thought were especially attractive to the cultivated Jews of Alexandria, then the cultural center of the Western world. The Old Testament was translated into Greek to avert the danger of apostasy through ignorance. But to people accustomed to the Greek philosophers and poets the Hebrew books seemed lacking in subtlety and sophistication and it was to answer these criticisms that in about 40 A.D. Philo, a scholarly Jew of Alexandria, evolved a new way of reading the Old Testament. He explained much of it in allegorical terms, so making it more acceptable to the urbane and cosmopolitan Jews of the period. Indeed it appealed to Gentiles too, and many Gentiles, Greek and Roman, rich and poor, were converted to Judaism, attracted by its high moral tone and deep sincerity. But the Jews' weakness lay in the exactions of their faith. They could not readily mix with Gentiles because the dietary rules of Judaism forbade their eating in other men's houses, and one-sided hospitality is not conducive to social mingling. Nor could they pay even lip service to the state religion, since Yahweh, a jealous god, forbade all rivalry. The rite of circumcision, which was incomprehensible and unpleasant to the Greek, was an added peculiarity in a day of superstition. Nor did the Jews share in public sports or go to the public baths, which were the social centers of the day. This was probably due to the strong objection to nakedness which was prevalent among the strictly orthodox Jews. The story of Noah the vintager (Genesis 9-20) is an expression of this feeling. Noah is found naked by his son Ham, who tells his brothers. They, walking backwards so as not to see their father, put a cloak over him. Ham and his seed are cursed for their sin in looking on their father naked.

This exclusiveness and separateness gave the Greeks a feeling that the Jew thought himself better than his fellows, since apparently what was good enough for them was not good enough for him. There were, therefore, constant sources of friction, and more and more Jews tended to congregate in groups about their synagogues, to be near their fellow believers. Differences and separateness breed suspicion and suspicion breeds fear. At times and in certain regions the Jews were tolerated, but there were instances of persecution which increased in number and violence as the years went on. In Palestine, the homeland of the race, there was constant conflict, not only with the occupying forces but also among themselves, and in about 70 A.D. Titus in exasperation razed the Temple to the ground, so crushing once more all prospects for the immediate future.

Through all their times of trouble a strong vein of hope

persisted in the Jewish people, and at the lowest ebb of their fortunes it was always most intense. They looked for a Messiah (Anointed One) who would deliver them from their persecutors and set up a Jewish kingdom. Over the centuries this expectation crystallized more and more. The Messiah was to be of the house of David, and only absolute obedience to the Law would assure his coming. Indeed some declared that if every believer would obey every detail of the Law for twenty-four hours the Messiah would come at once. Such a belief tended to increase the formalism of Judaism, or the Law came to be everything, overshadowing even the spiritual meaning which underlay it.

Returning to earlier times, the two contrasting lines of thought which have already been traced, the priestly and the prophetic, persisted throughout the centuries preceding the Christian era. In the century immediately preceding that era, they came to be represented by two distinct groups, the Sadducees and the Pharisees. The Sadducees were narrow, aristocratic and very conservative. They insisted on careful observance of the Law as ordained in the Old Testament, and rejected the commentary and explanations of later teachers and preachers. The Pharisees were largely of the educated middle classes, liberal in their observance of rules and stressing conduct rather than ritual. They accepted with the Old Testament much of the oral tradition which had grown up about it, and although the Gospel language sometimes reflects upon them, nevertheless they represented the more humane and more liberal aspect of Judaism in Gospel times. When, in about 30 A.D., Jesus began his ministry in Palestine and preached what seemed more radical liberalism than the most extreme of the Pharisees, the Sadducees were offended.

The Beginning of Christianity

Jesus was the son of a carpenter, a poor man, with no political influence. We know little of his life and antecedents, for all our information is contained in four short accounts, the Gospels of Matthew, Mark, Luke and John, the earliest of which—the Gospel of St. Mark—was not put in writing until at least thirty years after Jesus' death. According to the Gospels, he was a simple, unassuming man, conversant with the Law, as were most Jews, and burning with zeal to bring to life again the high ethical and spiritual ideas implicit in the faith. He apparently had no program of reform, no special doctrine to promulgate. There were no political views in his teaching. He was thoroughly democratic, mixing with rich and poor alike, and even with the hated tax collectors who were in the pay of Rome. The only difference between his teaching and the teachings of the great prophets of Israel was that Jesus spoke to the individual, and preached about man's personal relationship to his fellow man. Hillel's negative command he made positive and active: "Therefore all things whatsoever ye would that men should do to you, do ye even so to them: for this is the law and the prophets" (Matthew 7:12).

Jesus' popularity threatened the always unstable equilibrium between the Jews and Rome, and the power and safety of the Sadducean priestly party depended upon Rome. The preaching of John Wesley, seventeen hundred years later, was not as abhorrent to the Church of England as was Jesus' preaching to the Sadducees, for Wesley's preaching offended only the conservative taste of the Church, whereas Jesus' preaching threatened the very life of the Sadducees and the destruction of their ambitions.

The salvation of Orthodox Judaism lay in obedience to the letter of the Law; and in this man who broke the Sabbath, consorted with sinners, preached righteousness before ritual, and swayed crowds with his preaching the conservative party saw a dangerous influence. They tried in every way to trip him into treasonous statements which they could report to Rome. One such attempt was the incident mentioned in Luke

20:22, wherein the chief priests, in other words, the Sadducees, asked him about the tribute money.

The attempt failed, and it was only when people began to talk of Jesus as the Messiah that the Sadducees had their chance. This could be reported to Rome as treason. At the order of the chief priests, Jesus was seized and brought before the Sanhedrin, or Jewish court, to be questioned. The Sadducees, who controlled the priesthood, also controlled this court, which heard Jewish civil and criminal cases, but under Roman law had become merely an investigating committee, without power to impose penalties or inflict punishment. When the priests felt that they had grounds for charging him with an attempt at political power, they followed the statutory course of handing him over to the Roman procurator, Pontius Pilate, for final trial and judgment. The Romans crucified him ignominiously between two malefactors, and put over his head the mocking inscription, "The King of the Jews."

His followers, fearful of consequences, deserted him in the hour of need, but such was the force of the man that they could not forget him. Three days later a group of them went to his tomb. To their amazement it was empty. And then word began to go about that he had been seen here and there by this one and that among his disciples and friends, alive and well. For a few days only these appearances continued, and then he was gone.

The Pharisees had long believed in life after death, but no one had ever seen proof of the resurrection before. To the followers of Jesus the news came as a revelation, and as the glad tidings spread there grew up the conviction that Jesus was divine—the son of God. Hundreds were convinced, and a new sect arose among the Jews which believed in Jesus the Messiah, who was the son of God, and who, having risen from the dead, assured all mankind of redemption and resurrection. The resurrection, bringing with it hope for the future of the Jews suffering under oppression, was what drew the people, but these early converts still held to Judaism, only adding to it a belief in the saving Messiah, Jesus.

Paul's Ministry

It was under the leadership of Paul that Christianity spread into the Gentile world. Paul, or as he was originally called Saul, was a tentmaker in Tarsus in Asia Minor, and in spite of his Jewish and Pharisaic antecedents, a Roman citizen. The story of his miraculous conversion may be found in the Acts of the Apostles, and seems to have occurred within fifteen years after the death of Jesus, and when most of the disciples were still alive. On fire with the new faith Paul determined to spread it to all men, Jews and Gentiles alike, and from this time on devoted his life to missionary work. He traveled back and forth, up and down Asia Minor, into Greece, and over to Rome, preaching and teaching. The extraordinary appeal of the new faith and Paul's ability as a proselytizer are evidenced by the fact that Romans as well as Jews were alarmed at the phenomenal spread of the new religion, to such an extent that even in Paul's lifetime persecution of the Christians began, and both Paul and Peter were, according to tradition, executed in Rome for their subversive activities.

To understand the special appeal of Christianity to the world in the first century A.D. it is necessary to look at the political and religious situation at the time. Rome had conquered Greece politically, but intellectually and spiritually had been conquered by her. At the time of Alexander (356 - 323 B.C.) Greece had ceased to be a collection of small city-states and had become a nation, imbued with a world spirit. The Greek language had become the lingua franca of the known world, and Greek soldiers and merchants had traveled far and wide disseminating Greek language and thought and in exchange bringing home the luxuries of the Orient and, far more important, the religious mystery cults. There were many of these—practically one for every agricultural country. For the mysteries—Isis worship, Cybele worship, Mithraism—were all fertility cults, based on the propitiation of the god who ruled the crops, and who, dying in the fall, came back to life in the spring. Starting as crude and barbarous cults of sympathetic magic and licentious orgies, these mysteries gradually changed, becoming more spiritual, and in most cases extending the rebirth of the god in the spring to a rebirth for the worshiper, using the old agricultural rituals to symbolize the resurrection of the individual. To many, seeking some faith to cling to, these mysteries came as an answer to prayer. The ritual was elaborate and beautiful, the doctrine gave hope for the future and appealed to rich and poor, ignorant and learned alike. For in both Greece and Rome during the last few centuries before the Christian era, faith in the gods of Olympus had ceased; the poor and ignorant followed underground cults ruled by fear and superstition, and the educated and well-to-do tried to make philosophy or a half-cynical acceptance of life combined with an ethical outlook satisfy their spiritual and emotional longings. The mysteries spread far and fast, first in Asia Minor and Greece and then on into the western part of the empire, Rome itself and her provinces, Gaul, Spain and Britain. By the opening years of the Christian era they were largely established as accepted religions provided their followers did lip service to the cult of the emperor.

The Rome that had succeeded Greece in world dominion had become an empire. The old simple and dignified days of the republic were gone. The city was full of foreigners all claiming citizenship. Eastern luxury had softened and corrupted manners, family solidarity was a thing of the past, responsibility for one's neighbor was nonexistent, the poor grew poorer and the rich richer. Soon even the hope of salvation was denied the poor, who had first welcomed and practised the mysteries, but now found them grown too elaborate and expensive for the poor in purse. Who could afford a lamb for sacrifice at initiation, let alone the bull that Mithra required? As the empire grew and nations and races mingled more and more, the sense of group solidarity, of the tribe or family as a unit, lessened and men became conscious of themselves as individuals, standing alone in a hostile world, with no hope for the future. The letters and books of this period give a vivid picture of the times. The man who could afford it joined one mystery after another, hoping in this way to be sure of a future after this life. The cults were all secret and so well was the secret kept that to this day we have no exact knowledge of how the rites were performed. Undoubtedly some were crude and unrestrained, others in the bits and pieces that have come down to us show great spiritual development and high moral tone. The search for salvation, for a future life, for hope for the individual is the central idea of them all.

Into this world, where the rich sought feverishly for a salvation denied the poor, came Paul preaching a faith which to the casual observer seemed another mystery. For Paul preached a god who died to save mankind and to give his followers eternal life. This was the central thought of early Christianity. The new cult was secret, just as the mysteries were, for the government was opposed to Christianity as subversive, and the only protection from persecution was secrecy. But the puzzled and hopeless masses who had been disappointed in the mysteries, the poor, the ignorant, slaves and freedmen alike found that this new faith was different. Paul preached, not a mystical god lost in the mists of the past, not an allegorical figure, but a god who had become man and who within the memory of men now living had died and risen again. Furthermore, this god required no elaborate initiation, merely baptism by water, no sacrifice, but a communal meal of bread and wine; he came to rich and poor, saint and sinner, and offered salvation to all who believed in him. The mysteries had prepared the world, and the world found its answer in Christianity.

The early development of Christianity may be read in the Acts of the Apostles and the Epistles of Paul. The Gospels were not in use and probably not written until many years after all the eyewitnesses of the events recorded in them were dead. It was Paul who explained, expounded, exhorted, traveling untiringly and writing as he went. In the Epistles he gave the answers to all the burning questions asked by the converts. Were the Jewish ritual laws part of the new faith? No. Was circumcision necessary? No. The communal suppers had become disorderly, a scene frequently of greed and drunkenness. Paul deals with the matter (I Corinthians 11). He makes decisions about marriage, about behavior, preaches on death and the future life. He builds a whole religion based on the words and example of the Jesus he has never seen. He faced the criticism of the Jews, even of the Jewish Christians, the persecutions of the Romans, but hardest of all to face must have been the slow waning of hope in the imminence of the day of judgment. The disciples and the early converts expected the end of the world at once, and many ceased to be concerned in this world or in material things, supposing that they would have no further need for them. What must have been the feelings of the little band of missionaries when year after year went by and there was no second coming? The Epistles of Paul to the Thessalonians, perhaps the earliest Christian writings we possess, give a hint of the doubts which had begun to assail the minds of even the faithful as the months and years went by and the last day did not come. The most cogent proof of the lasting influence of Jesus and the genius of Paul lies in the fact that Christianity survived this crisis and continued to grow.

Its growth and the postponement of the Second Coming made further organization and a definition of belief essential.

So far there had been only scattered groups of believers meeting in private houses or in the upper rooms of public houses to eat a communal meal, and perhaps listen to a letter of instructions from Paul, or it might be to receive a new member through baptism. The community more or less pooled its resources to take care of its poor and of widows and orphans and some of the congregations had chosen leaders, presbyters, to guide and manage their affairs. But the congregations grew larger and more numerous; Paul and Peter and the others could not be everywhere at once; furthermore, they were growing older, and were in constant danger, liable at any time to be jailed or put to death. It was in response to these conditions that regular church officers, bishops, priests and deacons, were appointed. At first the deacons distributed alms and managed the business affairs of the group. The presbyters administered the sacraments and preached. And over the congregations of each region was appointed a bishop. The most important bishoprics of the early years were Antioch, Alexandria, and Jerusalem. But the two bishoprics or sees which were eventually to be supreme were those of Rome and Constantinople.

The story of the life of Jesus as we have it in the Gospels of Mark, Matthew and Luke was introduced at this time to keep before the people the facts upon which Christianity rested. Liturgies began to spring up, perhaps even an early creed took form out of the original Roman baptismal symbol. As richer and more important people joined the church, it was felt necessary to have a greater body of tradition to add to the authority of the Epistles and Gospels and so the holy book of the Hebrews, the Old Testament, with its Messianic prophecies, prefaced the slowly forming New Testament, to make up what came to be the Bible. Probably by the middle or end of the second century A.D. the nucleus of the Christian government and services, the hierarchy of bishops, priests and deacons, and the definition of the sacramental doctrine was formed. There was, of course, not entire agreement on some of the points. Heresies were forever cropping up and had to be contravened. There was much the same variation of thought then as now, and the germs of most of the modern sects may be found in those early days of Christianity.

The Early Church

The church did not develop without opposition. The empire, jealous of its failing powers and fearful of opposition, persecuted the new faith in a vain effort to stamp it out. But the Christians throve on persecution, seemed almost to welcome martyrdom. Some of the best minds of the period had gone over to the Christian ranks and were teaching the new faith, and as they taught were developing its dogma, giving it form and authority.

For a long time the growth of the church was chiefly in the East. Here, where the first apostles had taught and preached, were their successors the apostolic fathers, Clement, Ignatius, and still later Origen and Eusebius who wrote and discussed, formulating the dogma of the new church. And here also started the hermits who fled from the world's temptations into the Egyptian deserts until there were so many living there that they found it necessary to form groups, which became the first Christian monasteries.

By the third century the church had become a formidable power in the West also, with centers at Carthage, Rome, Milan, and even in Gaul and faraway Britain, and it was in the course of this time that Rome came to be the most important of these, rivaling the greatest of the Eastern bishoprics. For, according to the Gospel of St. Matthew (16:18) Peter had been chosen by Jesus to be the founder of the Christian church, and since traditionally he became the first Bishop of Rome (or pope, as the Bishop of Rome came to be called) the Western Church early claimed pre-eminence and authority over all the other metropolitan centers, and demanded a position of leadership. So as the great empire decayed the church seemed to be springing out of its ruins.

However, it was not until many years later that Rome was acknowledged even as the head of the Western Church and that her bishop came to be regarded as the equal of the bishops of Antioch and Alexandria. Rome as the center of empire was slowly losing ground, as the eastern boundaries of the empire were threatened by marauding hordes from the steppes of Asia. By the end of the third century A.D. there was little of the old imperial spirit left in the city, and the emperor, Diocletian, ruled from Nicomedia on the Bosporus. To be sure, the senate still sat in Rome, and life went on much as it always had, but the city was living on the memory of the past, and in present fear of the barbarians who were infiltrating from the north and as they received Roman citizenship were changing and undermining the cultural tone of Roman life.

Paganism had lasted longer in Rome than in the East, partly, no doubt, because Rome was farther from the centers of the mystery cults and so had never been as fully steeped in mysticism as the East; partly because of the temper of the people, and partly because the older men of the senatorial class clung to tradition, to the state worship of gods and emperor, and to stoicism—that gospel of self-help and resignation. It is interesting to observe that as it died paganism in Rome reached its highest ethical development and that leading Christians of the time were often close friends and admirers of the leading pagans. But to the younger people the new Christian faith of hope and salvation came as a boon in time of need, and rich as well as poor seized upon it. There is a charming and touching incident of a proud old patrician pagan sitting in his study with his granddaughter on his knee, hearing her recite a Christian hymn taught her by her mother. To him, trained on the sounding lines of Virgil and the elegant verse of Horace, the vulgarized Latin of the Christian hymn must have been as painful to the ear as free verse to the Victorian. Christianity was bound to triumph, but it reconciled much of the pagan element by compromise. There could be no fete for Bacchus or Ceres, but there could be harvest festivals. A favorite deity became a Christian saint, the temples were used for public halls.

Establishment of Christianity as the State Religion in the Empire

Unfortunately the new religion itself was by no means united. Almost from the beginning there had been difficulties of doctrine and procedure. The writings of the early fathers are full of discussions of heresies and schisms, and the question most discussed is that of the nature of Christ. Was He divine? Was He human? If He was both, which nature, human or divine, predominated? About the year 300 the followers of Arius, a deacon of Alexandria, went to the extreme of denying His divinity altogether, and it was just when Constantine accepted Christianity as the state religion that the controversy over the Arian view had reached its height. Almost as soon as the faith had been recognized, therefore, it was necessary in the year 325 to call a general council of the church at Nicaea to settle the dispute.

Although the decision of the council went against Arius, it did not convince his adherents, and the Arian doctrine continued to spread among the barbarian converts. Nevertheless, it was out of this council that the Nicene Creed developed, to become with the Apostles' Creed one of the great expressions of the Christian faith. In it there is developed in detail and at length the belief in the divinity of Christ.

To us today, the questions with which the church fathers concerned themselves sometimes seem trifling or even absurd. Tolerance, even the imperfect tolerance which we have achieved, is a late development. There was, furthermore, some excuse for the anxiety of the early church over heresy. A faith which is to be preached and taught, especially one designed for nonbelievers or uneducated people, must have definite articles of belief, and these must be consistent. The Gospels did not lay down rules and formulate a creed. They simply showed a way of life which anyone could follow even while belonging to another faith. If Christianity was to be differentiated from the mysteries, stoicism, neo-Platonism, or even the state religion, it had to be formulated, and the long, and to us futile, arguments about the Trinity, the sacraments, the real or seeming divinity of Christ, which went on year after year, century after century, were in the end what made Christianity a living faith rather than a dry system of ethics and morals. Even in Constantine's time the victory of Christianity was not assured, and in the reign of his nephew Julian, an effort was made to restore paganism to power. Constantine's instinct was right when it inspired him to unify the church and by calling the Council of Nicaea to give it cohesion and a bent for co-operation.

To the emperors of this period the eastern part of the empire seemed more important than the western, and Constantine withdrew finally from Rome and founded the new city of Constantinople in an effort to ward off the barbarian hordes pushing in from the east and northeast. But as he strained off the last vestige of power from Rome he laid open his northwestern and northern boundaries to invasion from the barbarians beyond the Rhine.

Much of Western Europe had been thoroughly Latinized during Rome's pre-eminence, and by the fourth century Christianity had followed Latin culture into Gaul, Spain, Britain, and Northern Africa. There were bishoprics in most of the chief Latin and provincial cities, and some of the best minds of Europe held the sees. On them fell the burden of guarding the culture of the West against the crude and untaught invaders who were pouring in from all directions. As Gaul, Spain, Britain, northern Africa, and even Italy were overrun by Goths, Vandals, and all the other tribes of barbarians, it became a race against time to civilize and Christianize the newcomers before all the vestiges of culture should disappear.

Four great men were largely responsible for accomplishing the almost impossible task: St. Ambrose, who died in 397, St. Augustine (430), St. Jerome (420), and Pope Gregory I (604). St. Ambrose, Bishop of Milan, strengthened the power and dignity of the church in the eyes of the barbarians, and took part in the conversion of St. Augustine, who as Bishop of Carthage later laid down the basic doctrines of the Western church. St. Jerome translated the Bible into Latin, which had become the universal language of culture in the West, and St. Gregory, who was pope from 590 to 604, proselytized and converted the heathen with the help of the newly formed monastic orders.

The development of monasticism in the West took a very different course from its development in the East. There were in Europe no warm dry deserts where living was comparatively easy and one could retire to live a life of prayer and contemplation with no thought of clothing or shelter. A few lone spirits managed to keep alive in solitude, but for the most part it seemed better for those who wished to retire to gather in communal groups and put up some kind of building in which to house themselves.

Monasteries and nunneries arose for men and women who wished to flee the world and its temptations and live in prayer, fasting and contemplation. Where there are groups living together, rules are necessary, and someone to enforce them. It was St. Benedict, with the help of Pope Gregory, who developed the rules which were adopted by most of the monasteries in Western Europe. The first of the Benedictine monasteries was founded early in the sixth century at Monte Cassino in southern Italy.

Benedict prescribed work as well as prayer and contemplation for the monks, and Pope Gregory added missionary activities to their duties. Monasteries began to spring up in the utmost confines of the continent, and with them went the Latin language, some elements of Latin culture, and Christianity.

It is more than probable that Gregory was himself a Benedictine monk, and under his wise and farsighted guidance the monasteries in the West became, not the self-contained units of world-weary men which they originally were, and which in the Eastern Church they continued to be, but active and outgoing organizations of missionaries. True, there were abuses even in these early days, the more so since the monks were not yet required to advance to priestly orders, a ruling made only in 1311; and any man could join an order, provided that he took the vows of celibacy and obedience. Many ignorant as well as many worthless men took monastic vows as a way to escape responsibility and assure themselves of an easy living.

For the most part, however, monasticism in the West became less and less an escape and more and more a life of devoted service. The head of the monastery, the abbot, was the decisive factor, for the monks were under his absolute control. If he was a man of force and idealism, he could make his house a great power, not only in the immediate neighborhood, but as far as his monks could travel. By the ninth century they had traveled far and wide and had set up monasteries even in the remote and trackless forests beyond the Rhine.

Gregory was a realist and did not expect too much from his heathen converts. He did not tear down temples and shrines, but told his missionaries simply to reconsecrate them, substitute relics for idols, and redirect sacrifices and pagan festivals into pleasant communal feasts. So the change from paganism to Christianity was almost imperceptible to the people, and though superstition and magic continued, there was a new Christian element added which education could eventually strengthen. Until the middle of the seventh century there was one center of missionary activity in Western Europe quite independent of Rome. When the Romans withdrew their legions from Britain in the fifth century, they left the country Latinized and Christianized, but defenseless against the invaders from the north and east. In time, driven by the savage Picts and Scots, Danes and Norsemen, and finally overrun by the Angles and Saxons, the Britons withdrew westward to Ireland, Wales, Cornwall, and the islands of the coast. Here they practised their religion, studied and wrote, cut off from the seething Roman melting pot and unconscious of the changes and developments going on in the mother church. While the rest of Western Europe was coming under papal rule, and dogma and form were being crystallized, even while eastern England was being re-Christianized from Rome (596), this Irish and west British Church developed quite independently and sent out missionaries into Gaul and the wild forests of Germany, braving all kinds of hardships and dangers in their zeal to spread the gospel and to establish seats of learning. St. Patrick and St. Columban were two of the early British missionaries and there were many others. The scholarship of these British and Irish monks was known everywhere and many of them were invited to preach and teach in European monasteries and churches. It was after the Synod of Whitby in 664 that the power of the Roman Church began to prevail, and this early British Church gradually faded away.

The task with which the church fathers and the missionaries were faced during the first five hundred years of Christianity was gigantic, and their success—imperfect as it seems from here—astonishing. They had not only to convert, but to civilize, and not only the barbarians who had invaded the Roman Empire, but also those still living in the forests and fastnesses of the wilderness beyond the Rhine. There the savage German tribes had never been touched by Latin culture, and they might at any time move down into the welter of peoples already struggling for foothold in the crumbling Western Empire. Some of the invading tribes, moreover, had already been converted, but to the Arian heresy instead of to orthodox Trinitarianism. To them the true doctrine must be taught. It was in answer to all the questions that arose during these first five centuries that dogma had to be more and more definitely stated and elaborated. Where it had been simple it grew increasingly complex and began to diverge from the teachings of the Eastern Church, as was but natural, since the problems which faced the two halves of the Empire were quite different.

In the East the succession of emperors continued. Often they were weak, sometimes they were of barbarian origin, they were all too frequently corrupt; but they centralized power and gave at least some semblance of law and order. In the West one puppet emperor after another was set up, only to be overthrown by a new invader. Rome itself was twice sacked by the Vandals; in 476 the Heruli overran the empire and set up their leader Odovacer as king; in 493 the Ostrogoths under Theodoric seized the power. All these emperors and usurpers paid nominal allegiance to the Emperor of the East, but he was either preoccupied with his own affairs or not interested in his western domain. After a few half-hearted efforts to quell the disorder he established an exarch at Ravenna, whose power, however, was short-lived. When the Lombards entered Italy in 566 there came a general political breakup in Italy and even lip service was no longer given to the East.

During this time of trouble and anarchy the popes had

gradually been building up their power. The barbarians came to respect them, and since many of the barbarians had been Christianized or had at least heard of the Christian teachings, they acknowledged the pope's spiritual power and even turned to him for help and advice or to settle disputes. Gradually he took over the position of moderator and became the one stable factor in the kaleidoscopic changes of the time.

Fortunately the pope who occupied St. Peter's throne when the final breakup came was that singularly able man Gregory I, who had already been so active in missionary work, and was known and loved throughout Western Europe, in which he finally made the Roman Catholic Church the great central power, and over which he assumed for his office the supreme control. Milan and Carthage, also seats of bishoprics, sank into secondary importance.

In Gregory's time, the movements and readjustments of barbarian invasion in Western Europe seemed for the moment to have reached some kind of stable equilibrium. In fact the first foreshadowings of nationality were beginning to show as people stayed settled in one region long enough to become identified with it. Latin in a somewhat debased and vulgarized form was still the language of the church and so the common medium of speech for the educated throughout the West, but for ordinary use various sections of the country were speaking in different dialects which would later develop into German, French, English, and the other modern tongues.

It was at this juncture that Islam sprang up in Arabia and threatened to submerge the world. Mohammed (570-632) derived certain aspects of his religion from Judaism, but Islam is very different from the restrained and puritanical faith of Judaism in its later development. According to the central tenets of Mohammedanism, there is one God, Allah, and Mohammed is his prophet. Their holy book was the Koran, in which were contained all the rules of life and conduct. Almost at once they set out to conquer the world for the new faith, and they nearly succeeded. When the flood finally receded, the whole political and religious face of the Mediterranean basin was changed. Northern Africa, which had been Christian, was in the hands of the Arabs, as was Spain. Only by the barest chance had Islam been prevented from submerging Europe entirely.

Yet out of the cataclysm came some good results. The power of Christianity had strengthened, and both Eastern and Western churches had hardened and gained in stature from the conflict. But never again would there be one Christian church. From the outset, East and West had developed in different directions, and though the final break did not come until 1054, the Eastern and Western churches were virtually separate from the period of the Moslem invasions onward. The original differences had seemed trivial—whether one should eat eggs in Lent, whether priests should be shaven, whether they should marry, whether there should be images in churches—but they were of vital importance at the time, and indicative of radically divergent viewpoints.

With the Arabs controlling the Mediterranean what little contact there had been between East and West decreased almost to the vanishing point. Some of the Italian cities continued to trade with Constantinople and with the new Arabian centers, but for the most part the West turned back on itself and for the next four hundred years lived practically a self-contained life. Once the language of the civilized world, Greek was forgotten and Latin took its place, except again in Italy, which, having once been the hub of the world, and having still the papal court as its center, always retained some vestiges of the culture and cosmopolitanism of the past.

The first five centuries of the Christian era had been spent on establishing and defining Christianity and civilizing and converting the barbarians. The next four were to be devoted to organizing and expanding the church.

The Dark Age in Europe

The growth of the individual and that of the human race are, as I said before, very much alike, and the Dark Age, about A.D. 600-1000 may be compared with the very early years of childhood, when the child, having learned to walk and talk, is adapting himself to his environment, absorbing inherited and traditional knowledge and custom, and accepting blindly the beliefs and prejudices of his family. So during these centuries the church, serving as guide and mentor, set up the pattern and began the almost impossible task of making the barbarians conform to it, at least outwardly.

The scholars and churchmen of the time were themselves hampered by a lack of teaching material. They had, therefore, to make their own textbooks out of the bits and pieces that they could find, fitting them together as best they could. The confusion of wars and invasions had destroyed most of the libraries of classical Rome, and in the provinces, ignorance of the Greek language closed many avenues of learning. Outside of the church few if any could read Latin, and even some of the priests and monks could not do more than recite the services by heart. And yet from this unpromising material teachers and preachers must be made to carry on the work of the church and spread her doctrines. And her work was important, probably the only constructive work in a world of chaos and confusion. The monasteries were a refuge for the homeless, hospitals for the sick, hostels for travelers; they even undertook relief work, sending wagon trains of supplies to ravaged areas, often at a distance. And as the missionary work proceeded the power and prestige of the pope who promoted it increased. Even when he was a weak man, as he sometimes was, respect for his office continued, for the men about him carried on the work.

Men like Bishop Isidore of Seville spent their lives "making excerpts from copies" and gathering them in encyclopedic volumes, in an effort to save and give to the world the scant salvage from the treasures of classical and early Christian writings. On the one section of Aristotle's philosophy which had survived from the past was based the whole educative system of the day. Of the making of books there was no end, but for the most part they were restatements or copies of older books, or anthologies of unrelated sections fitted together with commentaries and adapted for teaching Christianity. For the teacher was the church, and the end and aim of learning was to attain salvation.

To the great mass of people, rich and poor alike, the theological discussions and hair-splitting arguments of their spiritual guides meant little or nothing. They accepted the results without question, worshiping in the prescribed way at the appointed times, confessing, doing penance, attending mass, paying tithes. The church grew to be an ever-present factor in their lives as it acquired more and more land and assumed greater power. One could not marry or die without a priest; indeed, so essential was baptism that it was hard even to be born without one.

Europe was at this time agricultural and very poor. There was no industry and very little trade and owing to the absence of roads very little communication between different sections of the country. For the landholders—the feudal lords—fighting was the chief occupation, and as the natural divisions of land and language grew increasingly distinct, the fighting became more and more definitely the effort of war lords to establish their control, each of one special region.

England, for example, gradually changed from a group of warring states in the seventh century to a kingdom by the opening of the eleventh. France, too, first under Clovis, later under Charlemagne, and finally under the Capetians became a kingdom. In Spain the little region in the northwest which the Moors had not conquered slowly grew larger as the Spaniards expanded, pushing the Moors south. Italy and Germany alone remained groups of small states, unable to develop a central power that would give them a cohesive nationalism.

The fighting between these groups and between the various kings and their subjects was continuous and the land was ravaged and desolated, the peasants crushed and impoverished. Only the church was able to enforce any order at all, and often kings and princes defied even the church as represented by the pope. If the pope was strong he could check such rebellion by excommunication—a powerful weapon in a world which was uniformly Catholic and very ignorant. For a ruler who was excommunicated could no longer demand the obedience of his subjects; and if his subjects also defied the pope, there was always the ban which could be put on a whole region, and which, by depriving the people of all the church rites, could take from them the hope of heaven. For a country under a ban was dead. No church bells rang, no priests baptized or married or gave extreme unction—such a land was lost.

As the conflict went on, the pope instituted the Peace of God and the Truce of God, which limited fighting to certain days and periods only. But even these rules were not obeyed. Only another invasion of barbarians from Asia was able at last to relieve the situation.

The Crusades and the Middle Ages

During all these centuries Palestine had been a shrine of Christian pilgrims who came from all over the then-known world to worship at those spots where Jesus had lived and worked. The Arabs, a highly cultured and, after their first invasion, a peaceful group, had permitted and encouraged the pilgrimages, even allowing the Christians to set up a church and hospital in Jerusalem. In 1076, however, the Seljuk Turks, from the Caucasus, poured into Hither Asia and overran the land, threatening even Constantinople and seizing the Moslem possessions. They were converted to Islam, but like most new converts were very intolerant, desecrated the Christian shrines and put an end to pilgrimages.

Urban II, who was then pope, saw in this crisis a solution of his difficulties. With the help of a popular preacher, Peter the Hermit, he advertised a Holy War to recover the Christian shrines from the Turks. Every man who took part in this crusade was promised remission of his sins and the direct protection of the pope. Urban hoped, and with reason, that such an expedition, promising adventure, glory, and eternal salvation, would attract the unruly and so syphon off some of the ringleaders of the fighting in Europe. This would give the land a chance to recover from the depredations of war.

All Europe was thrown into a frenzy of enthusiasm for the new enterprise. Quarrels were forgotten in the excitement of preparation. Men pawned or even sold their possessions to get money for equipment. Everywhere could be met men wearing a cross sewed on their clothing to show that they were joining the Crusade. Western Europe, led by the church, was at last united in a common cause.

This was in 1096, and with the First Crusade we can say, roughly speaking, that the Dark Age had closed and the great centuries of the Middle Ages had begun. Of course it is not possible to date historical periods so closely. For a hundred years before the First Crusade Europe had been emerging from the Dark Age, and it would be at least a hundred years longer before the great creative centuries of the Middle Ages would be in full swing.

I have dwelt at some length on these first ten centuries, because they really are the common heritage of the Christian world. All the Christian roots are there and even those sects who seek to return to the earliest Christian organization will find that some of their traditions nonetheless date from these ten centuries. Certainly had it not been for the untiring work of the church during these years of invasion, war and confusion, Christianity might have been long delayed in reaching parts of the continent and some it might never have reached at all.

The creeds, many of the church hymns, much of the dogma of some of the later sects grew up at this time in spite of the lack of material, the ignorance and superstition of the masses, the poverty and confusion of the world, and the threats of Arab conquest. These centuries are an amazing example of what man can do in the face of every kind of challenge, provided that his driving idea is in keeping with the forward surge of humanity.

There is neither time nor space in so short a review of events to go into the details of the various Crusades. In themselves they were of no great importance. They continued over a period of about two hundred years, but after the first two or three were very sporadic and often not against the Turks at all. In time the task of driving out the infidel was seen to be hopeless and religious enthusiasm waned, to be replaced by politics and greed. In about 1208 Pope Innocent III directed one crusade against the Albigenses, a heretic group in Provence. A bloody and frightful massacre ensued, which successfully blotted out the heresy, but also laid waste one of the richest and most cultured sections of the continent. This was the first organized persecution of heresy on a large scale, but it foreshadowed the future.

Far more important than the Crusades themselves were the effects which they had on Western Europe. They opened windows on the outside world which had so long been forgotten. People who had never before left home traveled to distant lands, saw other ways and manners and had a glimpse of wealth and luxury that they had never dreamed of. Just as the world war has made people of today aware of geography and of other ways of life from their own, so it was with the Crusades. The returning crusaders brought not only booty and souvenirs, but travelers' tales, new points of view, wider contacts. Some brought back books, precious manuscripts, and scraps of new and stimulating knowledge.

The Eastern Empire had never sunk to the barbarous depths of ignorance reached by the West. Greek was there the common language and the great classics of Greece were still available and in use. The Arabs, when they came in contact with Greek thought and science, had been quick to accept it and make it their own. They had early become one of the most learned and cultured peoples of the day and had carried science to new heights. By the introduction of simple numerals they had made possible addition, subtraction, multiplication and division in large amounts, and so opened the way to higher mathematics; their invention of algebra had further simplified arithmetic, in medicine they were supreme, and in philosophy they had translated and made commentaries on the whole of Aristotle's great work. Contact even in war with such an advanced culture must have had a profound influence on all who were exposed to it.

The Europe to which the first crusaders returned was ready for new ideas, and there followed three extraordinary centuries of intellectual, artistic and religious outflowering. These were the centuries when the universities were founded, Paris, Bologna, Salerno, Prague, Oxford, and a host of others. Bologna was primarily a law school, Salerno emphasized medicine, but the great universities of the more northern cities devoted themselves to theology and to harmonizing Christian and Greek thought. In the twelfth century the complete Aristotle became available through the Arabs, and it was on Christian tradition through St. Augustine, on the Bible and on Aristotle that St. Thomas Aquinas (1225-1274) constructed the foundations of the theology which became final in the Catholic Church, even superseding the work of Augustine himself. Men began to think and question, and the arguments of the theologians of the thirteenth and fourteenth centuries made religious history. No longer were scholars confined to "excerpts from copies," but could begin to range at will through the original documents, where they found new and often bewildering facts and theories.

Trade and commerce began to develop and cities to spring up. The world was no longer divided into nobles, clergy and peasants, for a merchant class of city dwellers was appearing, well to do and often well informed and with wide connections in other parts of the world. There was even a manufacturing class of artisans combined in guilds which was gradually making itself felt.

And in the narrow streets of the towns there arose churches of a new type, no longer the heavy, dark-interiored neoclassic or Romanesque churches, nor the wide and domed Byzantine, but airy, many-windowed churches with flying buttresses to hold up the walls, and delicate carvings from nature or from fancy for decoration; while pointed arches in succeeding tiers drew the eye up from the dark and filthy streets to the sky above. These were the Gothic churches and cathedrals which still amaze men by their spiritual beauty. Not only architecture but all art was changed by this innovation, for with less bare wall space to decorate, the old Byzantine mosaic work began to go out and stained-glass windows and paintings which could be used for altarpieces became the rule. Paint is an easier medium than mosaic, and in time the new pictures began to grow more varied in subject matter and more life-like in appearance, and were a factor in teaching Bible story to the people.

Out of the church ritual, by now very elaborate and stately, grew drama. It was a slow development, again enforced by the need to educate the great mass of the public. The church services were in Latin and therefore incomprehensible to the congregation, but at the great feasts certain events of the life of Christ, such as the nativity and the resurrection, came to be enacted by the priests, not only for the congregation but often on the church porch for the benefit of the crowds. Later these performances were taken over by the guilds and played on floats; dialogue was introduced, and not in Latin but in the dialect of the people. Old Testament stories were added to the repertory and then the lives of the saints. Next moral lessons were taught in allegorical plays, and then historical events. From there to the drama of later times was a very short step.

It was during these centuries too that the use of paper for books was introduced by the Arabs, and the Bibles of the Poor began to be published—books illustrated with woodcuts, each with a short description of the picture.

Education began to be more general and was no longer confined to the church; and with education came the desire to read the Bible, the acknowledged source of the Christian faith. By now Latin, the established language of the church, had become a dead letter to the common man and every section of Europe had its own vernacular, so that the Bible, still in the Latin version made by St. Jerome, was a closed book to the public. In the middle of the fourteenth century John Wycliffe, an Englishman, first translated the Bible into English and so opened the way to later translations and to a mass of questions and doubts which gathered size and momentum as time went on.

During the first ten centuries of her existence the Church had built up what was virtually a totalitarian state. Emperors, kings and noblemen might question the pope's power and even on occasion defy it, but they dared not disregard an institution which controlled the entrance to future life and whose demands and doctrines permeated life in this world. The church was everywhere. It owned vast domains and thousands owed it feudal allegiance as well as the pious awe of devout believers.

With so much wealth and power in their hands it is not surprising that there were many abuses among the clergy, even those in high places. There are constant references in the literature of the time to lapses among the priests and monks and even the higher clergy—immorality, extravagances of living, nepotism (giving favors to one's relatives), simony (selling church positions to the highest bidder), ignorance and sloth, and callous disregard of the poor. The church constantly attempted reforms, but in so large an organization as the church had become these were not long-lived nor wide-reaching.

Some of the most valuable reform work of the period was done by the friars, who originated in the twelfth century under the leadership of St. Francis and St. Dominic. These men preached a return to the simplicity of the early church, with its emphasis on poverty, obedience and humility. Not attached to a monastery, the friars traveled everywhere preaching and teaching as they went. By the fourteenth century they had attained pre-eminence in learning and many of them taught in the universities. Roger Bacon, the first modern scientist, was a Franciscan, St. Thomas Aquinas, the greatest theologian of his time, a Dominican.

Emergence of the Individual

But perhaps the greatest thing that emerged from these four centuries was the individual man. All during the Dark Age man had not thought and acted for himself but as a member of a group. Here and there a single figure emerged, Gregory, Isidore of Seville, Charlemagne, Alfred, Bede, but they were few and far between. Even in the twelfth and thirteenth and fourteenth centuries we meet few individuals. The church was totalitarian; the state as it developed was interested, not in the welfare of the people, but in the power of the ruler, and in the growing rivalry between church and state. The unit was not the individual, but the group which was part of the great mass.

Perhaps the best illustration of the development of the

individual is found in the poems of three men who lived and worked, one in the twelfth, one in the thirteenth, and one in the fourteenth century. In their development may be seen a picture of the changing spirit of the world.

One of the great hymn writers of all times, whose hymns in translation are known to everyone and found in Protestant as well as in Catholic hymnbooks was Bernard of Cluny, who wrote in about 1145. He was, of course, a monk and his was the great Jerusalem hymn, of which "Jerusalem the Golden," "For thee, or dear, dear country," "Brief life is here our portion," are parts. It was written in Latin. To him this earthly experience was of no interest, for all his thoughts were centered on the world to come. He considered the monk's ways of celibacy and self-denial the best for this life and looked forward to the next world as the sole objective of our stay on earth. In his hymn, therefore, the emphasis is on the evils and sorrows of this brief earthbound experience, and the beauties of life hereafter.

A hundred years later Dante (1265-1321), a layman but still an orthodox and devout Catholic, wrote *The Divine Comedy,* one of the greatest poems of all time. He wrote, not in Latin, but in Italian, which he molded into an instrument of amazing beauty. His theme is still the next world, Hell, Purgatory and Heaven and the ultimate destiny of man, but he no longer holds up the life of self-denial as the best, and his criticism of the church is outspoken. And all through his poems there is visible a feeling for nature, a consciousness of the beauty of this world, for his similes and descriptions of the world to come are taken from the world he lives in.

It was for Chaucer (1340-1400) to express most clearly the new spirit of man. He also wrote in the language of the people (English in his case) and there is no hint of a preoccupation with the next world in his frankly secular *Canterbury Tales.* He describes the world about him and the people in it with accuracy, affection and humor, and all of a sudden they stand out not as a baker, a nun, a knight, but as one special baker or nun or knight with characters and characteristics different from every other. He too was still a devout Catholic, but he had ceased to center his interest on the world to come. He loved the world he lived in and described its beauties and delights with no thought of heaven.

The Eastern Orthodox Church

With this emergence of the individual in the more practical West, we must turn for a little while to the Eastern Empire and more especially to the Eastern Church, which was the original seat of Christianity and had followed its own conception of the faith, quite different from that of the Western world. The divergence arose partly from differences of temperament, partly from the political division which set these two great portions of the old Roman Empire apart. Temperamentally the West was bound to have a more matter-of-fact approach to religion, the East a stronger leaning toward mysticism.

As we have seen, the Eastern Empire in its political aspect became increasingly important from the end of the third century on, and the removal of the emperor to its new capital Constantinople finally left Rome isolated and exposed to barbarian invasion, with only the pope to represent her former supremacy. Under these conditions discord inevitably arose between the pope and the patriarch of the Eastern Church in Constantinople, who after 588 assumed the title Ecumenical (general or universal) Patriarch. On the other hand, the pope, the successor of Peter, whom the Gospels (Matthew 16:18-19) had called the "rock on whom I will build my church," more and more claimed supremacy over all of Christendom.

The discord at first took the form of rifts arising out

of petty quarrels, one of which, over the question of images (icons) in the church, lasted for many years. Eventually it was patched up, and the final break in 1054 came over a question of doctrine, concerning the addition by the pope of the so-called "filioque clause" in the Nicene Creed. Both Eastern and Western Churches believed in the Trinity and therefore in the full divinity of Jesus and of the Holy Spirit. But the Eastern Church maintained that the Holy Spirit proceeds from the Father alone, while the Western Church held that the Holy Spirit proceeds from both Father and Son. Michael Arularius, the then patriarch, refused to accept the pope's position, and the papal legates formally laid on the altar of St. Sophia a sentence of anathema on the patriarch and his followers.

While this argument on the "filioque clause" was the apparent cause of the break, there were other underlying and more basic differences which made the schism inevitable. There was the growing rivalry, both political and ecclesiastical, between Rome and Constantinople. Furthermore, in the East the Slavic and Oriental races were beginning to predominate, and they had little in common with the Germanic tribes who had to a great extent prevailed over the Latin population of the old Roman Empire.

It is, however, barely possible that even this schism might have been healed had it not been for the Turkish invasion which overran Asia Minor and Syria and even threatened the Eastern Empire during the latter half of the eleventh century. The Crusades which Western Europe organized in response to the Turkish menace may have benefited the West, but were a source of misery to the East. For the Eastern world was the battlefield of the Holy War, and the motley crowd of crusaders pillaged and looted wherever they went, once even attacking and taking Constantinople. These operations, which took place over a period of many decades, instead of uniting

Christendom in a common cause of Christianity against the infidel, only served to cement the hatred between the Orthodox and Roman Catholic Churches.

The period of the Crusades, though debilitating to the Eastern Empire, did not destroy it, and the church continued to flourish until 1453 when the final blow came. In that year Constantinople fell to the Ottoman Turks, and the Eastern Church came under the domination of the Moslem rulers of the territory. It was not entirely annihilated, for the Greek population was allowed to retain its faith and the election of patriarchs and other officials was permitted. Whereas, however, the Orthodox Church had been an established church, supported by the government, the Turks withdrew all financial support, and furthermore taxed the Christians so heavily that nothing was left for donation.

The resulting poverty was devastating and had a profound effect not only on the church but also on the world of learning. During the early centuries of Christianity, great monasteries had grown up throughout the Eastern Empire. Unlike the monasteries of the West, which had been largely occupied with missionary work, those of the Eastern Church were devoted largely to study and the preservation of ancient and learned documents. To a larger degree than the monks of the West, the Eastern monks had copied and assembled great libraries of scholarly manuscripts and had also fostered artistic development by their painting of icons. Now, under the pressure of direst poverty, the treasures that the monasteries had amassed were thrown into the market place and sold to the highest bidder. Valuable collections were thus dispersed, many of them to find their way to the West, where they added to the humanistic fever which had seized all of Italy and was spreading north, later to end in the Reformation.

Though the Eastern Church during this desperate period lacked the time and money to continue its scholarly and artistic projects, it maintained its doctrinary integrity, and during the Reformation, when the Lutherans claimed that their doctrine, as expressed in the Augsburg Confession, was in agreement with the doctrines of the Eastern Church, the effort at reconciliation was refused by the patriarch Joseph. In 1574 another attempt to reconcile Lutheranism with the Greek Church was made by one Martin Crusius, who sent a Greek translation of the Confession to the patriarch Jeremiah II. The answer was that the way to union with the Orthodox Church was to "Follow the apostolical and Synodical decrees." The Eastern Church continued through the centuries on its independent course, though a large proportion of its members lived in conquered territory and remained poor and weak until 1821, when the Greeks were liberated from Turkish rule and began once more to build up both their ecclesiastical and their secular strength.

Meanwhile, from the time that the Eastern Church declined in the area held by the Turks, it began to increase in power in the Slavic lands to the north, and more especially in Russia. There are few records of the early Russian Church, although tradition has it that St. Andrew founded the church at Kiev, planting the cross on the spot where the cathedral now stands. Through him the Russian Church claims apostolic succession for its primates. It was only in the ninth century, during the time of the Princess Olga, that Christianity really began to exist in Russia. Her grandson Vladimir made it the state religion, and henceforth it spread rapidly through the country.

After the fall of Constantinople in 1453 the Russian Church tended to develop into a separate entity and became increasingly powerful; and as the church in Greece grew poorer, the church in Russia grew richer. The patriarchate of Moscow was founded at the end of the sixteenth century and lasted until Peter the Great, who did not wish any rival power to the throne, permitted it to lapse in 1700 by appointing no successor to the Patriarch Adrian upon the latter's death. In place of the patriarchate Peter organized "The Most Holy Governing Synod," which, though composed of bishops and priests, was presided over by a layman. The patriarchate was restored after the fall of the tsar in 1917, but when the Russian Church excommunicated the Soviet government, the position of Orthodox Christianity as the state religion ceased in Russia, as it had ceased in Greece four and a half centuries before.

Russia had not been alone in making the Orthodox faith a national religion. After their liberation from the Turks in 1821, the Greeks set up a synod to govern their church, and made the king the head of the synod. The organization was henceforth the Hellenic Orthodox Church. The Serbian church was also an independent national church, as were the Rumanian, the Albanian and the Bulgarian. There are also Orthodox churches supported by the Armenians and the Syrians. These churches, though separate in government and organization, are all strictly orthodox in doctrine and the direct descendants of the ancient Eastern Church.

For the sake of clarity it has seemed best to follow the evolution of Eastern Christianity without a break to the present day, even though the quest has carried us centuries beyond the West that we left behind. It is to this West that we must now return, the West that had already lost the otherworldly aspiration of Bernard of Cluny and was beginning to think and feel in Chaucer's terms.

Humanism

The world that Chaucer lived in was a very different world from that in which Bernard of Cluny longed for the New Jerusalem. In the old agricultural Europe commerce and manufacture were emerging; cities were growing up and shaking off old feudal ties; trade was active and widespread; money had taken the place of barter; moneylending, out of which developed banking, was becoming a respectable and highly profitable business. And in connection with business the knowledge of reading, writing and arithmetic was becoming common to all but the peasant class. A spirit of enterprise, inquiry, self-assertion arose; and slowly at first, but increasing in strength, a desire for freedom of thought, unhampered by the restrictions of the church.

For the church moved more slowly than the world about it. Religion is conservative, since it is founded on tradition handed down from the past and woven into the fabric of the present.

During these extraordinary centuries (1100-1500) took place the spiritual and intellectual awakening known as humanism, which reached its full flower in the Reformation and Renaissance. Western Europe was like the boy or girl just emerging from childhood and looking about with eager and inquiring eyes at a world full of charm and promise in which to exercise the new freedom just attained. The promise was greater than its fulfillment, for further development came not by evolution, but by revolution.

Dissatisfaction with conditions in the church grew increasingly strong over the years. At first kings and emperors fought her power and demands, and then, as the people began to think and reason they too grew increasingly restive, especially in those countries remote from Rome: Germany, the Netherlands, England. Italy always took religion more quietly than the north, and in the revival of interest in learning turned to art and letters rather than theology.

Since the pope lived in Rome it came about, quite without plan at first, that he should be Italian. Most of the papal court (the *Curia Romana*), which included the cardinals who elected the pope, were also Italian. Feeling against Italian rule became very strong in the rest of Western Europe and led to a schism in the church (1378-1417) which resulted in the removal of the papal seat from Rome to Avignon and a succession of French popes who ruled from there. This period was dubbed the "Babylonian Captivity" and focused the attention of the world on the very flagrant abuses prevalent in the system.

One of the chief complaints against the church was its expense. For the church, being a large landholder, taxed both as a feudal lord and as an organization, draining money from both rich and poor. The public suspected, and perhaps often rightly, that the money thus gathered was improperly used —not for church requirements or for charity, but for the private use of clergy and monasteries.

It is not my purpose to discuss in any detail the politics of the times, though they were so closely concerned with religious development as to make it hard to leave them out entirely. The growing spirit of nationalism made kings unwilling to acknowledge the sovereignty of an Italian pope, who himself had large holdings in Italy, the papal states which he was trying to extend, often at the expense of kings or emperor. Spiritual leadership might be conceded to the heir of Peter, but not political domination.

The fifteenth century, for all its advancement of learning, showed signs of stress and strain which constantly increased in force. In 1415 John Hus, the Bohemian reformer, was burned at the stake for heresy. Influenced by Wycliffe's teaching, he had not been content to stay in the church, but had organized a church of his own, an offshoot of which is the Moravian sect of today. During the first half of the century the Hundred Years' War between France and England was raging, and in the East the Ottoman Turks, who had followed the Seljuks, were in control of most of the Balkan peninsula and threatening Austria. In 1453 the Hundred Years' War ended and the English were driven out of the European Continent. In the same year Constantinople fell to the Turks, who thus established themselves firmly in Europe.

Spain was gradually driving the Moors out of the Iberian Peninsula, and before the end of the century would be a united kingdom under Ferdinand and Isabella. In Italy the papacy had been restored after the "Babylonian Captivity." The struggle for supremacy between popes and general councils occupied the first half of the century and was followed by the line of Renaissance popes more interested in art and letters than in religion. In England the second half of the century saw the Wars of the Roses, which ended in destroying the power of the barons and setting the Tudors on the throne.

Exploration by sea to find a route to the East Indies was very active from 1453 on, and before the end of the century would come the discovery of America, with all its implications for the future. Everywhere there was restless activity and eager curiosity, and nowhere more than in Northern Europe, where it centered itself more especially on religion.

It was in the north in Mainz, Germany, and Haarlem, Holland, that in about 1450 the greatest innovation since the invention of the alphabet was first perfected—the printing press. By 1500 presses had been set up in practically every country of Europe, and it has been estimated that there were about five million books in circulation, in contrast to less than one hundred thousand manuscripts before this time. The discovery of printing had come in answer to the growing demand for books, and in turn it stimulated an ever-greater demand. Within a short time of its invention books were pouring off the presses, and everyone who could read was able to keep in touch with the thoughts and events of the time.

In Germany the general tenor of the publications was religious. Parts of the Bible in translation, then the whole Bible, books of devotion by the mystics, Eckhart, Tauler and Thomas à Kempis, pamphlets on church dogma, attacks on the abuses in the church, classics and some secular books poured out, and at prices so low that they were within reach even of the poor. Schools were improved by having better textbooks, and with reading matter available to all, the desire to read increased. Furthermore, as people read they thought, and with thought came questions.

Was the church they knew the church envisioned by its founders? Were the doctrines they were taught to be found in the Bible? Were seven sacraments essential? What were the actual teachings of the Bible, and why had it been for so long a closed book to the laity? The Reformation had begun some time before the man who finally preached it appeared.

These criticisms, it must be remembered, were not from heretics or unbelievers, but from loyal members and officers of the church. The cry was still for reform within the organization. But Rome, who should have led the way, was more interested in secular than in spiritual matters. The popes and cardinals were bestowing their patronage and attention on arts, literature and building, and were unconcerned with the deep unrest in the more remote reaches of their heritage.

By the opening of the sixteenth century scholars like Reuchlin, Colet, More and the great Erasmus had entered the discussion, striving by diatribe, reason, allegory, satire and humor to rouse the church to a recognition and correction of the abuses which seemed to grow more flagrant daily. But by this time it was in any event too late, for a spark was set to the tinder which started the flame of something nearer a revolution than a reformation, and Martin Luther set the spark.

Luther and the Reformation

Luther was born at Eisleben, Germany, in 1483, the son of a miner. He went to the university of Erfurt, and in 1505 joined the Augustinian order of friars and shortly after was ordained priest. He then taught for some years in Wittenberg. At this time Pope Leo X was building the great cathedral of St. Peter's in Rome and found himself in need of funds to complete the work. To meet the need he instituted a special sale of indulgences. The theory of the indulgence was that the saints had by their lives and martyrdom acquired an extra supply of merit which the pope could sell for the remission of sins. The more a man paid the more merit he received, so that even sins not yet committed could be paid for at a sufficiently high price.

In some ways Leo's procedure was not unlike Urban's when he promised forgiveness of sins to all who went on a crusade. The theory was the same in both instances. But the temper of the times had changed and Tetzel, the Dominican friar who sold the indulgences, was not as good a salesman as Peter the Hermit. Furthermore, it was not bravery and a sense of adventure that Leo drew upon, but the purse strings. To the very realistic and hardheaded German burgher the whole project looked like a scheme for drawing off his hard-earned German money for foreigners.

Luther was the spokesman for all these comfortable burghers as well as for his own conscience when he denounced the sale of indulgences, and nailed on the church door (the public bulletin board of the day) his ninety-five theses against the evil practices current in the church. Tetzel was mobbed and his sales fell off to such a degree that the church authorities were alarmed and summoned Luther to the chapter of the Augustinian order. Here he was asked to retract his theses, but this he refused to do.

All Germany by now was in an uproar, with princes and people taking sides for and against the rebellious friar. Fortunately he had an influential patron, Frederick the Wise, Elector of Saxony, who protected him during the troubled years that followed. At one time he even kept Luther in hiding for a year, and it was during these months that the reformer made his translation of the Bible, which became the standard German text.

It is pretty clear that Luther at first had no idea of going so far as to break away from the Catholic Church. Like Wycliffe, More and Erasmus, he sought at first to do away with the corruption that all good churchmen deplored, to restore the Bible to the people, in fact to break down the "mystery" and bring back religion. Wycliffe came too early, Erasmus was too moderate to force matters to an issue. Nor did Erasmus with his exquisite Latin and indirect attack appeal to the man on the street as did Luther, who spoke a forceful and often vituperative German which all could understand. It was the German that he used which became the modern norm of the German language. Luther typified the north's intense seriousness and desire for truth, and voiced the antagonism to Rome which in Germany was becoming evident in all classes.

In the dispute which followed his first protest, and as he began to clarify and expand his views, he found himself increasingly in disagreement with the church. From his profound study of the Epistles of St. Paul he became convinced that man was justified by faith, whereas the church demanded works as represented by the sacraments. Luther attacked the sacraments and reduced them from the seven required by the church to three, which he said were prescribed in the Gospels—baptism, communion and penance (the last according to Matthew 16:19 and John 20:23); and although he later omitted penance as a sacrament, he always regarded it as especially sacred. He opposed the celibacy of the clergy, himself left the monastery and married a recusant nun. Each step led on to the next until his stand was so far from that of the established faith that any return or even compromise was impossible.

Germany at that time was still divided into scores of small states, each ruled by a duke or king who owed allegiance to the emperor of the so-called Holy Roman Empire. This was composed primarily of Austria, Bohemia, and the German States, but claimed and at times actually attained an even wider scope. The German princes each possessed a certain sovereignty in his own right and the only thing which held them together, outside of the emperor's authority, was a common language and origin.

As the protest against Catholicism grew and Lutheranism became a distinct sect, some of the princes adopted the new faith, some remained Catholic. The church called general councils, threatened and pled with the heretics, but the breach would not heal. Indeed the heresy spread into Holland, England and Scandinavia, and from it grew new heresies with alarming rapidity. Even Luther was appalled at the Anabaptists, who carried his principles to the lengths of communism; and the revolt of the peasants, who took church reform as a justification for social and economic changes, roused him to violent protest.

To the Protestants, as the reformers came to be called after 1529, tolerance was as foreign as to the Catholics, and Luther's attack on the extremists was bitter and savage, encouraging the stamping out of revolt by the severest means. From this time on Lutheranism became more especially the religion of the upper and middle classes while the poor took up simpler creeds.

In 1555 at Augsburg a tentative peace was made by which each prince was to decide the religion for his state. It was nearly a hundred years later that the decision was made final, but through all the wars and oppressions of the century the same pattern held. Northern Germany, Holland, and Scandinavia remained Protestant, while most of southern Germany and Belgium stayed in the Catholic fold.

Luther was not alone in his protest. In Switzerland, the little independent federation in the Alps, Zwingli in 1520 introduced even more radical reforms and succeeded in setting up a church in Zurich which soon spread through a large part of the country. Zwingli's influence, however, was not as far-reaching as that of the third great reformer of the day, Calvin. John Calvin (1509-1564) was French, and his mind worked with the logical clarity for which the French are famous. His book, *Institutes of the Christian Religion,* was as important for the development of Protestantism as was St. Thomas Aquinas' *Summa Theologica* for the Roman Catholic Church. Forced on account of his views to leave France, Calvin went to Geneva, where he eventually set up a theocracy strictly conforming to Old Testament doctrines and prescribing every minute detail of daily life. Tolerance was not a part of any of the reform doctrines.

Calvanism was the direct ancestor of Presbyterianism. It organized the church as far as possible according to the plan of the early church, accepted only two sacraments, baptism and communion, and preached predestination, by which only those chosen by God would be saved. This, of course, while proving the omniscience of God, denied free will to man. The chief end of man, according to Calvin, was not to seek salvation, since it was not in his power to attain it. Man's only and entire function was to know God and glorify Him.

The Counter Reformation

The Catholic Church, however, was not idle during these years of revolt and apostasy. At the Council of Trent (1545-1563), as at earlier councils, numerous attempts were made to correct abuses and so restore the failing prestige and power of the church. In addition to the decrees which were passed, persecution of heresy on a scale hitherto unheard of took place. The Spanish Inquisition, a much more terrible organization than the Roman, spread from Spain into other parts of Europe and burning for heresy not of single persons, but often of a large number at once became a commonplace. But it was not the terrorism that halted the spread of Protestantism so much as the real and very sincere improvement in the standards and officials of the church; and the great and far-reaching missionary efforts of the Jesuits.

This brotherhood, called the Company of Jesus, was organized and led by a Spaniard, Ignatius Loyola (1493-1556). Loyola had been a soldier in his youth, and organized his company along strictly military lines, making unquestioning obedience and rigid self-control obligatory on all who joined it. His followers went everywhere, teaching and organizing schools, which became so famous for their pedagogical methods that they were soon the most popular in Europe and attended even by Protestants.

Within some fifty years after the rise of Lutheranism the Roman Catholic Church was once more firmly established; Protestantism was contained, and its spread into other countries of Europe prevented.

Before turning to the English Reformation it is necessary here to take up a line of historical and religious development which went on parallel to the development of Christianity, affected by it and affecting it, and yet almost like the history of a different land.

The Jews in Christendom up to Reformation Times

During the early days of the Roman Empire the Jews were tolerated and even accepted. Rome and its provinces were thronged with newcomers from the Orient, many of whom had been given citizenship, and some of the most highly esteemed and public-spirited of these were Jews. Their high moral tone and devoted family life was something that a Roman of the old school could understand and admire. In Spain especially the Jews flourished. There they had beautiful estates and felt themselves a part of the community, enjoying a freedom and scope of action which they had nowhere else.

As Christianity spread in Europe, life grew harder for the Jews. Feudal tenure of land was not possible for them, partly because they were unable to fulfill the military requirements, and partly because, as I said at an earlier point, they were different and unable to mix easily with the invading barbarians. It is interesting to observe that for a long time their position in Spain and Italy was better than in the north. Barred therefore from land tenure (the chief means of livelihood in feudal France, Germany or England), barred also for religious reasons from membership in the artisan guilds and thus barred from the crafts and skilled trades, shut off from social and political life in a world where the Christian faith was fast becoming obligatory, the Jews were forced into peddling and moneylending. Usury was proscribed for Christians, but even in those days, when barter was the rule and commerce almost nonexistent, there were times when money was necessary, and the Jews, with their international family connections, soon became the bankers and moneylenders of the world. Kings took them under their special protection, since from them alone could they get money for their eternal warfare.

The lot of the Jews for some centuries was probably in many ways better than that of most of the Gentiles of Europe. Many of them were wealthy, in a world of desperate poverty; they traveled far and wide and had contacts everywhere at a time when life for most men was narrow and confined; though subject to demands for money which often amounted to confiscation, they had no feudal services to perform, no exorbitant feudal dues to pay; they were to a large degree educated and informed in a world of ignorance. Many of the great scholars of the time were Jews, and their work together with that of the Arabs had much to do with the later rise of humanism in Europe.

But with the Crusades and the rise of trade the whole situation changed. Before starting out for Palestine many of the crusaders had raised funds by borrowing from the Jews, and upon their return they turned upon their erstwhile benefactors as profiteers. Moreover, with the development of the cities and their markets and fairs, the peddler's services were less in demand. To the Jews, however, most ruinous of all was the revival of money exchange, because with it the practice of banking and lending money on interest became usual even among the Gentiles, and the need of the body politic for Jewish lenders was gone. Furthermore, as nationalism increased in this new moneyed age, the kings were able to tax instead of borrowing from the Jews, and so no longer gave them protection.

The Jew found himself without roots in the lands of his adoption, with no justification for remaining, and with no homeland to return to. Because of his wealth, which it was easy to explain to the ignorant had been dishonestly acquired, he soon became an object of envy and suspicion. No laws protected him, and it was easy for anyone who had a real or imaginary grievance against a Jew to stir up popular prejudice against him. He was an infidel, closely related to the Arabs against whom the Crusades had been organized. The church taught that it was the Jews who had crucified Jesus—that Jesus himself was a Jew was forgotten, in fact may never have been known to much of the public of the time. The Jews, who actually were one of the first people to do away with human sacrifice, and to whom blood was distasteful, were accused of murdering Christian children for sacrifice at their feasts. The very learning and education for which the Jew was noted, and which made him an asset to any community of culture, made him suspect in a world where only clerics were able to read. The Jew was accused of being a wizard and his books were books of black magic.

Under such conditions he was hounded from place to place, an outlaw, with every man's hand against him. Here and there pogroms were instituted and large numbers of Jews of all ages and sexes cruelly massacred. In 1290 England expelled the Jews, in 1394 France expelled them. In 1492 Spain, having recaptured and consolidated the Iberian Peninsula, drove out all Moors and Jews, and in 1497 Portugal followed suit. One of the most frightful exhibitions of mob madness occurred at the time of the Black Death which swept over Europe in 1348 and 1349. The Black Death was probably an epidemic of the bubonic plague which today is known to be carried by rats through fleas which harbor the germs. But in an age when germs were unknown it was the Jews who were accused of bringing on the misfortune.

The horrors which ensued were unbelievable. The pope, the emperor, even some city officials tried in vain to stem the tide and prevent the mob violence which, especially in Germany and Spain, burned alive and tortured hundreds and thousands of Jews. It is interesting to note that all the wealth of these victims was then confiscated and all records of Gentile indebtedness were destroyed.

Conditions were always worst in Germany and Central Europe because the Jews who were expelled from France and England and later Spain had no other place of refuge and, as city dwellers after centuries of commercial life, naturally congregated in the cities. Instinctively good businessmen, since for centuries all their energies had been channeled in that one direction, they were frequently more successful than their Gentile competitors, still comparatively new to the mechanism of money and exchange. Even without the special incentive of the plague and superstitious fear to incite the people to violence, feeling ran so high that special sections of the cities had to be told off for the Jews to live in, and gates were set up that could be locked at night, not to keep the Jews in so much as to keep marauders out.

In Holland, where many of the old Sephardic Jews from Spain had settled, there was less persecution. In England the Jews were readmitted in 1655 and in 1685 given freedom to practise their religion. In Italy, always more cosmopolitan than the north, there was comparatively little persecution and among the scholars and cultured classes the Jews were accepted as valuable and important coadjutors in the work of finding and translating old manuscripts. It is worthy of note here that without a knowledge of Hebrew, which had to be learned from the Jews, the translation of the Old Testament from the original could never have been made. And it was this translation which was an important factor in the Reformation.

Through all these centuries Hebrew scholarship had continued its work of collecting and studying the ancient manuscripts. All the oral tradition which had come down from the remote past by word of mouth had been painstakingly gathered, sorted, and with the comment and commentary of succeeding generations made into the Talmud, second only to the Old Testament in sacred value among the Jews. The Talmud was finally completed by the end of the fifth century A.D. It was the great scholar, Maimonides, who in the twelfth century clarified and codified the sacred book.

In Judaism as in Christianity there was change and development, and the Jewish faith today is probably as far removed from the faith of Bible times as is Christianity from the primitive church of the first century. Much of the change and development took place during these centuries of persistent persecution and under the constant threat of expulsion, which made life both precarious and wretched.

The Reformation in England

For the main roots of religious development in the United States, we must now leave the continent of Europe and follow the course of events in England. Whether her geographical position, cut off by the Channel from the continent of Europe, was responsible for the molding of English history along its unique channels, it is hard to say. Perhaps the character of the English people had something to do with it, and again perhaps their character was the result of isolation. Certainly as far back as history goes the island has held a singular position, almost as though it were a continent in itself. We have seen that the early church had become independently rooted in the western section of the British Isles before Gregory sent his missionaries to convert the Anglo-Saxon states in the south and east. Even after the church of Rome was accepted as the church of England at the Synod of Whitby, 664, the papal power was unable to assert itself in a land so remote and isolated, and England for another four centuries was too fully occupied with her own affairs to be much concerned with the pope in faraway Rome.

When, in 1066, the Normans conquered England and brought her into contact with European politics and warfare, conflict with Rome started almost immediately and increased in vigor until the final break came in the reign of Henry VIII nearly five centuries later.

A strong line of kings and freedom from invasion made a nation of England while the Continent was still a mass of warring states. Resentment of outside interference was strong, and a struggle between king and pope soon arose over the pope's claims to make appointments to English sees. With this was of course connected the question of moneys which Rome so constantly demanded. Neither the king nor later the people as represented in Parliament, wished to see so much English gold taken out of the country, and English history is full of acts restricting the financial demands of the church.

During the Hundred Years' War, which lasted off and on from about 1337 to 1453, the English people achieved a large measure of self-government through Parliament, and the cities learned to assert themselves by granting or withholding money necessary for the king's wars. A little later the internal conflict of the Wars of the Roses destroyed the power and wealth of the nobles and paved the way for the rise of a wealthy and informed middle class which was henceforth to be the representative group in England. During these centuries there was an increasing undercurrent of dissatisfaction among the people, who seem to have become articulate singularly early, perhaps as a result of the degree of self-government which they had achieved.

The complaints were by no means entirely of kings and nobles. In the writings of Langland, Chaucer, Gower, and the preaching of Wycliffe and the Lollards may be found together with laments over the misery of the neglected poor, criticisms of the extravagance and corruption of the church and the ignorance and licentiousness of the clergy. The Paston Letters, the correspondence of a middle-class family in the fifteenth century, show the conditions of England very clearly, and are an example of the high degree of culture and information and of independent thought among commoners in England a century and more before Luther's day.

In this same century, besides Wycliffe's translation of the Bible—which in spite of every effort at suppression had made its way into many households—there was in use a book of hours and occasional devotions, written in English and called the *English Prymer,* for the private devotion of the people. Though the actual Reformation came later in England than on the Continent, the country had been prepared for it long generations before the break came. Perhaps when it finally rose, the very gradualness of its development made it less of a cataclysm in England that it had been across the Channel.

It was after the old feudal nobility of England was destroyed by the Wars of the Roses that the new middle class came to power with the Tudor kings. Business and commerce arose, sheep growing increased to supply wool for England's staple export, and both ready money and land for grazing became essential to prosperity. Much of the land and great wealth were in the hands of the church, which had extensive holdings in England as on the Continent, and king and subjects looked on it with envy.

There seemed, however, no prospect of an immediate change until some years after Henry VIII came to the throne. However much he might wish for the broad acres held by the abbeys and monasteries, he was too devout a Catholic to steal them from the church. Seeping even into England, Luther's preaching shocked Henry to such a degree that in 1521 he wrote a Defense of the Seven Sacraments, which earned for him the title of Defender of the Faith from the pope.

Humanism had its exponents in England at this time, and the writings and teachings of Colet and More show an enlightened interest in religious reform within the church, but no desire for change in doctrine or in allegiance to Rome. Erasmus, also on the moderate and conservative side in the religious struggle raging on the Continent, found the English point of view so congenial that he spent some years as professor of Greek at Cambridge. The king was himself a man of some learning and encouraged thought and expression as long as it was not out-and-out heresy.

As time passed, however, and no heir to the throne of England was born, Henry began to consider ways and means to rid himself of his wife, Catherine of Aragon, and marry someone who would give him the very necessary son which all England wanted. Catherine had been the widow of his brother Arthur, and church law did not permit marriage with a deceased brother's wife. The pope had given a special dispensation in this case, but none the less Henry appealed to him to annul the marriage on the grounds that the dispensation should never have been given. The pope, fearing the Emperor Charles, nephew of Catherine, refused to do so.

It is not possible here to follow the details of the case, which became a *cause célèbre* in all Europe. In the end Henry threw off the pope's sovereignty, declared himself the head of the English Church, and so secured the divorce from Catherine and married Anne Boleyn.

There was not much objection to the break with Rome from a nation whose training and national development had long been tending in that direction. The move was further popularized when Henry disestablished the monasteries and redistributed their land and wealth where he felt they would do his cause most good. Priests and bishops retained their benefices, only transferring their allegiance from the pope to the king. By 1536 the English Church was separate from Rome and reorganized as the national church of England, with the king as its head.

In doctrine Henry permitted no changes, but none the less some of his acts prepared the way for such changes in the future. In 1543 the Bible in English translation was ordered set up in the churches where it was easily available to the public, and a chapter was ordered read without exposition every Sunday. One of the litanies was also translated for the use of the people.

Even at this time there were at work in the land Lutheran, Zwinglian, Calvinistic and Anabaptist influences, but the great mass of the people, the whole body of clergy and the king himself were stanchly Catholic in doctrine, though not in allegiance.

In the reign of Edward VI the Protestant element in England came to the fore. Somerset, who was regent for the boy king, was an ardent Protestant and so by now was Archbishop Cranmer, who had helped Henry break away from Rome. There was some purification of the churches, in which images, roods, and stained-glass windows were destroyed. These were depredations of extremists, not popular in the countryside, but an expression of a militant Protestantism developing in the towns. Next the liturgy was translated into English for use in the churches. This was the work of Cranmer, who adapted the Roman missal and breviary and by the beauty of his English style made of the English Prayer Book one of the great classics of literature. In 1552 the Prayer Book was revised and made really Protestant, the Canon Law reformed, and forty-two articles of religion published.

England must have been ripe for Protestantism, for when Edward died after six years and Mary came to the throne, she was unable, despite her fanatical Catholicism, to return the English church to the fold of Rome. All in all she executed about three hundred Protestants, a record so high in contrast to England's usual moderation, that she became known to posterity as Bloody Mary.

It remained for Elizabeth (1558-1603) finally to establish Protestantism on a firm and lasting basis. She fell heir to a kingdom weakened and impoverished by two decades of unwise rule. Civil war or unrest and discontent in the land might be fatal in face of the outspoken hostility of Spain. The church which she set up was Protestant, but moderate enough to appeal to the great majority who were neither violently Catholic nor fanatically Puritan. Conformity and attendance at church she demanded, but the fine for nonattendance was not excessive, and there was no persecution for religious convictions. The prayer book of Edward's time was again changed to suit a wider group, the forty-two articles were changed to thirty-nine and in 1571 settled in the final form in which they stand today. Two sacraments—baptism and communion—were recognized, and communion was administered in both forms. The Church continued and has always continued to consider itself part of the Catholic, or universal, church, because according to tradition the line of succession of the bishops of the English, as of the Roman and Eastern Churches, has been unbroken, bishop having been consecrated by bishop since the earliest bishops were consecrated by the Apostles. This is the theory of the apostolic succession.

Meanwhile, under the leadership of a stern and devout Calvinist, John Knox, a very much stricter and more radical form of Protestantism was growing up in Scotland, not yet united with her southern neighbor. After the expulsion of Mary Queen of Scots, the Kingdom (like Geneva) had become virtually a theocracy, in this case ruled by Knox as vicegerent of God and regent for the infant king.

When in 1603 the infant king, James VI of Scotland, succeeded Elizabeth as James I of England, many Scotch Presbyterians accompanied him to London, bringing with them the strict and uncompromising faith of Calvin and Knox and so adding to the growing Puritan element already existing in England. James himself, as head of the English Church, was of course obliged to conform to its doctrine and practice. He was a stupid and opinionated pedant with an exaggerated sense of his own importance and soon found himself in conflict with his new subjects.

The Reformation had not brought peace into the world, because as it developed it subdivided into more and more sects. There were as many shades of religious difference as there were kinds of people and the differences seemed more important than the likenesses. That people could vary in belief and still live in amity was unthought of. Uniformity was required and since, following in Rome's foosteps, most churches were state churches, supported by taxes on the whole nation, no independent organization could long survive even if its existence had been tolerated by public opinion and the ruling powers.

In England the main division was into Anglicans, Puritans and Independents. Elizabeth, partly by her personal popularity and partly by careful diplomacy, had managed through most of her reign to impose conformity on Anglicans and Puritans, but even Elizabeth could not force the radical left-wing Independents into line. With James's accession the middle- and right-wing Puritans and Anglicans tended to fall apart, and a struggle between these two forces began which was to last another century. Each way of religious thought proposed to make itself the established faith and force the other into its ranks, and in the back of everyone's mind was the fear of a return of Catholicism, a fear which deepened when James's son, Charles, married a French Catholic wife, and the Anglican Church began to emphasize ritual.

Two events of James's reign were of importance in their effect on the future. During the years since Luther's great translation of the Bible into German (1522-1534), many translations had been made, one for nearly every country of Western Europe. Among the English versions, that of Tyndale and Coverdale appeared in 1535, the Great Bible in 1539, the Geneva Bible in 1560, the Bishop's Bible in 1568, and the Catholic or Douai version in 1582, the latter still the authorized version for the Roman Catholic Church in England. It was in James I's reign that the greatest translation in any tongue, except perhaps Luther's, was made in England. It was really a careful revision of previous texts, and was the work of many men comparing and annotating over a period of years. In 1611 this authorized, or King James, version was at last completed, and has remained one of the great English classics and the preferred text to this day. An authoritative edition of the Bible, thus made available to everyone, necessarily stimulated further interest in religion and a greater independence of thought and inquiry.

The Transplantation to America

It was in James's reign too that the New World, so long talked of by travelers and adventurers, was at last open to settlement by the peoples of northwestern Europe. The first contacts between the Old World and the New had been made under the Spanish flag, and the first colonization had been by Spaniards, in the Caribbean and in Mexico, Central America and Peru. The colonists had brought their religion with them, and Roman Catholicism remains today the leading faith of the Americas south of the Rio Grande.

These early Spanish conquistadors found a barbarian world in varying stages of culture and religious development. The Aztecs had organized the peoples around their capital in a military state, with a state religion in which human sacrifice played a prominent part. In Peru the state religion was a highly developed sun worship with the reigning Inca as the earthly representative of the god. The sudden impact of the better equipped and more highly organized peoples of Christendom inevitably took the form of conquest, in which the old barbarian culture was swept away and the barbarian religions abruptly cut off in their development and submerged.

North of the Rio Grande, America was generally thinly populated by hunting tribes to whom agriculture was a minor means of eking out the food supply. Except among the pueblos of our own Southwest, this huge territory had none of the centers of population, the masonry structures and the barbarian pomp which the Spaniards found in Mexico and Peru, and did not attract the conquistadors, although in 1540 Coronado led an expedition to the pueblos and even penetrated as far as modern Kansas. It remained for the peoples of northwestern Europe to settle the northern part of North America, and to give it the religious impress of their own varying faiths.

Early in the history of colonization, the French came to Canada and spread into the upper Mississippi Valley, until in 1763 the French and Indian War resulted in the cession of the territory to Britain. Today French is still the language, and Roman Catholicism the faith, of eastern Canada. For the United States, however, it is the long British colonization and its strong religious impulses which have the greatest meaning for the transplantation of Old World religions to American soil.

During the sixteenth century England had been too busy fighting Spain and establishing her own sea power to have any energy or money left for colonizing the lands she held in the New World. In 1607, however, the first successful colony of English settlers was made in Jamestown, Virginia. Before long the new frontier would be the means of escape to freedom for all the outlaws from the Established Church and for victims of religious persecution all over the world.

In 1567, during the reign of Elizabeth, a group of the radical thinkers, or Independents, were beginning to organize in separate congregations under the leadership of Robert

Brown. By the end of the century there were probably as many as twenty thousand of these left-wingers of Protestantism, and feeling against them had risen so high that in 1608 a large number of them fled to Holland, the only country where there was no religious persecution.

In time they established themselves at Leyden, where they built a church. As their children grew up these transplanted Englishmen began to be concerned about the future. They did not wish their children to become Dutch, nor did they approve of the very lax observance of the Sabbath which was prevalent in Holland. Sabbath observance was one of the strictest rules of both Calvinists and Independents, and was often more emphasized among them than even in the Jewish religion, which was their model. When the exiles in Holland heard of the successful settlement in Virginia, they felt that a solution for their difficulties had been found.

It was some years before they were able to gather the money and necessary equipment for such a venture, and in the end it was only a small proportion of the Leyden congregation that emigrated. In September, 1620, after overcoming many obstacles, the little band of Pilgrims set sail for the New World in the *Mayflower,* and eventually landed in Plymouth, Massachusetts, where they fondly hoped that they would be free from religious conflict. From this time on, up to modern days, America has been regarded as a haven for the persecuted minorities of the world.

It was by no means such a haven at once. Virginia, for example, accepted the Established Church of England and for a long time did not willingly receive either Puritans or Catholics. In fact at a later time in her colonial life she expelled them from her borders. The Pilgrims too ran into difficulties in their chosen refuge. For conditions grew worse in England, and the struggle for control between Anglicans and Puritans set in, which was to sway back and forth until the end of the century. In the time of Charles I when the Church of England under the leadership of Archbishop Laud became very high and ritualistic, and life grew intolerable for the Low-Church nonconformists, the Puritans began to migrate to America and founded the Massachusetts Bay Colony, not far from the Pilgrim Colony at Plymouth.

The Puritans were strongly Calvinistic, tending toward Presbyterianism. In some respects their development was unique. They based their faith on the Old Testament, and made of it a self-denying ordinance that reduced life to an uncompromising and joyless fulfillment of duty. Government and religion were united, so that any escape from their narrow view of life was impossible. More numerous and better organized than the Pilgrims, they were able eventually to absorb the smaller group and impose their way of life upon them.

At first their object was not to leave, but to purify the Anglican Church of what they considered its papist tendencies. But as the Anglican Church after its temporary eclipse under Cromwell (1648-1660) grew more ritualistic instead of less, and the powers of the bishops increased, the colonists gave up the effort to purify from within and threw off all allegiance to the mother church. Their position was further strengthened by the addition to their ranks of large numbers of refugees from the Cromwellian and Independent parties after the restoration of Charles II to the English throne.

In spite of their own tragic experiences of the past, there was no tolerance of divergent opinion among the Puritans. So long, however, as there remained frontiers, empty lands to move to, the dissenter could still move on and found another settlement to suit himself. Pioneer life was not so easy that a few hardships more or less mattered much. One by one the nonconforming and independent spirits moved out and established themselves elsewhere.

One of the most famous and unusual of these dissenters was Roger Williams. He asked, not for religious tolerance, but for religious freedom, a state of society which even now we see but dimly as a thing to be desired and worked for. He moved through the trackless wilderness to what is now Rhode Island, and the church which he there founded became the ancester of the Baptist Church today. In Rhode Island real religious freedom was first practised.

Meanwhile the Puritans in Massachusetts were being affected by contact with the more liberal Pilgrims, and the Presbyterian tendencies were gradually modified. In time Congregationalism, a milder form of Calvinism, became the prevailing denomination. Church and state were slowly separated, and it was left to each congregation to choose its own form of worship. In the eighteenth century one group went so far as to deny the divinity of Christ and so founded Unitarianism, which gradually spread and finally came to share Massachusetts and much of the rest of New England with Congregationalism. However, this development was late and the organization of Unitarianism in its final form did not really emerge until the early nineteenth century.

Another group of refugees from England were members of the Society of Friends, commonly called Quakers. They were founded in England by George Fox, who taught that God through His spirit acted directly upon His believers, and that man had but to keep an open mind and act as the spirit directed. Excluded from citizenship in England, some of the Quakers sought refuge in Boston. There violent persecution ensued. One of the English Quakers, William Penn, purchased a grant of land in America and in 1681 set up a refuge for his coreligionists, who fled there in great numbers, founding the colony of Pennsylvania.

The Quakers, pacifists by conviction, were comparatively tolerant and, having a large grant of land, welcomed believers of other creeds. In 1683 the Mennonites, one of the Anabaptist sects, fleeing persecution in Germany, built their first church in Germantown, near Philadelphia. Later they congregated further west and built up a thriving community near Lancaster, Pennsylvania. From there they branched out into other sections of the country and in time became famous for their simplicity of living and their skill in agriculture and cattle breeding.

In 1718 Pennsylvania also received a large group of Scotch-Irish immigrants from Ulster, who settled among the Alleghenies. It was through them that the Presbyterian Church was finally brought to this country. From there it spread across Pennsylvania into New Jersey and New York, finally even threatening the hold of Congregationalism in New England.

New York was settled by the Dutch and so became a stronghold of the Dutch Reformed Church, a modified Calvinism. The oldest parish in this country is the Dutch Reformed Collegiate Church in New York City, founded in 1638. Among the settlers from Holland there were some Lutherans, but owing to the intolerance of the Reformed Church they were unable to worship freely until the English took over New Amsterdam in 1664, renaming it New York. In the new colony no effort was made to turn out the original settlers, nor to interfere with their various faiths. Dutch Reformed, Lutheran, and Church of England flourished side by side.

As early as 1638 Swedish Lutherans were colonizing New Sweden, later Delaware, but after the English took over the region most of these joined the Church of England. Lutheran refugees from Salzburg in Austria settled in Georgia in 1734, but most of them were killed or dispersed when the American Revolution broke out. By far the largest number of Lutherans during colonial times settled in eastern Pennsylvania. They later became the first organized group under Henry Melchior Mühlenberg, who founded a synod in Philadelphia in 1748 and began to draw the scattered groups of colonial Lutherans into a united body.

Maryland was set up as a refuge for Roman Catholics,

who were increasingly unpopular in England. As the Calvinists grew stronger during the reigns of James I and Charles I, feeling against the Catholics also intensified. They were prohibited from holding office or taking any part in political life and so held the anomalous position of being merely tolerated in their own country, with no share in running it. George Calvert, later Lord Baltimore, and his son Cecilius were able to obtain a grant of land in America, and there in 1634 they started the colony of Maryland, which was to be free from religious contention, a place where Roman Catholic and Protestant could live together in peace and amity. True, the terms of the charter were not at all times carried out, and there was trouble in the years that followed, but the fact that Calvert envisioned a land where Roman Catholic and Protestant might live together without friction was a stride forward.

North and South Carolina were, like Virginia, largely Church of England. Georgia, the last of the colonies to be founded (1732), was the project of a philanthropist, Oglethorpe, who made of it a refuge for men imprisoned for debt in English jails. Besides these the settlers included younger sons, adventurers and land-hungry men from South Carolina. The basis of the settlement was not religious, but there was a large stratum of Anglicans who were most in evidence.

In England, meanwhile, after the struggle between Anglicans and Puritans had subsided and the threat of Catholicism under the later Stuarts had been resolved by the expulsion of James II and the succession of the Protestant monarchs, William and Mary, Anne and the Hanoverians, religious fervor had cooled. Commerce and the first beginnings of industry began to absorb the attention of the nation. Life among the rich and prosperous grew increasingly extravagant and frivolous, among the poor it became unbelievably sordid and hopeless. The invention of gin made hard liquor available to even the poor, for it was very cheap, and soon took the place of ale, which had hitherto been the accustomed drink for the working class. In London the death rate during the height of the gin era (1740-1742) was twice the birth rate, and statistics in other cities, rapidly becoming crowded by the demand for cheap labor, were not much better.

The churches—both the Anglican, or Established, and the nonconformist, or dissenting, chapels which by now had come to be tolerated—seemed sunk in a kind of lethargy and did little or nothing to alleviate conditions. Work among the poor and ignorant was as yet an untried field. The duties of the clergyman or minister were to preach on Sunday, administer the sacraments, and visit the members of the parish. Social service, which later was to become a recognized part of the duties of the church, was unknown. Before the Reformation, when everyone belonged to one faith, the priest's duties were clear. All were members of his flock, and if he was a good priest he cared for them. Even after the Reformation, in an economy still agricultural and retaining part of the heritage of feudal times, the care of the poor and sick was the responsibility of the squire or landholder who looked after his tenants. But with the migration of country folk to the cities the dislocation of population found the social structure unprepared to deal with the situation, and greater and greater masses of people were deprived of any refuge or help in time of need.

Early in the eighteenth century some person or group here and there began to feel the need for a more living and personal religion, and signs of an awakening sense of responsibility for others were evident in the writings of such men as Fielding and Smollett, in the pictures of Hogarth, in the setting up of a foundling hospital, in Oglethorpe's efforts to do away with debtors' prisons, and in the founding of charity schools. "Methodism" as a way of life was older than the founders of the Methodist Church, and the Wesley boys were brought up in a home which practised self-discipline and work for others. It was a "method" of religious life which had so profound an effect on John and Charles Wesley that they carried the seeds of it with them to Oxford, and started a movement which was to affect not only England, but also the New World, and stimulate the Protestant churches everywhere into a new burst of energy—a new conception of the function of the church.

As usual the movement was not originally designed to break away from the Established Church. It was a "method of life" which emphasized regular and systematic prayer, and attendance at the sacrament and at church; planned reading and study; in short, an organizing of life to the ends of righteousness. Hence the name "Methodism," given as a joke, but accepted by the Wesleys as a name for the new faith which grew out of their preachings. For the Church of England looked with disfavor on the evangelism of John Wesley, and he was soon denied a pulpit and forced to preach in the fields to ever-growing congregations.

The "Society," as it was at first called, was organized in London in 1739, and rapidly gained headway in England, doing a great work, not only in winning converts, but also in inspiring the whole country with a revival of religious feeling. The Methodists were tireless in their work of propagandizing in England and America, and in October, 1768, a Methodist chapel was opened in New York City. It was not until 1771, however, that Francis Asbury, called the "Wesley of America," crossed the Atlantic and began the real organization of the church in America.

In this country the ground was prepared by the increase in religious feeling inspired by the preaching of Jonathan Edwards. The revival of religious fervor which occurred in the colonies in the second quarter of the eighteenth century, and which was at least in part due to Edwards, is known as the Great Awakening. Edwards was a Congregationalist, and was largely responsible for the nullification of the Presbyterian tendencies in Puritanism and the real organization of the

Congregational Church. His preaching was vivid and forceful, filled more with threats to the wicked than with comfort to the good, and he left a mark on the religious life of New England which was visible for generations to come.

By the time of the Revolutionary War and the consequent separation of the colonies from England, most of the creeds of the mother country had taken root in America, as well as one or two from the Continent. The Church of England, known after the American Revolution as the Episcopal Church, together with Roman Catholicism, Presbyterianism, Congregationalism, Unitarianism, Methodism, the Baptist Church, the Society of Friends, the Dutch Reformed, Lutheran and Mennonite churches had all been transplanted and found here a place to expand and develop. The first article of the Bill of Rights appended to the Constitution of the new nation guaranteed not toleration, but absolute freedom of religion to everyone. Small wonder that henceforth, more even than in the past, America should become the haven for all those who were religiously repressed elsewhere, as well as a breeding ground for new denominations.

Almost from the beginning of the settlements the Jews had sought asylum in America, and in nearly every state were to be found members of the unfortunate outcasts from Europe. Many of these early Jewish settlers were absorbed and became important and valuable members of their communities. In 1722 one Judah Monis was an instructor at Harvard, and in 1727 the Jews were naturalized in New York, where they set up their first synagogue in 1730. During the War of Independence they gave great financial aid to the land of their adoption, with which they were now identified.

In Europe their plight had grown worse, and would become even more terrible during the years. Only in England, Holland, and at times France were they tolerated. Though not enviable in the German states, their lot was at least mitigated by the great Jewish scholar Moses Mendelssohn, who translated the Pentateuch into German and brought his people into some cultural contact with the life around them. Elsewhere, and especially in Poland and Russia, their condition was frightful. The ghettos, which had been established for their protection, were crowded and filthy slums, and any popular discontent was easily diverted to an attack on the Jews, conveniently concentrated in one district. At times these attacks were full-scale massacres, called in Russia pogroms. By the opening of the nineteenth century the migrations of remnants to America was already large, and at such times as the great troubles of 1848 it amounted to a mass movement.

Judaism was the twelfth of the major sects existing in America at the time of the Birth of the Nation, and like the other eleven was benefited by the clause in the Bill of Rights which made real freedom one of the fundamental tenets of the land.

Perhaps it was the heady taste of the new freedom, perhaps only the strongly individualistic habit of mind of the Americans, that made for the great diversity of religious opinion which arose in the nineteenth century. Much of this diversity seemed to originate in the stretch of country from northern Vermont across New York State and west to Ohio, and several of the leaders of the new movements were born in Vermont. The region was agricultural, not yet touched by the industrialism which immediately after the Revolution began to spring up along the coast, and the population was of pioneer ancestry. In 1790 came the Dorrilites, in 1800 Winchell with his divining rod, in about 1815 Miller and the Millennianists, still later Davis, the Poughkeepsie seer, and then the Fox sisters and spiritualism. All came out of this "burnt district," as it has been called because so often swept by the fires of religion.

Joseph Smith, the founder of the Latter-day Saints, or Mormons, was also from this region. He was born in Vermont in 1808, but in 1816 his family moved to Palmyra, New York, and it was here that in 1820 he saw the vision of God and the Saviour, and had the revelation of the Book of Mormon. It was some time before Smith was able to gain many followers and the Mormon church was not set up until 1830. Even then its growth was slow until the church moved to Ohio and the Young brothers joined it. Brigham Young, with Joseph Smith, can be regarded as a founder of the faith.

From the outset the Mormons were proselytizers, sending missionaries out into Europe as well as to the States. It was in part this aggressiveness, in part their increasing wealth and prosperity, and in part their doctrine, especially their belief in polygamy, which made them unpopular in every community in which they settled. From Ohio they went to Missouri, from Missouri to Illinois. In Nauvoo, Illinois, the trouble finally came to a head, the Mormons were attacked, and Joseph Smith and his brother imprisoned and murdered. After this the whole church moved west to set up a Mormon state on the frontier, where they could be unmolested.

The story of the trek is one of the most thrilling of the pioneer stories. Six thousand Mormons, men, women and children, carrying their possessions in covered wagons and driving their flocks and herds, traveled for weeks through pathless country infested with wild beasts and hostile Indians until at last they reached Great Salt Lake in Utah. Here they set up their New Zion and literally made the desert blossom like a rose. Their settlement was originally outside the boundaries of the United States, but the Mexican War brought them back under the government. The region was, however, for many years so remote that they were undisturbed, and during that time were able to increase in population and wealth, until Salt Lake City with its gorgeous temple and well-planned and well-kept streets became an outstanding show place in the country.

Another important movement in the country during the early nineteenth century was in the direction of communism. Most of these enterprises were at least tinged with religion, basing their way of life on Bible teaching, and many were importations from Germany. The Ephrata Cloister in Pennsylvania, founded by Beissel, a refugee from Germany, was one such community. Another was founded by Jemima Wilkinson, who was from Rhode Island and set up centers in several parts of the country. Then there were the Rappites, again German, who settled in western Pennsylvania. William Keil followed them, but went farther west to Missouri and thence to Oregon. At Joar, Ohio, there was a group of German Separatists under Bimeler; in Buffalo, New York, later moving to Ohio, the Amana Society established itself; there was Janson at Bishop Hill, Illinois. The country was dotted with attempted ventures in communism. The most successful and enduring of these were the Shaker communities. The founder of the group, Anna Lee Stanley, came from England in about 1774. By 1825 the new sect had at least twenty settlements and a membership of about six thousand. They lived communistically, practised celibacy, avoided ease and luxury, and expressed their religious fervor in dancing which sometimes became so violent as to end in convulsive shaking. It was from this that the name Shaker originated.

Besides the advocates of communal life this period also produced a great many seekers after utopia. The settlements which these men founded were again based on theories, partly religious, partly economic, and socialistic verging to the left. Today they might be classed as ventures in Christian Socialism. There were Hopedale, Fruitlands, Brook Farm, Oneida, all American in origin; and New Harmony and Nashoba, stemming from England.

The communistic settlements were for the most part composed of plain, simple people, inspired by deep faith, but willing also to work with their hands. The utopias were founded largely by intellectuals, imbued with half-baked humanitarian ideas and an incomplete philosophy of life.

The whole trend of the nineteenth century was, however,

foreshadowed in these abortive movements. Man had begun to suspect that faith alone could not save him. He could be devout, go to church, take the sacraments, and yet be found wanting. Duty toward God was only half; the rest of the commandment was duty toward one's neighbor. It was in answer to this need that missionary societies sprang up—not foreign missions only, but home missions. The Methodists, for example, had circuit riders covering all the new territories in the West, men who gave themselves unsparingly to working in trading posts and mining towns. It was in these frontier settlements that the camp meeting originated, later to come back and play a part in the revivals which became so prevalent in the East as well as in the West.

The simple gospel of a plain man who lived two thousand years ago in a remote Jewish town had more to do than we realize with the great movements of the nineteenth century. His teaching is the rock on which abolition of slavery, trade unions, equal rights, socialism and communism are all based.

It was in New England, where American industrialism first developed, that in the early part of the nineteenth century there arose an attempted philosophy of life. Out of Germany came the teachings of the great philosophers, Kant, Fichte, Schelling, Hegel, and influenced by their thought there grew up in Boston and its environs a group of idealists, the Transcendentalists. The movement, to which belonged such men as Alcott (the father of Louisa M. Alcott), Thoreau, Hawthorne, and Emerson, was mystic and idealistic, and, characteristic of its time and place of origin, strongly individualistic. Consciousness, not sense experience, was the basis of the truth it preached. Man's spirit can consciously control his life and development, because man is divine, a part of God.

From this beginning it was not hard to reach the place where the mind of man was the measure of all things, and the material world negligible and, finally, nonexistent.

Mary Baker Eddy was born in 1821 in Concord, New Hampshire. She had a clear and logical mind, and for a woman of that period an excellent education. She was a delicate child, and during girlhood and early womanhood was subject to frequent illness. It was during one of her acute illnesses that she made the discovery that by the use of will and prayer she could at once be relieved from pain, and starting with this premise she built up a religion which became known as Christian Science. In 1896 the First Church of Christ, Scientist, was set up, and immediately began to spread throughout the country. It appealed in especial, not to the poor, but to the well-to-do and educated middle classes, and has continued to make many converts from their ranks. Christian Science and Mormonism are the two large religious sects entirely American in origin.

It would be impossible to consider in detail all the other sects in the United States. In the fourth chapter will be listed those of at least 50,000 membership, together with short outlines of their variations in form and dogma. In the long run it seems as if the variations were of less import than their fundamental identity of purpose. Some people like ritual, some do not; some are inclined toward mysticism, some are matter-of-fact; some like color and emotion, some prefer simplicity and quiet faith. But in the end, religion is a search for God, by which we mean a power greater and better than man, and making for a better world, leading in the end to perfection.

In this short survey of the growth of Western religious thought there is evident almost a regular and persistent cycle from the simple to the elaborate and back to the simple form. Judaism started as a very crude pastoral faith. Over the ages it developed a ritual and became formalized and dogmatic. Primitive Christianity reverted to a simple form, but in the West developed the dogma and ritual of the Roman Church. Again Protestantism returned to the early Christians as models, and stripped the church of much of its form and ceremony, only to develop its own form and to be faced in turn with successive reversions to the early simplicity of the church of Paul and the Apostles.

Each time the schism has caused a reform within the original church, giving it new life and vitality and restoring some of its early ideals. Perhaps schisms are necessary to keep religion alive and healthy. On the other hand, it would seem that the narrow sectarianism practised by so much of the world might give place to real freedom of belief if we could only realize how small the differences really are and how much they merely reflect differences of temperament and background.

The first creature who tremblingly offered a bloody sacrifice to the terrible being who ruled the inexplicable and menacing world was only a short distance in the history of time behind us. In these few millennia, moments in the measurement of the universe, we have made amazing progress. We have even begun to envision freedom of belief. But we have not yet realized that within the limits of that freedom our search is for the same thing, and only the forms are different.

CHAPTER THREE

Common Roots, and Symbols

IN THIS CHAPTER is a selection of material taken from liturgies and hymn collections dating from pre-Reformation times, some, indeed, from pre-Christian times. These are some of the many roots, buried deep in the past, of the religions of the Western world as we know them today. In the hurry and bustle and in the material interests of modern life, roots are too often forgotten or neglected as of no importance. But no tree can grow full and straight and tall without roots; no building can stand without foundations; no child can develop into a mature and well-rounded adult without the stability which a family and home and a knowledge of his relationship to others gives him.

It is well occasionally to become conscious of our common past, and to consider our gradual development. In this way we may gain a fuller realization of the basic unity of the believing world, which, like a family developing in different directions, is still aware of its oneness in background and heritage.

The Ten Commandments, given out according to ancient tradition by Moses, perhaps as early as 1280 B.C., are still the expression of the basic ethics of Jew and Christian alike. From them—the first four expressing duty toward God, the other six duty toward one's neighbor—Hillel and Jesus developed their simplified rules, both versions of the Golden Rule, Hillel's in the form of a prohibition, Jesus' in a positive form. Moses' blessing in the Book of Numbers is used in Hebrew and Christian congregations alike, and is probably one of the most beautiful benedictions known to either creed. The Beatitudes, taken from the Sermon on the Mount, are an expression of Jesus' teaching accepted by all Christendom.

The Shema—the Jewish creed—is acceptable to both Jews and Christians, and the Apostles' and Nicene creeds are used by all the Christian churches. The Athanasian Creed is not properly an ecumenical or general creed. It originated in the Western Church perhaps as early as the sixth century, and was never adopted by the Eastern Church. It is one of the three accepted creeds of the Roman Catholic and Lutheran Churches, and is still retained in the Prayer Book of the Church of England. The Jewish prayer "Grant us Peace," from the morning service for the Sabbath, is of the third century, and one of the loftiest expressions of the ideals of Judaism. St. Chrysostom's prayer came from the early Greek Church, where it was in use in the fifth century. The Te Deum originated in the Western Church at about the same time. The singing of metrical hymns originated in the Eastern Church and was introduced into the west by St. Ambrose, Bishop of Milan, in the late fourth century. Many of his hymns were in praise of the Trinity, due to the fact that they were written when the Arian heresy was at its height, and these hymns were devised to impress the doctrine of the Trinity upon the people.

There are other roots too numerous to mention which go back to the distant past, and join all seekers after God into one company of worshipers.

The Ten Commandments (simple form)

1. Thou shalt have no other gods before me.
2. Thou shalt not make unto thee any graven images.

3. Thou shalt not take the name of the Lord thy God in vain.
4. Remember the sabbath day, to keep it holy.
5. Honor thy father and thy mother.
6. Thou shalt not kill.
7. Thou shalt not commit adultery.
8. Thou shalt not steal.
9. Thou shalt not bear false witness against thy neighbor.
10. Thou shalt not covet.

Exodus 20:3-17

Do not unto others what is hateful to thyself; this is the whole of the law, all the rest is commentary.

Hillel (*c.* 60 B.C.-*c.* A.D. 10)

Whatsoever ye would that men should do to you, do ye even so to them; for this is the law and the prophets.

Jesus (*c.* A.D. 1-*c.* 33)
Matthew 7:12

The Shema, the early Hebrew declaration of faith

Hear, O Israel: the Lord our God, the Lord is one.

Deuteronomy 6:4
(quoted according to the 1917 translation of the Masoretic Text)

The Blessing of Moses

The Lord bless thee and keep thee; the Lord make his face to shine upon thee, and be gracious unto thee: the Lord lift up his countenance upon thee and give thee peace.

Numbers 6:24-26

The Book of Psalms

(A hymnbook of Jews and Christians alike, too long for entire inclusion here, but to be found in the Holy Scriptures of both faiths.)

SELECTED PSALMS

Psalm 1

Blessed *is* the man that walketh not in the counsel of the ungodly, nor standeth in the way of sinners, nor sitteth in the seat of the scornful.

2 But his delight *is* in the law of the LORD; and in his law doth he meditate day and night.

3 And he shall be like a tree planted by the rivers of water, that bringeth forth his fruit in his season; his leaf also shall not wither; and whatsoever he doeth shall prosper.

4 The ungodly *are* not so: but *are* like the chaff which the wind driveth away.

5 Therefore the ungodly shall not stand in the judgment, nor sinners in the congregation of the righteous.

6 For the LORD knoweth the way of the righteous: but the way of the ungodly shall perish.

Psalm 19

The heavens declare the glory of God; and the firmament sheweth his handywork.

2 Day unto day uttereth speech, and night unto night sheweth knowledge.

3 *There is* no speech nor language, *where* their voice is not heard.

4 Their line is gone out through all the earth, and their words to the end of the world. In them hath he set a tabernacle for the sun,

5 Which *is* as a bridegroom coming out of his chamber, *and* rejoiceth as a strong man to run a race.

6 His going forth *is* from the end of the heaven, and his circuit unto the ends of it: and there is nothing hid from the heat thereof.

7 The law of the LORD *is* perfect, converting the soul: the testimony of the LORD *is* sure, making wise the simple.

8 The statutes of the LORD *are* right, rejoicing the heart: the commandment of the LORD *is* pure, enlightening the eyes.

9 The fear of the LORD *is* clean, enduring for ever: the judgments of the LORD *are* true *and* righteous altogether.

10 More to be desired *are they* than gold, yea, than much fine gold: sweeter also than honey and the honeycomb.

11 Moreover by them is thy servant warned: *and* in keeping of them *there is* great reward.

12 Who can understand *his* errors? cleanse thou me from secret *faults*.

13 Keep back thy servant also from presumptuous *sins;* let them not have dominion over me: then shall I be upright, and I shall be innocent from the great transgression.

14 Let the words of my mouth, and the meditation of my heart, be acceptable in thy sight, O LORD, my strength, and my redeemer.

Psalm 23

The LORD *is* my shepherd; I shall not want.

2 He maketh me to lie down in green pastures: he leadeth me beside the still waters.

3 He restoreth my soul: he leadeth me in the paths of righteousness for his name's sake.

4 Yea, though I walk through the valley of the shadow of death, I will fear no evil: for thou *art* with me; thy rod and thy staff they comfort me.

5 Thou preparest a table before me in the presence of mine enemies: thou anointest my head with oil; my cup runneth over.

6 Surely goodness and mercy shall follow me all the days of my life: and I will dwell in the house of the LORD for ever.

Psalm 46

God *is* our refuge and strength, a very present help in trouble.

2 Therefore will not we fear, though the earth be removed, and though the mountains be carried into the midst of the sea;

3 *Though* the waters thereof roar *and* be troubled, *though* the mountains shake with the swelling thereof. Selah.

4 *There is* a river, the streams whereof shall make glad the city of God, the holy *place* of the tabernacles of the most High.

5 God *is* in the midst of her; she shall not be moved: God shall help her, *and that* right early.

6 The heathen raged, the kingdoms were moved: he uttered his voice, the earth melted.

7 The LORD of hosts *is* with us; the God of Jacob *is* our refuge. Selah.

8 Come, behold the works of the LORD, what desolations he hath made in the earth.

9 He maketh wars to cease unto the end of the earth; he breaketh the bow, and cutteth the spear in sunder; he burneth the chariot in the fire.

10 Be still, and know that I *am* God: I will be exalted among the heathen, I will be exalted in the earth.

11 The LORD of hosts *is* with us; the God of Jacob *is* our refuge. Selah.

Psalm 51

Have mercy upon me, O God, according to thy lovingkindness: according unto the multitude of thy tender mercies blot out my transgressions.

2 Wash me thoroughly from mine iniquity, and cleanse me from my sin.

3 For I acknowledge my transgressions: and my sin *is* ever before me.

4 Against thee, thee only, have I sinned, and done *this* evil in thy sight: that thou mightest be justified when thou speakest, *and* be clear when thou judgest.

5 Behold, I was shapen in iniquity; and in sin did my mother conceive me.

6 Behold, thou desirest truth in the inward parts: and in the hidden *part* thou shalt make me to know wisdom.

7 Purge me with hyssop, and I shall be clean: wash me, and I shall be whiter than snow.

8 Make me to hear joy and gladness; *that* the bones *which* thou hast broken may rejoice.

9 Hide thy face from my sins, and blot out all mine iniquities.

10 Create in me a clean heart, O God; and renew a right spirit within me.

11 Cast me not away from thy presence; and take not thy holy spirit from me.

12 Restore unto me the joy of thy salvation; and uphold me *with thy* free spirit.

13 *Then* will I teach transgressors thy ways; and sinners shall be converted unto thee.

14 Deliver me from bloodguiltiness, O God, thou God of my salvation: *and* my tongue shall sing aloud of thy righteousness.

15 O Lord, open thou my lips; and my mouth shall shew forth thy praise.

16 For thou desirest not sacrifice; else would I give *it:* thou delightest not in burnt offering.

17 The sacrifices of God *are* a broken spirit: a broken and a contrite heart, O God, thou wilt not despise.

18 Do good in thy good pleasure unto Zion: build thou the walls of Jerusalem.

19 Then shalt thou be pleased with the sacrifices of righteousness, with burnt offering and whole burnt offering: then shall they offer bullocks upon thine altar.

Psalm 91

He that dwelleth in the secret place of the most High shall abide under the shadow of the Almighty.

2 I will say of the LORD, *He is* my refuge and my fortress: my God; in him will I trust.

3 Surely he shall deliver thee from the snare of the fowler, *and* from the noisome pestilence.

4 He shall cover thee with his feathers, and under his wings shalt thou trust: his truth *shall be thy* shield and buckler.

5 Thou shalt not be afraid for the terror by night; *nor* for the arrow *that* flieth by day;

6 *Nor* for the pestilence *that* walketh in darkness; *nor* for the destruction *that* wasteth at noonday.

7 A thousand shall fall at thy side, and ten thousand at thy right hand; *but* it shall not come nigh thee.

8 Only with thine eyes shalt thou behold and see the reward of the wicked.

9 Because thou hast made the LORD, *which is* my refuge, *even* the most High, thy habitation;

10 There shall no evil befall thee, neither shall any plague come nigh thy dwelling.

11 For he shall give his angels charge over thee, to keep thee in all thy ways.

12 They shall bear thee up in *their* hands, lest thou dash thy foot against a stone.

13 Thou shalt tread upon the lion and adder: the young lion and the dragon shalt thou trample under feet.

14 Because he hath set his love upon me, therefore will I deliver him: I will set him on high, because he hath known my name.

15 He shall call upon me, and I will answer him: I *will be* with him in trouble; I will deliver him, and honour him.

16 With long life will I satisfy him, and shew him my salvation.

Psalm 121

I will lift up mine eyes unto the hills, from whence cometh my help.

2 My help *cometh* from the LORD, which made heaven and earth.

3 He will not suffer thy foot to be moved: he that keepeth thee will not slumber.

4 Behold, he that keepeth Israel shall neither slumber nor sleep.

5 The LORD *is* thy keeper: the LORD *is* thy shade upon thy right hand.

6 The sun shall not smite thee by day, nor the moon by night.

7 The LORD shall preserve thee from all evil: he shall preserve thy soul.

8 The LORD shall preserve thy going out and thy coming in from this time forth, and even for evermore.

The Lord's Prayer

Our Father which art in heaven, Hallowed be thy name. Thy kindom come. Thy will be done in earth, as it is in heaven. Give us this day our daily bread. And forgive us our debts, as we forgive our debtors. And lead us not into temptation, but deliver us from evil: For thine is the kingdom, and the power, and the glory, for ever. Amen

Matthew 6:9-13

The Beatitudes

Blessed are the poor in spirit: for theirs is the kingdom of heaven.

Blessed are they that mourn: for they shall be comforted.

Blessed are the meek: for they shall inherit the earth.

Blessed are they which do hunger and thirst after righteousness: for they shall be filled.

Blessed are the merciful: for they shall obtain mercy.

Blessed are the pure in heart: for they shall see God.

Blessed are the peacemakers: for they shall be called the children of God.

Blessed are they which are persecuted for righteousness' sake: for theirs is the kingdom of heaven.

Blessed are ye, when men shall revile you, and persecute you, and shall say all manner of evil against you falsely, for my sake. Rejoice, and be exceeding glad: for great is your reward in heaven.

Matthew 5:3-12

Jewish Prayer (third century A.D.*)*

Grant us peace, Thy most precious gift, O Thou eternal source of peace, and enable Israel to be its messenger unto the peoples of the earth. Bless our country that it may ever be a stronghold of peace, and its advocate in the council of nations. May contentment reign within its borders, health and happiness within its homes. Strengthen the bonds of friendship and fellowship among all the inhabitants of our land. Plant virtue in every soul, and may the love of Thy name hallow every home and every heart. Praised be Thou, O Lord, Giver of peace.

The Prayer of St. Chrysostom (c. 400)

Almighty God, who hast given us grace at this time with one accord to make our common supplications unto thee; and dost promise that when two or three are gathered together in thy Name thou wilt grant their requests; Fulfil now, O Lord, the desires and petitions of thy servants, as may be most expedient for them; granting us in this world knowledge of thy truth, and in the world to come life everlasting.

The Apostles' Creed

I believe in God the Father Almighty, Maker of heaven and earth:

And in Jesus Christ his only Son our Lord: Who was conceived by the Holy Ghost, Born of the Virgin Mary: Suffered under Pontius Pilate, Was crucified, dead, and buried: He descended into hell; The third day he rose again from the dead: He ascended into heaven, And sitteth on the right hand of God the Father Almighty: From thence he shall come to judge the quick and the dead.

I believe in the Holy Ghost: The holy Catholic Church; The Communion of Saints: The Forgiveness of sins: The Resurrection of the body: And the Life everlasting.

The Nicene Creed (fourth century)

I believe in one God the Father Almighty, Maker of heaven and earth, And of all things visible and invisible:

And in one Lord Jesus Christ, the only-begotten Son of God; Begotten of his Father before all worlds, God of God, Light of Light, Very God of Very God: Begotten, not made; Being of one substance with the Father; By whom all things were made: Who for us men and for our salvation came down from heaven, And was incarnate by the Holy Ghost of the Virgin Mary, And was made man: And was crucified also for us under Pontius Pilate; He suffered and was buried: And the third day he rose again according to the Scriptures: And ascended into heaven, And sitteth on the right hand of the Father: And he shall come again with glory to judge both the quick and the dead; Whose kingdom shall have no end.

And I believe in the Holy Ghost, The Lord, and Giver of Life, Who proceedeth from the Father and the Son; Who with the Father and the Son together is worshiped and glorified; Who spake by the prophets: And I believe in one Catholic and Apostolic Church: I acknowledge one Baptism for the remission of sins: And I look for the resurrection of the dead: And the life of the world to come.

The Athanasian Creed (fourth century)

Whosoever will be saved: before all things it is necessary that he hold the Catholick Faith.

Which Faith except every one do keep whole and undefiled: without doubt he shall perish everlastingly.

And the Catholick Faith is this: That we worship one God in Trinity, and Trinity in Unity;

Neither confounding the Persons: nor dividing the substance.

For there is one Person of the Father, another of the Son: and another of the Holy Ghost.

But the Godhead of the Father, of the Son, and of the Holy Ghost, is all one: the glory equal, the majesty co-eternal.

Such as the Father is, such is the Son: and such is the Holy Ghost.

The Father uncreate, the Son uncreate: and the Holy Ghost uncreate.

The Father incomprehensible, the Son incomprehensible: and the Holy Ghost incomprehensible.

The Father eternal, the Son eternal: and the Holy Ghost eternal.

And yet they are not three eternals: but one eternal.

And also there are not three incomprehensibles, nor three uncreated: but one uncreated, and one incomprehensible.

So likewise the Father is almighty, the Son almighty: and the Holy Ghost almighty.

And yet they are not three almighties: but one almighty.

So the Father is God, the Son is God: and the Holy Ghost is God.

And yet they are not three Gods: but one God.

So likewise the Father is Lord, the Son Lord: and the Holy Ghost Lord.

And yet not three Lords: but one Lord.

For like as we are compelled by the Christian verity: to acknowledge every Person by himself to be God and Lord;

So are we forbidden by the Catholick Religion: to say, There be three Gods, or three Lords.

The Father is made of none: neither created, nor begotten.

The Son is of the Father alone: not made, nor created, but begotten.

The Holy Ghost is of the Father and of the Son: neither made, nor created, nor begotten, but proceeding.

So there is one Father, not three Fathers; one Son, not three Sons: one Holy Ghost, not three Holy Ghosts.

And in this Trinity none is afore, or after other: none is greater, or less than another;

But the whole three Persons are co-eternal together: and co-equal.

So that in all things, as is aforesaid: the Unity in Trinity, and the Trinity in Unity is to be worshipped.

He therefore that will be saved: must thus think of the Trinity.

Furthermore, it is necessary to everlasting salvation: that he also believe rightly the Incarnation of our Lord Jesus Christ.

For the right faith is, that we believe and confess: that our Lord Jesus Christ, the Son of God, is God and man;

God, of the substance of the Father, begotten before the worlds: and man, of the substance of his Mother, born in the world:

Perfect God, and perfect man: of a reasonable soul and human flesh subsisting;

Equal to the Father, as touching his Godhead: and inferior to the Father, as touching his manhood.

Who although he be God and man: yet he is not two, but one Christ;

One; not by conversion of the Godhead into flesh: but by taking of the manhood into God;

One altogether; not by confusion of substance: but by unity of person.

For as the reasonable soul and flesh is one man: so God and man is one Christ;

Who suffered for our salvation: descended into hell, rose again the third day from the dead.

He ascended into heaven, he sitteth on the right hand of the Father, God Almighty: from whence he shall come to judge the quick and the dead.

At whose coming all men shall rise again with their bodies: and shall give account for their own works.

And they that have done good shall go into life everlasting: and they that have done evil into everlasting fire.

This is the Catholick Faith: which except a man believe faithfully, he cannot be saved.

Glory be to the Father, and to the Son: and to the Holy Ghost;

As it was in the beginning, is now, and ever shall be: world without end. Amen.

The Te Deum

We praise thee, O God; we acknowledge thee to be the Lord.

All the earth doth worship thee, the Father everlasting.

To thee all Angels cry aloud; the Heavens, and all the Powers therein;

To thee Cherubim and Seraphim continually do cry,

Holy, Holy, Holy, Lord God of Sabaoth;

Heaven and earth are full of the Majesty of thy glory.

The glorious company of the Apostles praise thee.

The goodly fellowship of the Prophets praise thee.

The noble army of Martyrs praise thee.

The holy Church throughout all the world doth acknowledge thee;

The Father, of an infinite Majesty;

Thine adorable, true, and only Son;

Also the Holy Ghost, the Comforter.

Thou art the King of Glory, O Christ.

Thou art the everlasting Son of the Father.

When thou tookest upon thee to deliver man, thou didst humble thyself to be born of a Virgin.

When thou hadst overcome the sharpness of death, thou didst open the Kingdom of Heaven to all believers.

Thou sittest at the right hand of God, in the glory of the Father.

We believe that thou shalt come to be our Judge.

We therefore pray thee, help thy servants, whom thou hast redeemed with thy precious blood.

Make them to be numbered with thy Saints, in glory everlasting.

O Lord, save thy people, and bless thine heritage.

Govern them, and lift them up for ever.

Day by day we magnify thee;

And we worship thy Name ever, world without end.

Vouchsafe, O Lord, to keep us this day without sin.

O Lord, have mercy upon us, have mercy upon us.

O Lord, let thy mercy be upon us, as our trust is in thee.

O Lord, in thee have I trusted; let me never be confounded.

Early Hymns

Come Holy Ghost, who ever One,
Art with the Father and the Son;
Come, Holy Ghost, our souls possess
With thy full flood of holiness.

In will and deed, by heart and tongue,
With all our powers, Thy praise be sung;
And love light up our mortal frame,
Till others catch the living flame.

Almighty Father, hear our cry
Through Jesus Christ our Lord most high,
Who with the Holy Ghost and Thee
Doth live and reign eternally.

St. Ambrose (340-397)

Christian! dost thou see them
  On the holy ground,
How the powers of darkness
  Rage thy steps around?
Christian! up and smite them,
  Counting gain but loss;
In the strength that cometh
  By the holy cross.

Christian! dost thou feel them,
  How they work within,
Striving, tempting, luring,
  Goading into sin?
Christian! never tremble;
  Never be downcast;
Gird thee for the battle,
  Watch and pray and fast.

Christian! dost thou hear them,
  How they speak thee fair?
"Always fast and vigil?
  Always watch and prayer?"
Christian! answer boldly:
  "While I breathe I pray!"

Peace shall follow battle,
  Night shall end in day.

"Well I know thy trouble,
  O my servant true;
Thou art very weary,
  I was weary too;
But that toil shall make thee
  Someday all mine own,
And the end of sorrow
  Shall be near my throne."

St. Andrew of Crete (660-732)

Come, ye faithful, raise the strain
  Of triumphant gladness;
God hath brought his Israel
  Into joy from sadness;
Loosed from Pharaoh's bitter yoke
  Jacob's sons and daughters;
Led them with unmoistened foot
  Through the Red Sea waters.

'Tis the spring of souls today;
  Christ hath burst his prison,
And from three days' sleep in death
  As a sun hath risen;
All the winter of our sins,
  Long and dark is flying
From his light, to whom we give
  Laud and praise undying.

Now the queen of seasons, bright
  With the day of splendour,
With the royal feast of feasts,
  Comes its joy to render;

Comes to glad Jerusalem,
  Who with true affection
Welcomes in unwearied strains
  Jesus' resurrection.

Neither might the gates of death,
  Nor the tomb's dark portal,
Nor the watchers, nor the seal,
  Hold thee as a mortal:
But to-day amidst thine own
  Thou didst stand, bestowing
That thy peace which evermore
  Passeth human knowing.

St. John of Damascus (749)

Jesus, the very thought of thee
  With sweetness fills the breast;
But sweeter far thy face to see,
  And in thy presence rest.

No voice can sing, no heart can frame,
  Nor can the memory find,
A sweeter sound than Jesus' Name,
  The Saviour of mankind.

O Hope of every contrite heart,
  O Joy of all the meek,
To those who fall, how kind thou art!
  How good to those who seek!

But what to those who find? Ah, this
  Nor tongue nor pen can show;
The love of Jesus, what it is
  None but his loved ones know.

Jesus, our only joy be thou,
  As thou our prize wilt be;
In thee be all our glory now,
  And through eternity.

St. Bernard of Clairvaux (1091-1153)

Jerusalem the golden!
  With milk and honey blest;
Beneath thy contemplation
  Sink heart and voice opprest.
I know not, O I know not,
  What joys await us there!
What radiancy of glory!
  What bliss beyond compare!

They stand, those halls of Sion,
  All jubilant with song,
And bright with many an angel,
  And all the martyr throng.
The Prince is ever in them,
  The daylight is serene;
The pastures of the blessed
  Are decked in glorious sheen.

There is the throne of David;
  And there, from care released,
The shout of them that triumph,
  The song of them that feast.
And they who with their Leader
  Have conquered in the fight,
For ever and for ever
  Are clad in robes of white.

O sweet and blessed country,
  The home of God's elect!

O sweet and blessed country,
  That eager hearts expect!
Jesus, in mercy bring us
  To that dear land of rest!
Who art, with God the Father,
  And Spirit, ever blest.

St. Bernard of Cluny (1145)

For thee, O dear, dear country,
  Mine eyes their vigils keep;
For very love beholding
  Thy holy name, they weep.
The mention of thy glory
  Is unction to the breast,
And medicine in sickness,
  And love, and life, and rest.

O one, O only mansion!
  O Paradise of joy!
Where tears are ever banished
  And smiles have no alloy;
Thy loveliness oppresses
  All human thought and heart,
And none, O Peace, O Sion,
  Can sing thee as thou art.

With jasper glow thy bulwarks,
  Thy streets with emeralds blaze;
The sardius and the topaz
  Unite in thee their rays;
Thine ageless walls are bonded
  With amethyst unpriced;
The saints build up thy fabric,
  And the corner-stone is Christ.

The cross is all thy splendour,
  The Crucified thy praise;
His laud and benediction
  Thy ransomed people raise:
Upon the Rock of Ages
  They build thy holy tower;
Thine is the victor's laurel,
  And thine the golden dower.

O sweet and blessed country,
  The home of God's elect!
O sweet and blessed country,
  That eager hearts expect!
Jesus, in mercy bring us
  To that dear land of rest;
Who art, with God the Father,
  And Spirit, ever blest.

St. Bernard of Cluny (1145)

Day of wrath! O day of mourning!
See fulfilled the prophets' warning,
Heaven and earth in ashes burning!

O what fear man's bosom rendeth,
When from heaven the Judge descendeth,
On whose sentence all dependeth!

Wondrous sound the trumpet flingeth;
Through earth's sepulchers it ringeth;
All before the throne it bringeth.

Death is struck, and nature quaking,
All creation is awaking,
To its Judge an answer making.

Lo! the book, exactly worded,
Wherein all hath been recorded:
Thence shall judgment be awarded.

When the Judge his seat attaineth,
And each hidden deed arraigneth,
Nothing unavenged remaineth.

What shall I, frail man, be pleading?
Who for me be interceding,
When the just are mercy needing?

King of Majesty tremendous,
Who dost free salvation send us,
Fount of pity, then befriend us!

Think, good Jesus, my salvation
Cost thy wondrous Incarnation;
Leave me not to reprobation!

Faint and weary, thou hast sought me,
On the cross of suffering bought me.
Shall such grace be vainly brought me?

Righteous Judge! for sin's pollution
Grant thy gift of absolution,
Ere the day of retribution.

Guilty, now I pour my moaning,
All my shame with anguish owning;
Spare, O God, thy suppliant groaning!

Thou the sinful woman savedst;
Thou the dying thief forgavest;
And to me a hope vouchsafest.

Worthless are my prayers and sighing,
Yet, good Lord, in grace complying,
Rescue me from fires undying!

With thy favoured sheep O place me;
Nor among the goats abase me;
But to thy right hand upraise me.

While the wicked are confounded,
Doomed to flames of woe unbounded,
Call me with thy saints surrounded.

Low I kneel, with heart submission,
See, like ashes, my contrition;
Help me in my last condition.

Ah! that day of tears and mourning!
From the dust of earth returning
Man for judgment must prepare him;
Spare, O God, in mercy spare him!

Lord, all pitying, Jesus blest,
Grant them thine eternal rest.

Thomas of Celano (thirteenth century)

O Saving Victim, opening wide
The gate of heaven to man below,
Our foes press on from every side,
Thine aid supply, thy strength bestow.

All praise and thanks to thee ascend
For evermore, blest One in Three;
O grant us life that shall not end,
In our true native land with thee.

St. Thomas Aquinas (*c.* 1225-1274)

Symbols

Through the ages mankind has expressed its emotions and hidden meanings in a more or less traditional and universal language, the language of symbols. As its name implies, it is a sign language, and the understanding of the symbol and its origin is essential to the understanding of the development of man and his thoughts and emotions. We today may think ourselves free of this early speech, but our daily life is loaded with symbols which have come down from a remote past and of which we have frequently forgotten the meaning. What soldier today, giving the military salute, remembers that his forebears in the Middle Ages raised their visors to friends with the identical gesture? What member of a ritualistic church is conscious when he crosses himself that he is using the secret sign of recognition common among the early Christians when they were being persecuted for their faith, some sixteen hundred years or more ago?

Religion is generally slow in discarding tradition, and the churches of today are in greater or less degree bound to the past by a host of customs and symbols, some of which are heirlooms of so remote a period that their origins can no longer be determined. The study of ecclesiastical symbolism could easily become a lifework, and might be of great service in explaining certain aspects of human growth and behavior. With this service in mind, and for the practical purpose of explaining certain features of church architecture, decoration and ritual, I am setting forth a few of the most common and obvious details of ecclesiastical symbolism in use today.

1. The Church Building.

This is generally built east and west, with the altar in the east end. The early Christians, many of them Jews, were accustomed to face Jerusalem when they prayed, and since

Christianity spread chiefly westward, the east was in the general direction of the Holy City. Today it is not always possible to orient churches in this way, but the altar end of the church is none the less called "the east end" in ecclesiastical usage.

The Nave. The word comes from the Latin word for "ship," and since it is the section of the church where the congregation sits, its symbolism is that of a ship on the sea of life, sailing to a safe haven with God.

The Altar. There have been altars since the dawn of humanity, when earliest man chose a sacred stone as God's resting place and on it offered propitiatory sacrifices. In many churches today the altar is merely a table, but the symbolic meaning of this center of attention and worship is still alive, and in the more ritualistic sects the memory of the sacrificial rites for which it was first intended still lingers.

The aisles, the chancel, the sanctuary, the furnishings, the least architectural detail of the church, such as the pillars, the number of steps leading to chancel, sanctuary and altar, the rood screen, the iconostasis, are all fraught with hidden meanings. Where there is a spire, it points heavenward; a tower speaks of strength; the cruciform ground plan of so many churches is in memory of Christ's death on the cross and the road that all who follow Him must travel.

The candles used in churches all have symbolic meaning. Basically they refer to Christ as the light of the world. Two at either side of the altar cross are Eucharistic and express the two natures of Christ, God and man. Elsewhere three candles represent the Holy Trinity; five candles, the five wounds of Christ on the cross; seven, a perfect number, symbolizes His perfect life. Why candles at all in this day of artificial light? Because the early Christians worshiped either underground in the catacombs, or in inner rooms or in caves, and candles were their one source of light.

2. Symbols of God.

The Hand, usually reaching down and with three fingers stretched out in blessing. The Bible is full of references to the Hand of God. The symbol means power or mercy, and is frequently surrounded by the nimbus of divinity.

The Eye, surrounded by a triangle, representing God's all-seeing power.

3. Symbols of Jesus.

The Good Shepherd. In John 10:14 Christ speaks of Himself by this name, and in Hebrews 13:20 He is spoken of as "our Lord Jesus, that great Shepherd of the sheep."

Agnus Dei, the Lamb of God. The lamb represents sacrifice, and in sacred art often carries a banner in token of victory.

The Fish. The letters of the Greek word for "fish," taken separately, are the initial letters of the Greek words meaning "Jesus Christ, Son of God, Saviour." In early Christian times, therefore, the symbol of the fish became a secret sign among believers.

I H S and I H C. These are the first three letters of Jesus' name in Greek, and were also secret signs. Similarly the Greek letters chi rho, which resemble XP in the Western alphabet, are the first two letters of the Greek transliteration of the name Christ.

The crown of thorns and three nails, or the three nails alone, stand for Christ the Sacrifice.

The star betokens His birth.

The pomegranate, which was used to adorn the robe of the Jewish High Priest, refers to Jesus in His priestly aspect.

4. Symbols of the Holy Spirit.

The Descending Dove recalls the form in which the Holy Ghost is described as descending on Jesus at His baptism.

The Cloven Tongues of Fire are another symbol of the Spirit, in accordance with Acts 2:3.

5. *Symbols of the Holy Trinity.*

The equilateral triangle.

Three interlaced circles. The circle, having no beginning and no end, stands for eternity.

The trefoil or clover leaf.

Two equilateral triangles superimposed to form a six-pointed star.

The triangle and circle interlaced, to denote the equality of the three Persons and their eternity.

6. *The Cross.*

Primarily the cross represents Christ, and therefore His redeeming sacrifice. Even in pre-Christian times it had symbolic meaning and had long been in use. Among Christians, however, it assumed and has always kept a very special significance, since it is identified with Christ's death. It soon became the most characteristic symbol of the new faith, so that the making of stone or wooden crosses during those first centuries of persecution was unsafe. The followers of Jesus therefore "signed themselves with the sign of the cross" as a means of confessing Christ and identifying themselves to each other.

The usual form of the symbol is the Latin Cross such as the Romans used for the Crucifixion. The Greek and Maltese Crosses and the Cross Fleurie, all square in design, are used chiefly for decorative purposes. St. Andrew's is a leaning cross and is so called because it is believed that St. Andrew was martyred on a cross of this form. The Celtic Cross, a form of the Latin, but with a nimbus at the crossing, is frequently used in cemeteries for its beauty of design.

The cross sometimes appears with the figure of Christ upon it, and is then a crucifix. The early form of crucifix shows

Christ clothed, crowned and triumphant, a reigning king. The asceticism of the Middle Ages introduced the figure of the suffering and dying Lord.

7. Other Symbols.

The Anchor, a variation of the cross and the symbol of hope (Hebrews 6:19: "Which hope we have as an anchor of the soul").

The Butterfly, a symbol of the Resurrection.

The Crown, the symbol of victory, sometimes used in combination with the cross.

The Phoenix, a very ancient symbol of the Resurrection, since the phoenix is said to rise from its own ashes.

The Pelican, who is said to feed her young with her blood, the symbol of Atonement.

The Vine, standing for the Church: "I am the vine, ye are the branches" (John 15:5).

The scepter or the crossed keys, the symbol of authority. The keys may also stand for St. Peter, who keeps the gate of Heaven.

Wheat, a sacramental symbol, standing for the Bread of Life.

The Palm, signifying rejoicing, in reference to Christ's triumphant entry into Jerusalem.

The Lily, the symbol of purity.

The Lamp, standing for Jesus as the "Light of the World." Burning before the host or on the altar, it represents the real presence of Christ. This is a very old symbol; the Hebrews kept a light burning before the Ark to show that Yahweh was present.

The Winged Man, Winged Lion, Winged Ox and the Eagle, symbols of the four Gospel writers, Matthew, Mark, Luke and John.

There is a special meaning attached to numbers, which

governs both architecture and ritual in ecclesiastical symbolism.

One is the symbol of unity and means God.

Two, Jesus Christ as God and man, or the Incarnation.

Three, the Holy Trinity.

Four, the earth. So one speaks of the four corners of the earth, the four winds, the four quarters, and so forth.

Five, the symbol of sacrifice, the five wounds of the Lord.

Seven, a perfect number. There are seven days in the week, seven petitions in the Lord's Prayer, seven archangels, and anciently the "seven stars of the sky" (sun, moon, Mercury, Venus, Mars, Jupiter and Saturn).

Ten, the complete number. The Ten Commandments express man's whole duty to God and his neighbor.

Twelve, the universal number, three times four, matter penetrated by spirit. There were twelve tribes of Israel, and twelve Apostles.

Much of this numerology is as old as the oldest stargazers in Babylon, and yet it is repeated again and again in Christian religion and art.

Christian art and architecture as well as Christian literature refer constantly to angels. The Greek word "angel" means messenger, and the angels are regarded as messengers of God. The earliest references to angels as such dates from the time of the Persian Empire (550-333 B.C.), and they begin to be mentioned in Hebrew literature during this period. Christian art and literature early adopted them, and they are frequently seen in stained-glass windows, carvings and pictures. According to tradition, the hierarchy of Heaven consists of seraphim, cherubim, thrones, dominions, virtues, powers, principalities, archangels and angels. The seraphs, or seraphim, are frequently represented with six wings; they are fiery and purifying ministers of God. The cherubs, or cherubim, are a somewhat lower order of angel and symbolize divine wisdom or justice. They are frequently pictured as heads with two wings. There are seven archangels, of whom St. Michael (Who is Like God), Gabriel (Hero of God), Raphael (Healing of God), Uriel (Flame of God) are the best known in Christian tradition. The remaining three, Barachiel, Jehudiel and Sealtahiel, are mentioned only in Jewish lore. Angels are not departed spirits. They have never been and never will be incarnate, are immortal and without sex.

To one who knows none of these symbols, entering a church must be a bewildering experience. He comes to worship God, and finds himself surrounded on every hand by eagles, lambs, keys, winged creatures of various sorts, and initials that have no obvious meaning; priests dressed in robes of another day and era do incomprehensible things and say words which seem to have two meanings; congregations rise, kneel, turn and bow for no apparent reason. When the significance of even a few of the symbols is known, the whole picture begins to fall into place. This is the communion of the past, present and future, the link that binds together the ages of religious thought and feeling.

CHAPTER FOUR

Denominations of the United States of America

IN THIS CHAPTER I shall take up the principal denominations of the United States for separate discussion. Owing to the limitations of space and time I have confined myself to an account of only those denominations which, according to available information, have a membership of fifty thousand or over. Were I to discuss any smaller groups, however interesting and important, I should lay myself open to charges of partiality, and were I to include all religious bodies and sects I should not be able to give more than a few words to each one, which would be contrary to the purpose of this book.

The account of the organization, doctrine and form of worship of each denomination has been prefaced by a short history of its origin and how and when it came to this country. Some of the religious bodies played a large part in the development of creeds and were described and discussed in the history which is contained in the second chapter of this book. Among these are Judaism, the Eastern Church, the Roman Catholic Church, the Church of England, Lutheranism and Calvinism. In these cases the prefatory paragraph is very short, only telling how and when they arrived in America.

Words which are very generally used and which may puzzle readers not accustomed to religious terminology, have been explained in a glossary at the end of the book.

The census of members of the various denominations is taken from the Year Book of American Churches, 1947, published by the Sowers Printing Company, Lebanon, Pa. Here and there the numbers have been further corrected by the denominations themselves.

In the group of religious beliefs selected for discussion there will be found nearly every type of church government, doctrine and form, under which general heads other denominations may be classed. By episcopal is meant governed by bishops. Many of the churches with this form of government, such as the Episcopal and Methodist churches are also controlled by synods or councils. In churches of the congregational type, the local congregation is in control, though even in these churches there is as a rule some kind of council acting in an advisory capacity and serving to hold the congregations together. Synodal government is the expression used to describe that form of church organization ruled by the convention or presbytery.

In the listing of the denominations I have followed to some extent a historical order. Christianity sprang from Judaism and it has therefore seemed reasonable to discuss the Jewish faith first since in it may be found many of the doctrinal antecedents of the Christian religion. Next in order I have placed first the Eastern Orthodox Faith, which in organization and ritual still clings to many of the forms of the early church. The Roman Church, for centuries the only faith in Western Europe and the mother church from which Protestantism sprang, is treated next in order. After that the various protestant denominations appear alphabetically, since it is impossible to place them in chronological order.

The study of the ancient forms and rituals used in the

Jewish and early Christian churches is of great interest to all, for in them may be seen the origin of many rites and customs of the post-Reformation sects. This is especially true of the Communion Service, which has been the center of the Christian ritual from time immemorial and has some of its roots in the Jewish Passover and some in the pre-Christian mysteries. Truly the "communion of saints" is by means of this long tradition made a reality and reaches from far into the past to the yet unseen future.

JUDAISM—4,641,000

Among the early settlers of this country, as early indeed as 1654, were a number of Jews fleeing from persecution in Europe. Some came with the Dutch to the New Netherlands, some with Oglethorpe to Georgia, and a scattering came with the other groups of settlers. By the time of the Revolution there were Jewish communities in Rhode Island, New York, Pennsylvania, South Carolina and Georgia. Most of the earlier settlers were Sephardic (Portuguese) Jews who had fled to Holland and England from the Inquisition in their own land, and now sought a permanent home where they would be free to believe and worship in their own way. At the beginning of the eighteenth century, Ashkenazic Jews from Germany and Poland began to join them, and since then most of the Jewish immigrants have been Ashkenazim. The first public synagogue in this country, the Congregation "Shearith Israel" ("The Remnant of Israel") was consecrated in New York City in 1730.

During the Revolutionary War the Jews, most of whom were patriots, gave generously to the war effort in both men and money, in this way identifying themselves with the common cause, and establishing their stake in the Republic.

ORGANIZATION:

Judaism in this country may be divided into three groups or "wings," though there is no sectarian schism between them:

1. *Orthodox.* These adhere to traditional Judaism and accept no significant changes from the custom and practice of the past. Their houses of worship are still called synagogues, since they still consider the Temple at Jerusalem the only center of sacrificial worship and look forward to its eventual re-establishment.
2. *Conservative.* They maintain that Jewish law is a living tradition subject to change, but insist that any changes must be made in accordance with the traditional canons for the interpretation and development of rabbinic law.
3. *Reform.* The rabbis of these congregations claim authority themselves not merely to interpret but also to amend Talmudic and even Biblical laws.

Reform Jews have omitted the prayer for the restoration of the Temple at Jerusalem from their liturgy, and as a rule call their houses of worship temples.

Judaism is a religious community and its central authority is the word of God as given by Yahweh to Moses in the Law and as explained and expounded by the priests, prophets, and some inspired teachers of later time. These laws and teachings are all contained in the Old Testament, the Talmud, and some later manuals. Any decision on religious matters is based on the Talmud.

Those who know the Old Testament, the Talmud and the manuals and are faithful to their teachings are chosen to be rabbis (teachers) and accepted as leaders. There is no synod, hierarchical organization or central government in Judaism. Any meetings which they hold, such for example as the Central Conference of American Rabbis, are for discussion only and are not in any way binding. Some rabbis, widely known for their exceptional learning in the Law, are often called on by common consent for the clarification of difficult questions, but their decisions need not be accepted as final. Today it is customary to ordain rabbis after they complete the course of study at one of the rabbinical schools.

Each congregation has the widest possible religious autonomy. It chooses its own rabbi, and once appointed, the rabbi is free to preach, interpret and expound without interference, according to his learning and convictions. American congregations generally have, besides the rabbi, who is primarily a religious leader, lay officers consisting of president, vice-president, secretary and board of directors, who control the material and financial welfare of the synagogue or temple.

DOCTRINE:

Judaism is really a way of life and so has no formal creed or mass of dogma. Its single tenet of belief is contained in the Shema (Deuteronomy 6:4-9), which begins, "Hear, O Israel: The Lord our God, the Lord is one." The only change in the faith over the centuries has been the increasingly spiritual and lofty conception of God, who, starting as a tribal god, primitive and anthropomorphic, has become universal, omnipotent, omniscient and pure spirit.

There is a well- known Jewish statement of faith by Maimonides, the philosopher and codifier of the Talmud (1135-1204), which is incorporated in the Jewish hymn Yigdal though not universally formulated as a creed. It attributes thirteen basic dogmas to Judaism, and embodies so much of its singleness of faith that it has seemed well to quote it in outline:

1. Belief in God's existence.
2. Belief in His unity.
3. Belief in His incorporeality.

4. Belief in His timelessness.
5. Belief that He is approachable in prayer.
6. Belief in prophecy.
7. Belief in the superiority of Moses to all other prophets.
8. Belief in the revelation of the Law and that the Law contained in the Pentateuch is that revealed to Moses.
9. Belief in the immutability of the Law.
10. Belief in divine providence.
11. Belief in divine justice.
12. Belief in the coming of the Messiah.
13. Belief in the resurrection and human immortality.

Orthodox and Conservative Jews in general follow the example of the ancient and medieval teachers in avoiding a generally adopted Jewish creed beyond the consensus of opinion found in the traditional writings. Reform Jews have tried to find a common platform, and in 1937 drew up what is known as the Columbus platform (named after its place of origin), which is a short statement in nine articles of the broad essentials of Judaism today. God, man, the place of the Torah (Old Testament Law), Israel's mission to the world, ethics and religion, social justice, peace, the religious life, are discussed and defined in terms broad enough to make the statement acceptable to all Jews, whether Orthodox or Reform.

All three wings of Judaism accept the fundamental religious, spiritual and ethical principles of the Law as given in the Old Testament and look upon the Babylonian Talmud as the common law of Jewish ethical discipline. The dietary laws of the Old Testament, interpreted and enlarged in the Talmud and later codes, are observed by the Orthodox Jews, but are not stressed in the Reform congregations.

According to these laws, Jews may eat all vegetable foods, fishes that have fins and scales, certain types of fowl, and those quadrupeds which have cloven hoofs and chew the cud. Warm-blooded animals may be eaten only if officially slaughtered. Butchers are specially trained for this work, and must obey certain rules and regulations. The knife used for slaughtering must be very sharp in order that the animal may not suffer unnecessarily. The butcher must be able to judge whether the animal is healthy. The blood must be thoroughly drained from the victim, to comply with the Jewish rules which forbid the eating of blood. There are other dietary regulations concerning the preparing and cooking of food and the utensils to be used.

In accordance with Mosaic law, circumcision is required of all male Jews.

Emphasis in modern Judaism is, as has always been true of the prophetic element since earliest times, on conduct rather than creed. The conception of Israel as the chosen people entails not privilege, but responsibility. Because God revealed Himself to them, they are chosen to lead the world into the ways of truth and righteousness. When all the world has seen the light and is at peace, then the Messiah will have come.

FORM OF WORSHIP:

Judaism so permeates the life of its members that it is hard to describe its form of worship by considering only the synagogue and temple services. In a very real sense each home is a place of worship, each head of the family a priest, and every meal a sacrificial meal. Prayer is an essential part of Judaism, and special prayers for every possible contingency and for use either at home or in public worship are included in the liturgical collections.

The liturgy of the Jewish synagogue is highly developed and has wide variation. Much of it is extremely ancient and was the basis of the later Christian liturgies. It is in part symbolical, in part commemorative. In the Orthodox synagogues it is conducted in Hebrew, in the Reform temples in

English, with the exception of a few Hebrew prayers and phrases. Though the liturgy and ritual of all three wings are fundamentally the same, that used by Reform congregations has been somewhat simplified and given a greater ethical appeal.

No human figures may be used to decorate synagogues, but the very strict rules of the second commandment have been so far relaxed as to permit a lion or an eagle to be depicted on the Ark and at other places in the building. The Ark is the center of worship. In it is kept the scroll of the Law and a light burns before it. A stand for the reader of the service faces the Ark, and there is frequently a second stand in the middle of the gathering for the reading of the Law.

In Reform and Conservative congregations, the old custom whereby men and women worshiped in separate parts of the synagogue has largely been given up.

Any adult male may lead the congregation in prayer, but in the larger congregations a leader, the hazzan, is generally appointed, sometimes with a choir to assist him. There may also be a special reader for scriptures, who must not only be able to read the Masoretic text, but also be an expert in cantillation (a system of chanting).

The seventh day of the week, Saturday, is celebrated as the Sabbath, according to the fourth commandment, which sets it aside as the day on which God rested after creating the world, and on which therefore man must do no work. The Sabbath begins at sunset on Friday and ends at sunset on Saturday. The chief Sabbath service takes place on the Friday evening. There are several variant Sabbath services of prayer and thanksgiving for both morning and evening. In the home also there are special services connected with the Sabbath: lighting the candles, which is the duty of the mistress of the house, and prayers to welcome the Sabbath, said by the master of the house. After the evening service there is also a special meal in the home, consisting of a flask of wine and two loaves of bread. Over the wine is recited a blessing, the Kiddush, or sanctification of the day.

The major Jewish feasts and fasts are:

1. The Passover, in memory of the escape from Egypt. It is a spring festival—the great festival of the rebirth of nature. During the seven days of its duration only unleavened bread (massah) may be used, and there is a ritual for searching the house for leaven before the Passover. Special cooking utensils and dishes are kept for the festival, so that there may be no danger of leaven touching the Passover food.
2. Pentecost, or Shabnot, toward the end of May or beginning of June. This is the feast of the wheat harvest and commemorates the revelation of God to Moses on Mount Sinai.
3. Feast of Tabernacles, or Sukkoth, in October. This is the late harvest festival and a traditional thanksgiving after the pilgrimage in the Wilderness. It lasts for nine days, during which pious Jews are supposed to live in huts made of boughs. Today the huts are symbolized.
4. Rosh ha-Shanah, September or October;
5. Yom Kippur.

The ten days which begin with Rosh ha-Shanah and end with Yom Kippur are ten days of penitence. Rosh ha-Shanah is the Jewish New Year, a very solemn festival when God judges all living things for their deeds during the past year. It is a season of prayer and repentance and ends with Yom Kippur, the Day of Atonement, when all seek forgiveness of their sins.

Two lesser feasts are Purim (in March), which is a day of joy and carnival, when presents are exchanged, and Hannukah (in December) in memory of the purification and rededication of the Temple by the Maccabees, which is again a season of joy and present giving. There are also some lesser fasts, Tisha b'Ab, Gedaliah, the tenth of Tebet and seventeenth of Tammuz, all of historical significance.

The Jewish calendar is based on the lunar month of twenty-nine and a half days, the beginning of each month coinciding with the new moon. An extra month is intercalated seven times in nineteen years.

THE EASTERN ORTHODOX CHURCH

This is the ancient church as it developed in the Eastern Empire, just as the Roman Catholic Church is the ancient church as it developed in the Western Empire. Each calls itself the Catholic, or Universal, Church. There is, however, no bond of union between them, for doctrine and polity have varied widely since the two branches of the church finally separated over eight hundred years ago. The third church which calls itself Catholic, the Anglican, has drawn closer to the Eastern Church of late years and some bodies of the Eastern faith in this country now recognizes the validity of the Anglican orders, though doctrinally the churches are separate.

The Eastern Orthodox Church is the accepted church of large portions of Eastern Europe and has several branches in the United States. It was originally composed of the patriarchates of Alexandria, Antioch, Jerusalem and Constantinople, of which the last named came in time to have jurisdiction over Christianized Russia. In 1589, however, the Russian Church became a patriarchate in its own right, equal in rank to the four original patriarchates. Peter the Great permitted the office of patriarch to lapse and in its stead set up a Holy Synod which governed the organization from 1721 to 1917. In the latter year, in spite of war and revolution, the Great Sobor, or council, was held and the Russian Church once more became one of the five patriarchates.

Before World War II there were also a number of autocephalous churches (free in government but compelled to hold the same dogma and doctrine as the mother church) and also of autonomous churches (having some liberty of government but dependent on the mother church) which were members of the Orthodox structure and had branches in America. Just what their status is today is still not entirely clear.

ORGANIZATION:

The ministry of the Eastern Orthodox Church is the threefold order of bishops, priests and deacons, as practiced in the early church. The patriarchs are bishops of the highest rank, the metropolitans of lesser. The bishops, united in a general council, represent the Church and under the guidance of the Holy Ghost decide infallibly all matters of faith and ecclesiastical procedure. Ministers of Christ must be regularly called and appointed to office and consecrated by the sacrament of holy orders. Priests may administer all the sacraments except that of holy orders, which may be administered by bishops only. Candidates for the diaconate and priesthood may marry, but after ordination marriage is forbidden. Bishops must be celibate. The monastic orders, so well known in Greece, Jerusalem and Sinai, do not exist in America.

DOCTRINE:

Eastern Orthodox doctrine is virtually the same for all branches of the Church. Its belief is based on Holy Scriptures, holy tradition and the decisions of the first seven Ecumenical Councils, I Nicaea (325), I Constantinople (381), Ephesus (431), Chalcedon (451), II Constantinople (553), III Constantinople (680-681), and II Nicaea (787). The Niceo-Constantinopolitan Creed is the accepted statement of belief. It differs from the Nicene Creed of the Western Church in omitting the *filioque* clause, which declares that the Holy Ghost proceeds *from the Son* as well as from the Father. By this omission, Article 8 of the Eastern version therefore reads, "And I believe in the Holy Ghost, the Lord and Giver of Life, who proceedeth from the Father, who with the Father and the Son is worshiped and glorified."

Infallibility is attributed only to the church as represented by its general synods. These cannot err, since they are under the abiding influence of the Holy Ghost.

The Church does not believe in the immaculate conception of the Virgin Mary, but does however honor her and believe in her perpetual virginity and the virgin birth of Christ. It reverences the nine orders of angels (Cherubim, Seraphim, Thrones, Dominions, Virtues, Powers, Principalities, Angels and Archangels), the saints, relics of the saints, pictures of holy subjects, and the cross; but forbids the use of carved images.

Seven sacraments are accepted: baptism, chrismation, communion, penance, holy orders, marriage and holy unction. Baptism by threefold immersion, in memory of the three days in the tomb, is recognized as the true form. After baptism, anointing with the holy oil (chrismation) makes the infant a full member of the Church. This sacrament takes the place of the confirmation usual in the Western churches, and immediately afterwards the child receives its first communion. Like the Roman, the Eastern Church accepts the doctrine of transsubstantiation (the changing of the bread and wine into the actual body and blood of Christ), but does not seek to explain the manner of the change, accepting it as a miracle.

Holy Unction is given not only to the dying but also to the sick for its healing properties. The doctrine of purgatory is rejected, though it is believed that there is an intermediate state in which the dead remain until the Second Coming. For the good this state is happy, for the evil it is unhappy, and for those who had repented before death but not proved their penitence by actions, it is one of temporary unhappiness. Prayers of the living to and for the dead and of the dead for the living are efficacious. According to ancient custom memorials of boiled wheat are prepared on behalf of the dead on certain days in the year (I Corinthians 15). Whereas God is omniscient and knows each soul's destiny, man may still exercise free will. Both faith and works are necessary for salvation.

FORM OF WORSHIP:

The service of the Eastern Church is elaborate and solemn. The ceremonies, of apostolic origin, are an integral part of worship and every motion and each garment and sacred object has a meaning. The language used in the liturgies is old Greek or Slavonic according to the nationality of the church, and is probably as near the spoken language of today as Chaucerian English is to modern speech.

The most important service is the Divine Liturgy celebrating the Holy Eucharist. There are four regular liturgies, of St. James, St. John Chrysostom, St. Basil and St. Gregory. The liturgy of St. James is very long, lasting for three hours, and differs in ceremonial from the others. It is used twice a year, on the Feast of St. James on October 23rd, and on the Sunday after Christmas. That of St. Basil is used ten times a year on great feast days, and the shorter liturgy of St. John Chrysostom at regular celebrations. On Wednesdays and Fridays in Lent the short order of St. Gregory is used. Some of the consecrated bread, the body of Christ, is reserved for use at these services.

The three great liturgies each consist of three distinct sections: the Office of Oblation, during which the bread and wine are prepared for consecration; the Liturgy of the Catechumens (those receiving instruction preparatory to becoming church members); and the Liturgy of the Faithful, which is the celebration of the Holy Mystery.

The whole liturgy reflects conditions in the early church, and seems to have come down from remote antiquity, in some cases pre-Christian. In the Liturgy of the Faithful there is an ancient prayer not found in the Roman Mass, asking that the Holy Ghost may change the elements—the bread and wine—into the body and blood. The manner in which this is done, the Church says, "none but God can understand." Communion is given in both kinds, the bread dipped into the wine after the blessing. Instead, however, of permitting the communicant to touch it, the priest dips up a morsel on a spoon and puts it into the recipient's mouth. This use of the spoon is said to have been instituted by St. John Chrysostom, since in his time a woman took a piece of the consecrated bread home to use as a charm in witchcraft.

Services are also held at vespers, vigils, matins, and the other hours, but these consist only of readings from the Bible, prayers and hymns, and have none of the liturgical ceremonial of the great liturgies. No "silent liturgies" or private masses are celebrated.

The altar and sanctuary as also the table of oblation are cut off from the choir and the rest of the chancel by the ikonostasis, a screen or thin wall on which are hung the sacred icons. There are three doors through this screen, the central one forbidden to anybody not an ordained priest. A curtain hangs within this door which is drawn or withdrawn as the rubrics direct. For a long time the music was all *a cappella,* but in this country today organs have been introduced into the churches.

The two largest Eastern Orthodox bodies in this country are the Greek Orthodox (Hellenic) and the Russian Orthodox.

The Greek Orthodox Church (Hellenic)—275,000

Between 1890 and 1914 there was a greatly increased emigration of Greeks to the United States. Most of the early arrivals came without their families, but later, when these also had come over and the immigrants had become permanent residents of the country, the need for a church of their own arose. In 1915 a serious attempt was made to organize the Greek Church in America, but it was not until 1922 that the Church was established and only in 1931 was the organization completed in its present form.

The Greek Orthodox Church (Hellenic) in the United States forms the Archdiocese of America and recognizes the jurisdiction of the Ecumenical Patriarch of Constantinople. Like all the churches affiliated under the Constantinopolitan patriarchate the Church is autonomous and governed by its own archbishop and synod. Its doctrine and dogma are necessarily those of the Eastern Orthodox Church, but all matters of discipline are referred to the Patriarchate at Istanbul.

THE RUSSIAN ORTHODOX CHURCH—300,000 VOTING MEMBERS

The Russian Orthodox Church is one branch of the Eastern Orthodox Church which has maintained missionary activity in modern times. In the eighteenth century it already had missions on the Aleutian Islands and in Alaska, which were then Russian territory. The cathedral built in Sitka in the middle of the nineteenth century still bears witness of their work.

After Alaska was sold to the United States in 1867 the see was removed from Sitka to San Francisco, where there were a large number of Russians, Serbs and Greeks. In 1891 it was found necessary to add to the Church a parish in Minneapolis, and in 1905 the see was transferred from San Francisco to New York, where an Orthodox Russian church had existed since 1876.

Until 1917 these churches were governed by the Holy Synod in Russia, and when in that year the patriarchate was restored by the Great Sobor they, like the Russian churches, went under the patriarch's control. With the establishment of the Soviets a change in polity and doctrine was forced on the Church; the newly appointed patriarch, Tikhon, was imprisoned and his associates were either exiled, imprisoned or executed. Bishops and clergy who would accept the new Soviet ideology were appointed, a married episcopate was established, and the oath of allegiance to the Soviet government was demanded of the Russian Orthodox clergy, including those in America.

This oath the clergy in America would not accept, and in order to protect themselves from further encroachment they convoked a sobor (convention) in Detroit in February, 1924, in which the Russian Orthodox Church in America proclaimed itself temporarily autonomous.

However, the U.S.S.R. claimed the cathedral in New York and installed there a priest who subscribed to its demands. Unable to expel the new incumbent, the ruling bishop of the Orthodox faith in America, together with a large number of the congregation, were forced to seek a new cathedral. Trinity Parish of the Episcopal Church offered them a chapel to use temporarily. In June, 1943, the Church bought property at 59-63 East Second Street in New York City, and its headquarters were moved to this new center on June 24, 1943.

The latest information on the growth of the Russian Orthodox Church in North America indicates that it numbers 206 congregations in the United States (of which 14 are in Alaska), and 34 in Canada, or 240 in all. These are served by a clergy numbering 264, including seven bishops. The church census includes only those, such as heads of families, who are entitled to vote in parish meetings.

THE ROMAN CATHOLIC CHURCH—24,402,124

The first Catholic congregation established in what is now the United States was in St. Augustine, Florida, in 1565. At that time Florida belonged to Spain and was the center of great missionary activity among the Indians. From St. Augustine missionary work spread west to Santa Fe and by about 1600 the Franciscans were proselytizing on the Pacific Coast. In the seventeenth century French priests were active along the coast of Maine and on the Great Lakes, and the Jesuits were moving down the Mississippi. The story of these early missions is one of the epics of American history. Priests and friars went with every trading party, sharing the hardships of life in the trackless wilderness, and the names of some of our midwestern towns still bring back the echo of the impression left by these selfless and devoted men.

To the English colonies the Catholic Church did not come until the immigration of the English Catholics to Maryland in 1634. Religious toleration was from the outset the law of the colony, but in later years the ruling was abrogated and the Catholics restricted. It was not until after the adoption of the Constitution and amendments in 1787 that religious freedom was granted to all forms of belief, and all restrictions were removed.

The Revolutionary War left the Catholic Church in America without any immediate hierarchical superior. The link with the English Church was of course broken, and a French superior did not seem a satisfactory solution of the problem. In the end John Carroll of Maryland was proposed and accepted as the superior, or prefect apostolic, of the thirteen original states and the Church in the United States became independent of the vicar apostolic of London.

Many problems arose during the next few years, for there was no precedent for setting up a Catholic Church in a new republic with no previously existing Catholic tradition. In several of the states, for example, Catholics could hold no office in the new government unless they renounced all foreign jurisdiction, civil or ecclesiastical; the rights of congregations to own church property and choose and dismiss pastors were sometimes questioned; there was no theological school to train new clergy. These and many other difficulties were eventually solved, and the Roman Catholic Church began to spread very rapidly so that today it is far and away the largest religious denomination in the country, outnumbering even the Baptists, who compose the largest single Protestant group.

MEMBERSHIP:

Membership begins with baptism, and all who are baptized into the Roman Catholic Church are counted as members unless they have formally renounced such membership.

ORGANIZATION:

The parish is the smallest unit and is the charge of a priest who may have other priests to assist him. The priesthood alone has authority to administer the sacraments. The priest is appointed by the bishop or archbishop and is subject to his rule. A number of parishes constitute a diocese over which is the bishop, who is assisted by a vicar-general, a chancellor or secretary and a council of consultors. The dioceses are further grouped in provinces of which there are twenty-two, each presided over by an archbishop. Four of the present archbishops are cardinals.

The general government of the Church throughout the world is vested in the Pope, or Bishop of Rome, who holds office for life. He is assisted by a complex machinery of administration, consisting of first the College of Cardinals and the Curia Romana. The College, restricted to seventy in number, stands next to the Pope in authority, has in its hands the election of a new pope when the see is left vacant by death, and serves as the papal advisory body. The Curia Romana, representing the general administrative mechanism, is composed of "congregations" and "tribunals," each with its particular functions and responsibilities. The "congregations" are composed of cardinals, and one of the most important is the Congregation of the Holy Office, which controls the Index and decides what books are permitted reading for the laity throughout the world. The tribunals, composed of lesser dignitaries, deal with much of the administrative routine.

The orders of ministry are: priests, deacons, subdeacons and those in minor orders. Candidates for orders who are studying in one of the recognized divinity schools are called "seminarians." When he is ordained subdeacon, the seminarian makes a solemn pledge to observe chastity for life; after a time of service, if approved, he is ordained deacon, and then priest. The priest conducts church services, administers the sacraments and alone may celebrate the Mass. A deacon may be specially authorized to preach and administer certain sacraments. Bishops, archbishops and cardinals are chosen from the ranks of the priests.

There are two kinds of religious orders—the monastic orders, who take the vows of obedience, poverty and chastity, and the religious congregations of priests and the brotherhoods and sisterhoods, who take simple, not perpetual vows. Priests who live in religious communities are called regular clergy because they live by a regula, or rule; parish priests, diocesan or secular clergy. The clergy are all who are tonsured. Most of the teaching, nursing, almsgiving, etc., is done by these religious orders.

There is a fully organized system of ecclesiastical councils which are an important factor in church polity. The diocesan synod is a gathering of the priests of a diocese. Over this is the provincial council composed of the bishops in the territory of a metropolitan or archbishop. A plenary or national council is an assembly of all the bishops of the country. Highest of all is the general, or ecumenical, council convoked by the Pope and including all the Catholic bishops of the world.

It is this general council which settles doctrinal and disciplinary matters, and its acts to be binding must be confirmed by the Pope.

The laity has no voice in the conduct of the church nor

in the choice of a priest but take some part in the management of parish affairs. Church property is held officially, not personally by the archbishop, and passes to his successor.

The salaries of priests are settled on a uniform basis for each diocese. The income of the church is from pew rents, plate collections and offerings for baptisms, marriages, masses, etc. Of this money the priest may keep only his salary. The rest is used for the church and the various charities which it supports.

In 1870 a decree of the Vatican Council, the first ecumenical council since the Council of Trent in 1545-1563, pronounced the Pope infallible when, in his capacity as supreme teacher for the Universal Church, he defines a question of faith or morals.

DOCTRINE:

The Apostles' Creed, the Nicene Creed and the Athanasian Creed are looked upon as containing the essential truths accepted by the Church. Over and above these there is a "profession of faith" to which must agree all who enter the Church. It includes, besides the rejection of doctrines condemned by the Church, and a promise of obedience to church authority in matters of belief, a statement of faith as follows:

"Only one God, in three divine Persons, distinct from and equal to each other—that is to say, the Father, the Son, and the Holy Ghost.

"The Catholic doctrine of the Incarnation, Passion, Death and Resurrection of our Lord Jesus Christ; and the personal union of the two Natures, the divine and the human; the divine maternity of the Most Holy Mary, together with her most spotless virginity.

"The true, real and substantial presence of the Body and Blood, together with the Soul and Divinity of our Lord Jesus Christ, in the most holy sacrament of the Eucharist.

"The seven sacraments instituted by Jesus Christ for the salvation of mankind; that is to say: Baptism, Confirmation, Eucharist, Penance, Extreme Unction, Orders, Matrimony.

"Purgatory, the resurrection of the dead, everlasting life.

"The primacy, not only of honor, but also of jurisdiction, of the Roman Pontiff, successor of St. Peter, Prince of the Apostles, Vicar of Jesus Christ; the veneration of the saints and of their images; the authority of the apostolic and ecclesiastical traditions, and of the Holy Scriptures, which we must interpret and understand, only in the sense which our holy mother the Catholic Church has held, and does hold; and everything else that has been defined and declared by the sacred Canons, and by the General Councils, and particularly by the Holy Council of Trent and delivered, defined and declared by the General Council of the Vatican, especially concerning the primacy of the Holy Pontiff and his infallible teaching authority."

The sacrament of baptism is administered by the pouring on of water. Confirmation is the laying on of hands by the bishop through which "the Holy Spirit is received" by the candidate. In the Eucharist the Body and Blood of Jesus are received through the sacred species under the appearance of bread and wine. It is to be received fasting and given to the laity only in the form of bread. In penance the sins committed since baptism are forgiven. Extreme unction is the anointing by oil of those in danger of death. Holy Orders give to bishops and priests and other ministers power to perform their sacred duties. Matrimony is the sacrament which unites a man and woman in marriage. Such a marriage "cannot be dissolved by any power."

The chief commandments of the Church to the laity are:

1. To hear Mass on Sundays and holy days of obligation.

2. To fast and abstain on the days appointed.
3. To confess at least once a year.
4. To receive the Holy Eucharist during Easter-time.
5. To contribute toward the support of the pastors.
6. To observe the regulations in regard to marriage.

FORM OF WORSHIP:

The church services are highly ritual and strictly follow a liturgy which is read in Latin in the greater portion of the world, although there are a number of other liturgies followed by churches in communion with Rome. Low Mass is spoken, High Mass is sung. When officiating priest, deacon and subdeacon all take part it is known as Solemn Mass. That part of the Mass which changes according to season is called the proper, the rest the ordinary. The ordinary consists of the Kyrie, Gloria, Credo, Sanctus et Benedictus and Agnus Dei.

The officiating priests and deacons wear elaborate vestments, each part of which has an old symbolical meaning, as have also the gestures and such acts as censing, ringing the bell, lighting candles. Altarcloths and hangings as well as church furnishings have their origins also in the remote past.

The Roman Catholic Church carries on a large educational work, which includes elementary and grade schools, normal schools, universities, and theological seminaries as well as schools of social work. It has orphanages and hospitals in the most remote sections of the country and many of the religious orders are devoted to charitable and welfare work both in Catholic institutions and in the homes. Such wide activities are made possible by the centralization of government, the rule of strict obedience to the Church, and the celibacy of the clergy and monastic orders, who have no family ties to hold them in any one place.

THE ANGLICAN (PROTESTANT EPISCOPAL) CHURCH—2,155,514

During colonial days the Church of England was established over a large part of the country, and was especially strong in Virginia, Maryland and New York. After the Revolutionary War the Colonial Church separated from the Church of England, and in 1789 took the name The Protestant Episcopal Church in the United States of America. For its liturgy as an independent body, the prayer book was slightly changed and modified, to adapt it to a nation under a republican form of government. Today the Episcopal Church is frequently called the Anglican Church, because it is one of a group, including the established Church of England, the Episcopal Church in Scotland, Ireland and Wales, and the Church of England in the colonies and dominions of the British Empire, which constitute a family of churches known as the Anglican Communion. A meeting of the bishops of the entire Anglican Communion is held every ten years at Lambeth Palace in London, at the invitation of the Bishop of Canterbury.

ORGANIZATION:

The Episcopal Church derives its name from its form of government, inherited from the Roman Church and carried over by the Church of England when it broke with the papacy in the sixteenth century, again to be carried over when the American body began its independent existence on this side of the Atlantic. Its ministry is the historic threefold order of bishops, priests and deacons, in descending order of rank. After a prescribed course of training and active duty, the deacon is normally ordained a priest, and the bishops are selected from the priesthood. Women who wish to devote themselves to work in the Church may become deaconesses, but cannot enter the priesthood.

Each congregation is served by one or more priests, sometimes with a deacon or a lay reader, or both, to assist the priest. There may also be one or more deacons to help with parish activities and visiting. The church is the center of the parish, and its control and government are in the hands of the rector and vestry, the latter a body of laymen chosen from the congregation. A group of parishes constitutes a diocese, under the direction of a bishop; in a very large diocese he may be assisted by a bishop coadjutor or a suffragan bishop. Matters affecting the diocese as a whole are settled at the annual Diocesan Convention, over which the bishop presides, and every three years there is a general convention which is the supreme governing body of the entire Church. This is composed of two houses, the House of Bishops and the House of Deputies, the latter made up of both clergy and laymen. The General Convention elects, and is presided over by, the presiding bishop.

It is interesting to see the close resemblance of this organization to the form of government set up in this country by the Constitution. The men who planned the government of the Episcopal Church were many of them either instrumental in drawing up the Constitution, or were deeply interested in it, and the similarity between the two forms, church and state, is therefore not an accident, but a deliberate choice, by the founding fathers of the Church, of what seemed to them likely to allow most freedom within the law.

DOCTRINE:

The articles of belief are contained within the Apostles' Creed and the Nicene Creed. They are further enlarged upon in the Offices of Instruction, which are based upon the ancient catechism of the Church of England. The Offices expound the purpose and meaning of baptism, the Apostles' Creed, the Ten Commandments, Christ's summary of the Law, the Lord's Prayer, the Church and the sacraments.

For membership in the Church, baptism and confirmation are required. Knowledge of the Offices of Instruction is a prerequisite of confirmation—a laying on of hands by the bishop—and confirmation itself is a prerequisite of admittance to Holy Communion. Only two sacraments are generally necessary, baptism and Holy Communion. A sacrament is defined as "an outward and visible sign of an inward and spiritual grace," and the special Episcopalian position on the Holy Communion is contained in the phrase, "the real presence of Christ." The Church does not attempt to define the exact form of the presence more precisely. The other five ancient sacraments acknowledged by the Roman Church are not expressly denied as sacraments, and in some degree are accepted by certain Episcopal parishes, more especially by those known as "high" churches. The Thirty-nine Articles as established in 1801 are still included in the Book of Common Prayer, but subscription to them is no longer required.

FORM OF WORSHIP:

Church services are conducted in accordance with the liturgy contained in the Book of Common Prayer, as revised in 1928. The form varies according to the preferences of the individual congregation, or rectors of congregations. Some churches, known as "high," adopt a more elaborate ritual, with use of the word "mass" instead of Holy Communion, and in some instances reservation of the sacrament and auricular confession. Some are very "low," with a table instead of an altar, and as little ceremony as is compatible with the prescribed service. The liturgy is capable of wide variation in use, and the majority of Episcopal churches have placed themselves between "high" and "low," observing a moderate form acceptable to all. In many congregations, especially those in the "middle" and "low" groups, members of other denominations are invited to receive the sacrament at the service of Holy Communion.

The desire to sacrifice one's whole life to Christ and to His church is found in some members of nearly every denomination. It was recognized in the early church and resulted in the monastic orders which played so large a part in church development. When the Church of England broke from the Roman Church and became independent, and still more when the Puritan element prevailed, the monastic orders with their practices of chastity, poverty and obedience were frowned upon and crushed. In about 1840, however, as an outgrowth of the Oxford Movement in England, the demand arose for restoration of orders of the kind, and eventually sisterhoods and brotherhoods vowed to celibacy and service were established within the Episcopal Church, which have done valuable work in preaching, education and rescue. The Holy Cross Fathers and the Sisters of St. Mary are famous for their devoted activities.

THE BAPTIST CHURCHES—over 14,000,000

The Baptists acknowledge no human founder, no human authority, and subscribe to no man-made creed. They look to the Bible as the one source of authority and to the New Testament in particular as a guide to faith and right living. The Reformation was hardly under way before people holding these views began to spring up everywhere, encouraged by Reform doctrine to suppose that every man would be free to interpret the Word of God according to his own lights.

ORIGIN:

In the early part of the sixteenth century, when Luther was still formulating his creeds, the Anabaptists, or rebaptizers, arose in Switzerland and Germany, and from these centers spread rapidly into Holland and England. The Reformers, dismayed at what seemed to them religious license, did their best to stem the tide which they themselves had released, but to no avail. Even persecution could not stem it, indeed seemed only to swell it. Having thrown off the papal rule, these new "heresies," as they were considered by the established churches of the various countries, grew and spread and again subdivided into new varieties of religious belief until it began to look as if all unity of faith were gone and the very authority of government destroyed. In those days, church and state were looked upon as interdependent, and whatever threatened the one seemed a menace to the other also.

Anabaptists and Baptists alike received their names from their views on baptism. Searching the Scriptures, they could find no justification for infant baptism (pedobaptism). According to their reading, this sacrament presupposed repentance for sins and a desire to do better, and since such a state of mind was obviously impossible for a baby or even a young child, it followed that a person must have reached a certain maturity before baptism could be efficacious. They therefore required the rebaptism of all proselytes and prescribed adult baptism as the accepted practice.

In England the Anabaptists were known as Separatists, but it was not until 1607 that the English Baptist movement really started, when an independent congregation left England to seek religious freedom in Holland. At this time sprinkling was still the accepted form of baptism, and it was not until 1640 that further reading of Scriptures convinced the leaders of the Church that immersion, symbolizing a death, burial and resurrection, was the form practiced in the New Testament. In Romans 6:4 Paul says: "Therefore we are buried with him by baptism into death: that like as Christ was raised up from the dead by the glory of the Father, even so we also should walk in newness of life." From this time on, baptism by immersion became the rule among Baptists, and in the eyes of the world one of their distinguishing characteristics.

The first Baptist church in America was probably that founded by Roger Williams in Providence, Rhode Island, in 1639. But the greatest Baptist advances were made in and around Philadelphia and in the neighboring regions of Delaware and New Jersey. In 1707 these churches came together into the Philadelphia Association, which was soon followed by other Baptist associations, notably in South Carolina and Rhode Island. Before many years there were Baptist churches spread widely over all thirteen colonies. Some of those in the North were Particular, or Calvinistic, and acknowledged only a partial atonement for sins in Christ's death. They did not, however, go as far as Calvin, who claimed that the atonement was only for the elect. Many others accepted a larger measure of human freedom in the achievement of salvation. The southern Baptists of these early colonial times were of the General Baptist conviction, claiming that the atonement offered by Christ was universal.

The freedom of faith which Roger Williams had preached, and on which the Baptists laid so much stress, soon led to numerous subdivisions in the Church itself. The Bible was the only authority, and every man read it and interpreted it in his own way, with the result that by the time of the Revolution there were already six main groups of Baptists as well as several smaller divisions in the country.

The Great Awakening in 1740 influenced the Baptists just as it did all other Protestant denominations, and the evangelistic work of the Baptist Church, as well as their expansion into the frontier country, may be said to have begun at this time. About a hundred years later the Baptists started their work in the foreign mission field, for which they have always been famous.

The Baptist Church, because of its avoidance of set creeds and its insistence on freedom of belief and separation between church and state, has given wide room for variation within the faith and remained a living and growing force. It was early accepted by the Negroes, and even in Revolutionary times they had set up a church in South Carolina which was followed by others in various parts of this country and Canada. For the most part, however, until after the Civil War the slaves attended their masters' churches, where they sat in the galleries.

After the Civil War the Negro congregations in all parts of the country broke away and set up churches and church organizations of their own, which have become active and living forces in the country. It is interesting here to observe that in Russia, where all religion has been, to say the least, discouraged, the Baptists are growing in strength and their membership despite government control has been estimated at 2,000,000, perhaps as much as 3,000,000.

Along educational lines too the Baptists have not been idle. Besides publishing houses, seminaries, and other denominational institutions, the University of Rochester, Brown University and the University of Chicago are all Baptist foundations, as are the University of Richmond, Wake Forest, Furman, Mercer, Mississippi College, William Jewell College, Denison, Oklahoma Baptist University and Baylor University.

DOCTRINE:

Baptists, as has been said, have no formulated creed, basing their entire faith and practice on the Holy Scriptures. Their interpretations of the Bible vary to such a degree that fundamentalists and higher critics as well as all intermediate shadings may be found among Baptist congregations.

The New Hampshire Confession, a modification of the Westminster Confession, has become a platform for a large section of Baptists, but it is by no means binding or in any way final. A condensed version of it follows:

1. The Scriptures are divinely inspired and adequate as a foundation for faith (II Timothy 3:16, 17).

2. God is glorious, omnipotent and uniquely divine.

3. Man fell and has transmitted the original sin to his descendants.

4. The way of salvation lies through grace through the mediation of Jesus, the Son of God (John 3:16).

5. Man's justification is by the grace of Christ through faith in Him.

6. Salvation is free to all by faith alone.

7. To be saved man must be regenerated by the Holy Spirit.

8. Man stands in need of repentance, grace and faith in Jesus Christ.

9. Election is the eternal purpose of God, but election is in some way consistent with man's free agency.

10. Through sanctification, a progressive work, we are made partakers of God's holiness.

11. Those who are truly regenerate, born of the spirit, will endure to the end (John 8:31).

12. Man is originally born in sin.

13. The visible church of Christ is a company of baptized believers, associated by covenant in the faith and fellowship of the Gospel. The only Scriptural officers of the Church are bishops or pastors and deacons.

14. Baptism is the immersion in water of a believer in Christ. The Lord's Supper commemorates the dying love of Jesus, and its observance is to be preceded by self-examination.

15. The Lord's day is sacred.

16. Civil and divine government are, and should be, separate.

17. The distinction between good and bad men holds both in life and after death.

18. There will be a last day with a final judgment.

The beliefs held by all may be summed up as follows:

1. Religious freedom.
2. The validity and inspiration of the Bible.
3. The divinity of Christ.
4. The immortality of the soul.
5. The brotherhood of man.
6. The future life.
7. The need of redemption from sin.
8. The coming of the kingdom of God.

Within these limits there is a wide variation of individual belief.

As ordinances all Baptists accept baptism and the Supper of the Lord, and insist on the baptism of adults by immersion as the Scriptural and therefore a prescribed method.

FORM OF WORSHIP:

The form of worship is decided by each congregation, whence there is no fixed ritual or liturgy, but on the contrary room for great variation. Some of the modern city churches have lighted altars and a vested clergy and follow a liturgical form.

SUBDIVISIONS:

There are today nine major Baptist sects in the country as well as a large number of small independent groups. The nine are the Northern Baptists; the Southern Baptists; the National Baptist Convention, U.S.A., Inc. (colored); the National Baptist Convention of America (colored); the Free Will Baptists; the United American Free Will Baptists (colored); the American Baptist Association; the Primitive Baptists; the National Baptist Evangelical Life and Soul Saving Assembly of U.S.A. In all, these number nearly 15,000,000 members. For the sake of brevity they may be classed in six groups according to their differences in minor points of belief, procedure and polity.

I
The Northern Baptists—1,592,349
The Southern Baptists—6,079,305

The first general organization of Baptist churches was not made until 1814, when a General Missionary Convention was formed for the purpose of permitting members of the faith to express themselves in missionary activities. In 1845 the southern branch broke away on the slavery issue and organized the Southern Baptist Convention.

In 1907 the Northern Baptists incorporated themselves under the laws of the state of New York, thus making it possible to co-ordinate their wide activities more closely. Their organization is very practical and efficient. The local church is the unit and is of course independent of every other church of the Convention, except in so far as it agrees with any given policy. The Convention is composed of delegates from the churches and from certain national and state church organizations. There is a managing body called the General Council, which is continuous when the Convention is not in session. In the Southern Baptist Church the organization is practically the same, but the continuing body is the Executive Committee.

Northern and Southern Baptist Churches are essentially in harmony with each other and interchange both membership and ministry on terms of equality.

II
National Baptist Convention, U.S.A., Inc.—4,122,315 (colored)
National Baptist Convention of America—2,575,621 (colored)

The first African slaves were brought to this country in 1619, but it was over a hundred and fifty years before there was a colored church or a trained colored preacher. What was probably the first Negro Baptist Church was set up on the South Carolina side of the Savannah River a few years before the Revolutionary War, and it may well be that this was the seed from which the faith spread among the Negroes. Today the colored Baptist churches are an active and growing organization all over the country; and are also strong in the foreign and home mission fields.

The National Baptist Convention, U.S.A., Inc., is the older and parent convention of the two. It was incorporated under the laws of the District of Columbia in 1915. The National Baptist Convention of America is usually referred to as the "unincorporated" body. Both conventions are in general agreement with the Northern and Southern Conventions described under Section I above, but represent a more strictly Calvinistic element. Their churches unite in county and district associations and also in state conventions. The National Baptist Convention, U.S.A., Inc., has held its meetings annually since 1880 in cities as widely scattered as New York, Chicago, Dallas and Atlanta. The proceedings of their sixty-sixth annual convention, held in Atlanta, Georgia, in 1946 show a wide range of membership and interests.

DOCTRINE:

The doctrines of the Southern and Northern Baptists and of the two Conventions are very similar. The Southern Baptists and the Negro Conventions are sometimes more Calvinistic than the Northern Baptists and hold more firmly to the New Hampshire Confession. The Southern Baptists as a rule practice close communion (permitting no one not of the "same faith and order" to attend Communion). However, these differences are by no means universal.

III

American Baptist Association—115,022

HISTORY:

This is not a distinct sect, but comprises a separate and distinct group who were opposed to conventions as an unjustified innovation among the Baptists. They look upon the Association in which they are joined as a co-operation of the churches comprising it, and therefore like the association of the primitive churches. They have annual meetings to which each church elects three "messengers," and where all questions are settled by the majority vote of the messengers present, except on major questions, for which a two-thirds majority is required. These annual meetings are called "The meeting of the messengers composing the American Baptist Association."

DOCTRINE:

The American Baptist Association accepts the New Hampshire Confession, previously summarized.

IV

Primitive Baptists—69,157

Like the American Baptist Association, these were opposed to the increasing organization of churches and Church, and more especially to the formation of missionary societies. They consist therefore of a loosely knit group of congregations throughout the country, held together only by fraternal visits. These are the so-called "Hard-Shell" Baptists. They are extreme in the autonomy they give to the individual congregation.

ORGANIZATION:

The ministry is not trained in theology, and ordination is by the laying on of hands of pastors and elders called by the church to which the candidate belongs.

DOCTRINE:

The Primitive Baptists are strongly Calvinistic and "fundamentalist." They believe in

1. Man's total depravity.
2. That man cannot of himself attain grace.
3. That God chose His people in Christ before the foundation of the world.
4. That sinners are justified only through Christ.
5. That the saints—the elect—will all be preserved.
6. That baptism and the Lord's Supper are divinely ordained.
7. That the institutions of the day (church societies) are not to be countenanced.
8. That Christ will come again to judge the world, condemn the wicked to eternal punishment and the righteous to eternal bliss.

They also accept as literally true and inspired the whole Old and New Testament.

In some sections the Primitive Baptists believe in the practice of foot washing in connection with the Lord's Supper.

V

FREE WILL BAPTISTS—221,317
UNITED AMERICAN FREE WILL BAPTISTS (colored)—75,000

ORIGIN:

In 1701 a Welsh Baptist group emigrated to Pennsylvania where in 1703 it was given land known as the "Welsh Tract." The colony prospered and sent out missionaries, one of whom, Elder Paul Palmer, organized a church in North Carolina.

For some years after the Civil War the line between white and colored Free Will Baptist churches was not strongly drawn, but as the Negroes increased in numbers and activities they felt the need for a church of their own, and in 1901 were organized as a separate denomination.

ORGANIZATION:

The Free Will Baptists are distinctly congregational, but for business purposes hold quarterly meetings of the state bodies in which all members may participate, and also annual conferences representing the whole denomination. The officers of the church are pastor, clerk and treasurer; deacons, who care for alms distribution and preparations for the Communion service; and elders who look after spiritual interests and settle controversies between brethren.

In the United American Free Will Baptists the local churches are not as autonomous as in the parent group. The conferences have authority over the local churches in both doctrinal and business matters.

DOCTRINE:

Both groups accept the five points of Arminianism, as against the five points of Calvinism. They believe that

1. Election and condemnation are conditioned upon the faith or unbelief of man and not arbitrarily determined by God.

2. Atonement is for all, but only believers enjoy its benefits.

3. Man, unaided by the Holy Spirit, is unable to come to God.

4. Grace is not irresistible, but those who desire Christ's help will be kept from falling.

5. Man may relapse from a state of grace.

They accept the New Hampshire Confession.

They acknowledge four ordinances: Baptism (by immersion only), the Lord's Supper, which is uniformly open Communion; foot washing; and anointing the sick with oil.

VI

National Baptist Evangelical Life and Soul Saving Assembly of U.S.A.—70,843

MEMBERSHIP:

Membership consists of those who feel it their duty to seek daily to save lost souls and reclaim backsliders.

ORIGIN:

The sect had its origin in Kansas City where it was founded by A. A. Banks. It was at first affiliated with the National Baptist Convention, unincorporated, but in 1936 became an independent organization. The Assembly has always done relief work, and is especially interested in "soul saving," setting as its goal one million souls annually.

Beside the main bodies of Baptists listed above there are numerous small independent groups, both white and colored, each with some individual belief or practice.

The General Six Principle Baptists take their name from Hebrews 6:1, 2, which they look upon as binding:

> "Therefore leaving the principle of the doctrine of Christ, let us go on unto perfection; not laying again the foundation of repentance from dead works, and of faith toward God, of the doctrine of baptisms, and of laying on of hands, and of resurrection of the dead, and of eternal judgment."

In accordance with this teaching they insist on the laying on of hands when members are received into the Church, as a sign of the reception of the gifts of the Holy Spirit. This may be said to correspond with the rite of Confirmation in some of the other denominations.

The SEVENTH DAY BAPTISTS keep the seventh day of the week instead of the first as the Sabbath.

The GENERAL BAPTISTS believe in general atonement, that is, that Christ died for all men, and not only for the elect.

The SEPARATE BAPTISTS also preach the gospel of general atonement. They celebrate the Lord's Supper in the evening.

The DUCK RIVER BAPTISTS take very much the same stand as the General Baptists—a liberal Calvinism.

TWO-SEED-IN-THE-SPIRIT PREDESTINARIAN BAPTISTS are named in accordance with their faith. The "two seeds" mean one seed of good and one of evil, one from God and one from the devil. Both seeds are predestined and cannot change. The atonement was for the good seed who are children of God and will be saved in the last day.

The INDEPENDENT BAPTIST CHURCH OF AMERICA is a Swedish group centered in the northern Middle West. They are opposed to war.

The CHRISTIAN UNITY BAPTIST ASSOCIATION acknowledges three ordinances: baptism by immersion, the Lord's Supper, and foot washing. They also believe in the redemption of the body of saints, infants and idiots, the latter two not being responsible for sin and not in need of regeneration of the spirit.

The history of the SEVENTH DAY BAPTISTS (German) is very interesting and closely related to the development of the Dunkards. Conrad Beissel came to this country from Germany in 1720 and settled in Pennsylvania. For a while he lived with Becker, the founder of the Dunkards, and learned from him the art of weaving. Later he and a friend moved to Lancaster County, where they built a cabin and retired to a life of prayer and contemplation. Their fame spread and young men were sent to them for religious instruction. In time Beissel and some of his followers and pupils formed a congregation. Their adoption of the seventh day as the Sabbath brought persecution upon them, but they continued strong in their faith and in 1728 organized themselves as Seventh Day Baptists.

In 1732 Beissel withdrew and formed the Ephrata Society, based on communistic lines. Celibacy was adopted as a rule of life and a brothers' house and sisters' house were set up. Toward the close of the eighteenth century celibacy was given up and the group returned to the fold of the Seventh Day Baptists, building a church in 1829. In 1900 the property held by the Society was transferred to the congregation.

The distinguishing doctrines of this group are baptism by trine forward immersion, foot washing, anointing the sick, the blessing of infants, observance of the seventh day as the Sabbath, and nonresistance as implied in the sixth commandment, "Thou shalt do no murder."

Every five years Baptists of all shades of belief and from all over the world gather for the Baptist World Alliance.

THE CHRISTIAN REFORMED CHURCH—134,608

The Christian Reformed Church, like the Reformed Church in America, is an offshoot of the Reformed Church in Holland. During the eighty years of Holland's war for independence (1568-1648) the Dutch learned much about religious toleration, and when political freedom was attained a large measure of religious freedom ensued. The chief forms of belief in the tiny country were Catholicism, Lutheranism and Calvinism. From the Calvinistic roots grew the various Reformed elements, two of which are largely represented in the United States.

The Reformed Church was the established church of Holland until the time of the French Revolution. In 1816

Holland became a kingdom and the new monarch, William I, reorganized the church under the state in a way that many of the members thought contrary to the Presbyterian order. In 1834 there was open secession of a large group on the grounds of:

1. A falling away from the pure doctrine of the Reformed Church.
2. A hierarchical form of church government and arbitrary regulations.
3. The use of unsound hymns.
4. A new form of subscription by which doctrine was to be taught, not *because,* but *in so far as* it was contained in the Word of God.
5. Unfaithfulness of preachers regarding their ordination vows.

In about 1864, in part as a result of persecution and perhaps still more because of hard times, several groups of the seceders set sail for the United States. Most of them eventually settled in Michigan and Iowa, where place names like Holland, Zeeland, Vriesland, still persist. At first the struggle for survival was so hard and settlements were so widely scattered that any kind of denominational organization was out of the question. For the older people the absence of a church, while a deprivation, was not dangerous as it was to the children who were receiving no formal religious training. When, therefore, living conditions grew easier the new settlers began to look about for a church affiliation of some kind.

Their relationship with the Church in Holland had been severed, and their closest and most natural tie was with the Reformed Church on the east coast, which dated back to the early days in Holland before the secession. The newcomers, who by now had increased in number largely by immigration, connected themselves with this Dutch Reformed Church with the reservation that they could leave it if at any time they found themselves at variance with its principles and practices. Apparently the union was too hasty, and basic differences soon appeared. The newcomers felt that the Dutch Reformed Church in America was in error because:

1. It departed from the Calvinism of standard doctrine.
2. It neglected catechistical preaching and teaching.
3. It used eight hundred hymns, not all of which were doctrinally sound.
4. It tolerated Freemasons as members in good standing.
5. It administered private baptism.
6. It permitted open communion.
7. It neglected family visiting.

In 1857, therefore, the midwestern settlers organized a new church called first the Holland Reformed, then the True Dutch Reformed, the Holland Christian Reformed, and finally in 1880 the Christian Reformed Church. The new denomination spread slowly at first. For some years it was involved in fresh dissensions, and furthermore it had difficulty obtaining pastors, since it had to depend on men sent from Holland.

In 1875, however, it started a theological school in Grand Rapids, Michigan, and was soon training its own ministry. At about this time, as the older immigrants died and a new generation sprang up, the use of English began to creep into the churches, until by 1920 it was general. It was in the latter years of the nineteenth century that the Christian Reformed Church started missionary work, which expanded from home missions to work among the Indians in the Southwest, and finally to active work in China and Nigeria.

MEMBERSHIP:

Membership includes all those children who have been baptized in the Church, as well as adult communicants.

ORGANIZATION:

The organization is strictly Presbyterian. The ministers are of equal rank, and each congregation is under the joint rule of its minister and elders, forming the governing body, or consistory. The elders and deacons are chosen by the congregation. Groups of congregations are represented in a classis formed of delegates from each, and in turn each classis sends four delegates (two ministers and two elders) to a synod, the highest church court in the organization.

For purposes of inspection of all phases of teaching and work, every classis appoints at least two ministers for church visitation.

DOCTRINE:

The church lays great emphasis on creeds, and in *The Christian Reformed Church in North America* Dr. Henry Beets gives five reasons for creeds, which are in some degree an explanation of the need so many people find for a formal statement of faith:

1. A creed gives a résumé of the leading teachings of the Bible, which is, of course, the basis of all Christianity.
2. It is a bond of union between like-minded people.
3. It gives outsiders an official statement of faith.
4. It keeps the church from being torn by dissension.
5. It is a standard of orthodoxy.

The Christian Reformed Church accepts three statements of faith:

1. The Heidelberg Catechism (1653), which is a compendium of doctrine.
2. The Belgic Confession, which was approved by the Synod of Dort (1618-1619) and is an exposition of the chief doctrines of grace.

3. The Canons of Dortrecht (1619). This is strongly Calvinistic and states the Church's views on controversial subjects such as "Divine Predestination," redemption through Christ's sacrifice, total depravity, and the "Perseverance of the Saints."

The basic doctrine of Calvinism is the sovereignty of God, from which it follows that man's first duty is to do God's will. In Adam's fall the power to do God's will was destroyed and all were condemned. God, in Christ, redeems the elect and gives them saving grace through the Holy Spirit. God's purpose moves to a predestined end, but at the same time man is represented as a free moral agent responsible for all his acts. Moreover, the sincere offer of salvation to all who hear the gospel is also emphasized.

The Church accepts two sacraments, baptism and the Lord's Supper.

FORM OF WORSHIP:

The Christian Reformed Church is semiliturgical. It has a liturgy with forms of prayer for optional use in public worship. The use of the liturgy for the administration of the sacraments and for ordination is obligatory. The sermon is the important feature in public worship, and in all the churches a section of the Heidelberg Catechism is expounded every Sunday. For this purpose the catechism is divided into fifty-two parts. Formerly only psalms were sung, but in 1935 a Psalter Hymnal was introduced which contains 327 psalms and 141 hymns. The use of the psalms is obligatory, that of the hymns optional.

The Christian Reformed Church still preaches the old orthodox gospel, whereas the Reformed Church in the East has grown more liberal. The Christian Reformed Church has been able to hold to the old forms the more steadily because it has kept much of the training of its children in its own hands, setting up schools owned and operated by societies of Christian parents.

The Church is active in missionary work, especially among the Indians. It also maintains beneficent institutions and several hospitals in this country.

THE CHURCH OF THE BRETHREN—196,000

The German Baptist Brethren originated in Westphalia, Germany, in 1708. As the new Protestant churches in the seventeenth century grew more and more formalized, and as dogma, ritual, ceremony and organization developed and seemed to become essential for church membership, dissatisfaction was felt in many quarters. To many, and especially to the pietistic group, the personal element in religion, direct communication with God, seemed to be lost, and the Protestantism on which they had founded their hopes was coming to seem barren and sterile.

In 1708, at Schwarzenau, eight persons (five men and three women) led by Alexander Mack, one of the pietist group, baptized each other by trine immersion in the River Eder, probably the first baptism of the kind in the Protestant Church. This was the first step in the organization of a new congregation, which became the German Baptist Brethren, often called Tunkers or Dunkers from their mode of baptism. Since 1908 the official name of the church has been the Church of the Brethren.

As the Church grew and spread, the members everywhere suffered hardships from the state churches. The Treaty of Westphalia (1648), which ended the religious wars for Roman Catholics, Lutherans and Calvinists, had not given religious freedom to the other forms of faith, and the governments insisted that everyone should support the state church. In 1719 the congregation at Creyfeld, led by Peter Becker, moved to Germantown, Pennsylvania, and set up a new church. Their example in moving to America was followed by other congregations, and in time the German Baptist Brethren (now the Church of the Brethren) became a vigorous and growing denomination in the new country.

MEMBERSHIP:

A personal profession of faith and baptism by trine immersion are the requirements for membership.

ORGANIZATION:

For the first two centuries of the Church's existence ministers were elected by vote of the local congregation, and after being called sought to prepare themselves for their work; but during the last half century a rapid change has been taking place in the procedure. The tendency is for young men to decide on the ministry as a life vocation, pursue a college course, and then complete three years of professional training in a well-recognized divinity school, usually Bethany Biblical Seminary, which is the seminary of the denomination. The ministry is rapidly becoming a paid one, with a well-trained pastor in charge of the local church.

The local congregation is the unit, presided over by an elder and governed by a council of all members. There are three degrees in the ministry, licentiate, ordained and elder. In most instances an experienced minister who has proven his worth is ordained as an elder, which entitles him to serve as the administrative head of his local congregation, or a neighboring congregation. The congregation elects members to a state district meeting, with which is connected an "elders' meeting" composed of the elders of the district. One of the elders is chosen annually to serve as moderator of the meeting and as head of the district for his year of office. Above the district meeting is the General Conference, embracing the entire brotherhood. Each district sends one or more elders to serve on the Standing Committee of the General Conference, and the local congregation elects one or more delegates to the delegate body. The conference elects a moderator annually who serves as head of the denomination during his period of office. At the general session there is free discussion and all delegates vote, for democracy and brotherhood are distinguishing characteristics of the denomination.

DOCTRINE:

The Church is orthodox Trinitarian. It has no formal creed, but takes the New Testament in its entirety as its creed. When any question arises as to doctrine and practice, the Brethren ask, "What does the New Testament say on this question?" All decisions made by the General Conference must be in harmony with the teachings of the Scriptures as the Brethren interpret them.

There are three main ordinances of the Church. First is baptism by trine immersion, following repentance and confession of faith, the person baptized being confirmed while kneeling in the water. Second is the threefold Communion service, commonly known as the Love Feast, or Agape. This comprises the feet-washing service (John 13:1-17), which symbolizes humility, cleansing, service and equality; the common meal, which symbolizes fellowship, love and peace; and the Communion, partaking of the bread and wine, which symbolizes communion with Christ. The feet-washing service and the fellowship meal represent communion between man and man, which the Brethren feel prepares them for more effective communion with Christ through partaking of the bread and wine. An effort is made to portray the Last Supper in this service. Sisters wear the prayer veil at the Love Feast. Third is the anointing service, based on James 5:14-16. This is not a last rite before death; its main emphasis is rather on healing, employing spiritual power along with medicine for the healing of the patient.

The Brethren insist on temperance, the simple life, rigid honesty, clean living and the doctrine of peace. They believe in translating their faith into general holiness of living, right living being genuine evidence of conversion. No class distinctions are recognized, and legal oaths are opposed. The New Testament rites and ordinances which they practise, and the church forms which they observe, are regarded as aids to the realization of a life of prayer, fellowship and love worthy of the followers of Jesus. The Brethren ideal has always been "Live like Jesus," or, as sometimes phrased, to live according to the Sermon on the Mount.

FORM OF WORSHIP:

Worship is almost entirely in the nonliturgical tradition. There is variety in the services and considerable freedom. Congregational life is a warm fellowship of sincerity and earnestness. From its foundation the Church has been widely known as one of the "historic peace churches."

WORK:

Emphasis during the twentieth century has been on home and foreign missions, stewardship of life and possessions, Christian education, the importance of home and family life, evangelism, and relief and rehabilitation work. In recent decades preaching has been largely exhortation to these "good works," the continued exposition of the Scriptures, and insistence on the simple New Testament tradition upon which the Church was originally founded.

The headquarters of the Church of the Brethren are at Elgin, Illinois, where their publishing house is located and where a staff of trained secretaries carries on much of the administrative and promotional work of the General Brotherhood.

THE CHURCH OF CHRIST, SCIENTIST

The Church of Christ, Scientist, was founded by Mary Baker Eddy in 1879.

ORGANIZATION:

The First Church of Christ, Scientist, in Boston is The Mother Church, and the local churches throughout the world are regarded as branches. Though, in a town where there are several Christian Science congregations, one of the churches calls itself First, the article *the* may not be used, and it remains simply First Church of Christ, Scientist. The officers of The Mother Church are The Christian Science Board of Directors, a President, First and Second Readers, a Clerk and a Treasurer. The governing board of the denomination is The Christian Science Board of Directors. Each branch church has its own self-government.

MEMBERSHIP:

To become a member of The Mother Church, the applicant must be a believer in the doctrines of Christian Science as contained in *Science and Health with Key to the Scriptures*, by Mary Baker Eddy, and must not be a member of any other denomination.

DOCTRINE:

The beliefs of the church are contained in the Bible and in *Science and Health with Key to the Scriptures*. In the 89th edition of the Church Manual there are furthermore six basic tenets of the Church as follows:

"1. As adherents of Truth, we take the inspired Word of the Bible as our sufficient guide to eternal Life.

"2. We acknowledge and adore one supreme and infinite

God. We acknowledge His Son, one Christ; the Holy Ghost or divine Comforter; and man in God's image and likeness.

"3. We acknowledge God's forgiveness of sin in the destruction of sin and the spiritual understanding that casts out evil as unreal. But the belief in sin is punished so long as the belief lasts.

"4. We acknowledge Jesus' atonement as the evidence of divine, efficacious Love, unfolding man's unity with God through Christ Jesus the Way-shower; and we acknowledge that man is saved through Christ, through Truth, Life, and Love as demonstrated by the Galilean Prophet in healing the sick and overcoming sin and death.

"5. We acknowledge that the crucifixion of Jesus and his resurrection served to uplift faith to understand eternal Life, even the allness of Soul, Spirit, and the nothingness of matter.

"6. And we solemnly promise to watch, and pray for that Mind to be in us which was also in Christ Jesus; to do unto others as we would have them do unto us; and to be merciful, just, and pure."

God is "the divine Principle of all that really is" (*Science and Health,* p. 275). This is the basic idea of Christian Science. God is further defined as Mind, Soul, Spirit, Life, Truth, Love. Jesus is the Way, or Way-shower, and His atonement is "the exemplification of man's unity with God" (*Science and Health,* p. 18). The Holy Ghost is the divine Comforter and spiritual man is made in God's image and likeness. This does not, however, mean the flesh and blood man as he is seen by others, for matter is not real, and only Mind and Spirit are real substance. All else is seeming, produced by error. This distinction between the real and the seeming but unreal is especially emphasized and repeated again and again in different forms. "Truth is real and error is unreal" (*Science and Health,* p. 368). "All reality is in God and His creation, harmonious and eternal. That which

He creates is good, and He makes all that is made. Therefore the only reality of sin, sickness, or death is the awful fact that unrealities seem real to human, erring belief, until God strips off their disguise" (*Science and Health,* p. 472). Man must learn to overcome evil, sickness, even death, because they are not real. To do this he must have spiritual understanding and to this end must know the truth according to the words of Jesus: "If ye continue in my word, then are ye my disciples indeed; and ye shall know the truth, and the truth shall make you free" (John 8:31, 32).

Upon this text, the miracles of Jesus, and Jesus' words to His disciples as He sent them out to carry on His work (Matthew 10:5-10, 28:16-20, Mark 16:14-18, John 14:12) Christian Science bases its healing powers. The practice must be spiritual, for the human mind cannot attain either harmony or health. The power of truth and right thinking is valid not only in matters of health but in every circumstance of life.

Prayer is a very important element in the practice of Christian Science, and every member of the church is instructed to use the following prayer daily: " 'Thy kingdom come;' let the reign of divine Truth, Life, and Love be established in me, and rule out of me all sin; and may Thy Word enrich the affections of all mankind, and govern them!" (*Manual,* p. 41)

Baptism and Holy Communion are received in a spiritual sense with no material symbols. Baptism is defined as "Purification by Spirit" (*Science and Health,* p. 581). Communion commemorates not the Last Supper but the joyous morning meal taken by Jesus and His disciples after the resurrection (John 21:9-13).

(The foregoing quotations from the writings of Mrs. Eddy are included, by permission of the Trustees under Mrs. Eddy's Will, to whom grateful acknowledgments are due.)

FORM OF WORSHIP:

The services are nonliturgical, but there is an order of service given in the *Manual* and followed by all the churches. The principal part of the Sunday service is the Lesson-Sermon which is prepared by a special committee and read in every branch church. Two Readers, usually a man and a woman, read alternately, one from *Science and Health with Key to the Scriptures,* the other from the Bible. The prescribed passages are read without comment. The services open and close with suitable music.

Communion is not observed in The Mother Church, but in branch churches is appointed for the second Sundays in January and July. After the congregation has knelt in silent communion, the Lord's Prayer is repeated in unison. At all Sunday services the scientific statement of being (*Science and Health,* p. 468) is read together with the correlative Scripture (I John 3:1-3).

Testimony meetings are usually held on Wednesday at which experiences, testimonies, and remarks are given.

CHURCH OF GOD (ANDERSON, INDIANA)—95,325

The Church of God (Anderson, Indiana), so called to distinguish it from any other "Church of God," is the result of a movement which started in about 1880 in some of the midwestern states. Its originators felt that the Church was hampered by too much organization and ecclesiasticism and demanded that it be more directly under God's rule. The sect regards itself rather as a movement within the Church than as a separate denomination.

MEMBERSHIP:

Those who profess union with Christ alone.

ORGANIZATION:

The local churches are congregational in form. The ministers meet in state or regional conventions, but these act merely in an advisory capacity. A General Ministerial Assembly meets in June in connection with the annual convention and camp meeting at Anderson, Indiana. This assembly oversees the business and co-operative aspects of the church work, but has no authority in doctrinal matters. Ministers are ordained by other ministers.

DOCTRINE:

1. The divine inspiration of the Holy Spirit.
2. The Bible is both divine and human and grew out of human life in touch with God.
3. The Holy Trinity.
4. The Holy Spirit gives gifts by which man may do God's work in the world but these gifts do not necessarily prove the presence of the Holy Spirit.
5. Sin separates men from God.
6. Sin is forgiven by virtue of Christ's atonement and by repentance and faith.
7. The necessity of the experience of holiness.
8. The personal second coming of Christ. There is no thought of a millennial reign, for the Kingdom of God is here and now.
9. The final judgment, the resurrection of the dead, the reward of the righteous and punishment of the wicked.

The sect accepts three sacraments: baptism (by immersion), foot washing, and the Lord's Supper. It considers the Church the body of Christ made up of all Christians who are one in Jesus Christ, and looks upon denominationalism as a hindrance to this unity and therefore unscriptural. It seeks a restoration of the New Testament ideal of the church, and regards personal spiritual experience rather than general agreement of belief as the foundation of this restoration.

THE CHURCH OF JESUS CHRIST OF LATTER-DAY SAINTS—911,279

(*The Mormons*)

The "Mormons," or Latter-day Saints, are members of a religious organization calling itself the Church of Jesus Christ of Latter-day Saints which was founded at Fayette, New York, in 1830 by Joseph Smith, Jr. In his history of the Church he describes in detail the visions which guided him to the discovery of the *Book of Mormon,* an ancient record which he believed to contain the fullness of Christ's gospel as it had been made known by Mormon to the ancient inhabitants of America. The "Angel Moroni," who made the revelation to Joseph Smith, was Mormon's son. The name Mormon is derived from this man, and the Church represents itself as the "Restored Gospel" of Jesus Christ.

The adherents of the Church were gradually forced westward by persecution: from New York to Ohio, then to Missouri, then to Illinois. It was in Illinois that the Prophet Smith was killed by a mob in 1844. By this time the Mormons numbered about 200,000. In the confusion which ensued upon the death of their prophet, some of the Mormons scattered, some followed Smith's son, Joseph Smith III, but about 20,000, under the leadership of Brigham Young, moved still farther west into what is now Utah. At that time the region around Great Salt Lake was a barren wilderness, but, free from persecution at last, the settlers were able to devote their energies to constructive work, and by the time Utah was included in the United States in 1896, Salt Lake City had become the center of a thriving agricultural community.

ORGANIZATION:

The smallest church unit is the "ward," which corresponds to a parish. It has a meetinghouse and is in charge of a bishop and two counselors. A group of wards is a "stake," and at its head are a president and two counselors. The church also supports missions which may consist of a group of states or part or all of a foreign country. In these missions active proselytizing is carried on by missionaries called for two-year periods. Over each mission is a president.

There is a general church conference twice a year, in spring and fall, composed of officers and members from all parts of the Church. At these meetings instructions from the general authorities are received, and church business is transacted.

Priesthood in the Church is looked upon as the power delegated from God to man, and authorizes the bearer to officiate in the name of God. There are two priestly orders, the Melchizedek and the Aaronic, of whom the former holds the power of presidency and therefore the supreme authority, spiritual and temporal, over the entire Church. This authority is vested in the First Presidency of three high priests, one of whom is president and two are counselors. The president is looked upon as a prophet, seer and "revelator," clothed with all the authority given when the Church was restored by the heavenly beings who communicated with Joseph Smith. The Melchizedek order includes high priests, seventies, and elders. The Aaronic order, under a presiding bishopric of three, has chiefly to do with temporal matters—collection of tithes, distribution of alms, care of the church properties and administration of the outward ordinances of the Gospel, such as water baptism and the bread and water of the Lord's Supper. Its officers are priests, teachers and deacons. Special callings in the higher priesthood include the apostles and patriarchs of the Church. There are twelve apostles, forming a governing quorum directly under the First Presidency.

There is no paid ministry. Every faithful man is ordained to the priesthood and is then subject to "orders," which may send him anywhere to preach or proselytize. In a very real sense he is a minuteman prepared at any time to obey the call of duty. Many women also accept calls as missionaries. Since there are no salaries except for those who give full time to the general organization, every man who serves has his own profession or trade by which he earns his living, and out of his income pays a tenth, or tithe, to the Church. This money is used to build and maintain the churches, sustain missions and support church charities and needs. Since there are few "poor" Mormons, many of these gifts benefit people outside of the Church.

DOCTRINE:

The Mormons do not accept any of the formal creeds, though their teaching is very much that of the Apostles' Creed, with certain original additions of their own. Two sources of doctrine are recognized:

1. The Scriptures, consisting of:

(a) The *Bible,* Old and New Testaments, "correctly translated."

(b) The *Book of Mormon.*

(c) The *Doctrine and Covenants*—a collection of revelation given in the present day.

(d) The Pearl of Great Price—a collection of fragments from the writings of Moses and Abraham, translated to Joseph Smith.

2. Direct revelation from God. This may come by voice or through angel messengers, or by impressions on the mind by God's spirit. Only one man on earth at any time may

receive revelation to guide the church—the president of the church.

Their articles of faith as expressed by Joseph Smith are:

1. We believe in God, the Eternal Father, and in His Son, Jesus Christ and in the Holy Ghost.

2. We believe that men will be punished for their own sins, and not for Adam's transgression.

3. We believe that through the Atonement of Christ, all mankind may be saved, by obedience to the laws and ordinances of the Gospel.

4. We believe that the first principles and ordinances of the Gospel are: first, Faith in the Lord Jesus Christ; second, Repentance; third, Baptism by immersion for the remission of sins; fourth, Laying on of hands for the gift of the Holy Ghost.

5. We believe that a man must be called of God, by prophecy, and by the laying on of hands by those who are in authority, to preach the Gospel and administer the ordinance thereof.

6. We believe in the same organization that existed in the Primitive Church, viz., apostles, prophets, pastors, teachers, evangelists, etc.

7. We believe in the gift of tongues, prophecy, revelation, visions, healing, interpretation of tongues, etc.

8. We believe the Bible to be the word of God as far as it is translated correctly; we also believe the Book of Mormon to be the word of God.

9. We believe all that God has revealed, all that He does now reveal, and we believe that He will yet reveal many great and important things pertaining to the Kingdom of God.

10. We believe in the literal gathering of Israel and in the restoration of the Ten Tribes; that Zion will be built upon

this (the American) continent; that Christ will reign personally upon the earth; and, that the earth will be renewed and receive its paradisiacal glory.

11. We claim the privilege of worshiping Almighty God according to the dictates of our own conscience, and allow all men the same privilege, let them worship how, where, or what they may.

12. We believe in being subject to kings, presidents, rulers and magistrates, in obeying, honoring and sustaining the law.

13. We believe in being honest, true, chaste, benevolent, virtuous, and in doing good to all men; indeed, we may say that we follow the admonition of Paul—we believe all things, we hope all things, we have endured many things, and hope to be able to endure all things. If there is anything virtuous, lovely, or of good report or praiseworthy, we seek after these things.

Mormons hold firmly to the belief that man can become like unto God. This doctrine they express in the words "As man is, God once was; as God is, man may become." God Himself in Mormon philosophy is ever changing and progressing through all eternity. In the end this doctrine of man's perfectibility makes for a plurality of gods, with relative degrees of eternal aptitudes.

The Mormons believe that there are many worlds and world spheres inhabited by spirits in different stages of development. There is in the hereafter a celestial glory for those who have accepted and lived God's message in all particulars. There is a terrestrial glory for those who believed in Jesus and His mission but failed to abide by the terms of the Gospel. The telestial glory is for those who are also heirs of salvation, but their glory is that of the stars, contrasted with that of the moon and sun. But so marvelous is the afterlife that even in the telestial glory the joy will be greater than mortal man can imagine.

God's purpose is to bring about the immortality and eternal life of man. Man, by failing to react to God's intention, may for eternity have to remain in a lesser degree of glory suited to his limited capacity.

Baptism and the Lord's Supper are accepted as sacraments. Furthermore, it is possible to assure the salvation of those who have died by being baptized for them by proxy here on earth. This is a solemn duty for believers. Marriage is for eternity and all family ties are continued in the next world if they have been "sealed" in this world. It is possible to "seal" husband and wife or parent and child by proxy for those who have passed on.

FORM OF WORSHIP:

No gentile is permitted to enter the Temple in Salt Lake City, and the service there is consequently a sacred ritual. The other churches, or tabernacles, are open to attendance by anyone. In the *Book of Mormon,* in that portion designated as the Book of Moroni (Chapters 3, 4, 5, 6), directions are given for ordination, the Lord's Supper and baptism, and the prayers to be used in carrying out the ordinances. Bread and water (not wine) are the material symbols of the Lord's Supper.

Outside of the prayers thus prescribed there is no set ritual or form of worship. The service consists of prayer, praise and preaching. Any man in the congregation may be called upon to preach and must answer the call.

The first Sunday of every month is observed as a fast day upon which believers abstain from food and drink. Smoking, liquor, tea and coffee are forbidden according to a special revelation from God. Celestial marriage, known more generally as polygamy, was adopted in 1852 as a matter of revelation, which the Mormons ascribe to Joseph Smith. In 1890, however, it was prohibited by a manifesto which enjoins the church membership to conform to the laws of the land.

The church enters into every phase of the life of its members. It helps the sick and poor, looks after education, amusements and social activities. It has started many economic and commercial ventures, such as coal mines, farms, knitting factories, sawmills, and building and housing projects. Many of the enterprises are co-operative and in almost every line of endeavor have proved successful, owing to the unifying influence of the Church. Compensation for work on welfare projects is not by a daily wage, but according to need.

THE CHURCH OF THE NAZARENE—201,487

The Church of the Nazarene originated in New England in 1886, during a period of Wesleyan revival. It is one of those sects which stress Christian perfection or holiness as a "second blessing" which follows justification. At first it consisted of a few ardent Wesleyans who wished to return to the fervor and simplicity of the great Methodist's early teaching. They met at first in homes, then in a rented store. All over the country other men and women were doing much the same thing during the closing years of the nineteenth century. There seemed to be a crying need for some special religious element not to be found in the existing churches. It was not until 1907, after over twenty years of growth that a number of the Holiness churches, from regions as far apart as California, Texas and Rhode Island, united as the Pentecostal Church of the Nazarene. In 1919 the Quadrennial General Assembly removed the term "Pentecostal" from the title, in order to mark a distinction from those sects which stress the gift of tongues.

MEMBERSHIP:

Consists of those who have been publicly received into the Church after declaring their experience of salvation and their belief in the Church. They are then baptized, generally by immersion, though pouring and sprinkling according to the choice of the applicant are permissible.

ORGANIZATION:

Each church is governed by a church board elected by the congregation. Churches are divided into groups according to area, and form assembly districts, in which each church is represented. The district assemblies are held annually for the management of district matters. A general assembly representing the districts is held every four years. A council of pastors and delegates at the district assemblies passes upon the fitness of candidates for the ministry and ordains them after four years of study. Ministers are licensed, and ordained. The ordained ministers are elders. A feature of the Nazarene ministry is the commissioning of evangelists, who are active in revival work.

DOCTRINE:

In all essentials the church agrees with early Methodism as founded by Wesley. The basic doctrine was expressed by the General Assembly as follows:

"We believe that entire sanctification is that act of God subsequent to regeneration, by which believers are made free from original sin, or depravity and brought into a state of entire devotement to God, and the holy obedience of love made perfect.

"It is wrought by the Baptism with the Holy Spirit, and comprehends in one experience the cleansing of the heart from sin and the abiding, indwelling presence of the Holy Spirit, empowering the believer for life and service.

"Entire sanctification is provided by the blood of Jesus, is wrought instantaneously by faith, preceded by entire consecration, and to this work and state of grace the Holy Spirit bears witness.

"This experience is also known by various terms representing its different phases, such as 'Christian perfection', 'perfect love', 'heart purity', 'the baptism with the Holy Spirit', 'the fulness of the blessing', and 'Christian holiness.' "

The Nazarenes have fifteen articles of belief which are included in the constitution which may be found in their church manual. They have also an agreed statement of belief.

"Recognizing that the right and privilege of persons to church membership rest upon the fact of their being regenerate, we would require only such avowals of belief as are essential to Christian experience.

"We therefore deem belief in the following brief statements to be sufficient:

"1. In one God—the Father, Son and Holy Spirit.

"2. In the plenary inspiration of the Old and New Testament scriptures and that they contain all truth necessary to faith and Christian living.

"3. That man is born with a fallen nature, and is, therefore, inclined to evil, and that continually.

"4. That the finally impenitent are hopelessly and eternally lost.

"5. That the atonement through Jesus Christ is for the whole human race; and that whosoever repents and believes on the Lord Jesus Christ is justified and regenerated and saved from the dominion of sin.

"6. That believers are to be sanctified wholly, subsequent to regeneration, through faith in the Lord Jesus Christ.

"7. That the Holy Spirit bears witness to the new birth, and also to the entire sanctification of believers.

"8. In the return of our Lord, in the resurrection of the dead, and in the final judgment."

There are besides general rules of behavior, both of omission and of commission. Among these are prohibitions against swearing, desecrating the Sabbath, drink, tobacco, quarreling, dishonesty, extravagance in dress, and dancing, theaters, secret orders or fraternities: and positive injunctions to be courteous, kind, helpful to others, loving, churchgoing and charitable.

There are besides some special rules, as, for example, the giving of tithes to the Church and using only unfermented wine and unleavened bread for the Lord's Supper. The Church refuses remarriage to a divorced person, except the innocent party in a divorce for adultery. It advocates divine healing and prayer for the sick, as taught in the New Testament; and acknowledges two sacraments, baptism and the Lord's Supper.

FORM OF WORSHIP:

Rituals are prescribed for the Baptism of Believers, the Baptism of Children, the Dedication or Consecration of children whose parents do not wish them baptized, the reception of church members, the Lord's Supper, Matrimony, and the Burial of the Dead.

THE CONGREGATIONAL CHRISTIAN CHURCHES—1,140,824

The Congregational Christian Churches are formed from a merger made in 1931 of the Congregational Churches of the United States and the General Convention of the Christian Church.

The Congregational, like the Baptist Church was the direct descendant of the Independents in sixteenth-century England. From the outset they demanded separation from the Established Church and finally a group of them (the Pilgrims) came to America to set up a colony where they might establish their own form of worship and belief. They were the founders of Plymouth Colony, which was in time merged with the Puritans of Salem and Massachusetts Bay. It is interesting to note that, though the Pilgrim-Puritans left England to escape the dominance of an established church, their own depth of religious conviction soon made church membership an essential qualification for citizenship in the new colony. Roger Williams and Anne Hutchinson were both obliged to leave as a result of the narrow political and religious sectarianism of the Pilgrim-Puritan rule, and Roger Williams became the founder of the Baptist Church in Providence, Rhode Island.

In time, greater tolerance arose and a gradual separation between church and state developed. The Church itself began to move away from rigid Calvinism toward the more liberal thought of the early founders of Plymouth Colony. In the middle part of the eighteenth century, during the "Great Awakening," the fiery preaching of Jonathan Edwards did much to break the "old order," for a growing number of people, finding his teachings too violent, withdrew still further toward a more liberal faith.

Congregationalism received its name from its form of organization, by which each congregation was autonomous. From the Pilgrim-Puritans it inherited the conception of a covenant between God and man, the covenant of grace, on which, rather than on general creeds, it based its faith. So loose a bond of union has resulted in great variation in both doctrine and polity and it is not surprising, therefore, to find that the Unitarians were an offshoot of the Congregational Church.

In 1801 westward expansion brought Congregationalists and Presbyterians into close contact and a "Plan of Union" was adopted to permit an interchange of ministers for both in the new settlements. But the closer-knit Presbyterian organization proved more effective in maintaining ministerial standing for presbyterially ordained ministers than the loose-knit Congregational association of autonomous churches, and the net result of the union was that the Presbyterians gained ascendancy in much of the Northwest Territory.

The Plan of Union showed the weakness of the Congregational organization in placing too much emphasis on the autonomy of the local church, and in 1852 a convention of ministers and delegates of the Congregational Churches was called in Albany. The purpose of the meeting was only to gain support for benevolent and missionary work, but it was the beginning of a wider voluntary church co-operation. In Oberlin in 1871 the National Convention of Congregational Churches was officially organized and a constitution adopted which provided for triennial meetings and a provisional committee with interim duties.

It is evident from what has been said that Congregationalism for a long time had no denominational platform. There was from the outset a general consensus of belief among the majority of the churches based in large part on the Westminster Confession. Several other platforms were suggested for adoption in the eighteenth century, but not until 1913 was a generally acceptable statement of belief set forth. The section on faith reads as follows:

"We believe in God the Father, infinite in wisdom, goodness and love; and in Jesus Christ, His Son, our Lord and Savior, who for us and our salvation lived and died and rose again and liveth evermore; and in the Holy Spirit, who taketh of the things of Christ and revealeth them to us, renewing, comforting, and inspiring the souls of men. We are united in striving to know the will of God, as taught in the Holy Scriptures, and in our purpose to walk in the ways of the Lord, made known or to be made known to us. We hold it to be the mission of the Church of Christ to proclaim the Gospel to all mankind, exalting the worship of the true God, and laboring for the progress of knowledge, the promotion of justice, the reign of peace, and the realization of human brotherhood. Depending, as did our fathers, upon the continual guidance of the Holy Spirit to lead us into all truth, we work and pray for the transformation of the world into the Kingdom of God; and we look with faith for the triumph of righteousness and the life everlasting."

The Christian Church was a union of many elements, Presbyterian, Methodist and independents, who had for one reason or another broken off from the parent stems. Some of these remnants were in Virginia, some in the Cumberland Valley of Tennessee and Kentucky, some in New England. For a long time the union was very loose, but by 1890 it had become a separate denomination known as Christians (Christian Connection) which later changed to Christian Church (American Christian Convention) and in 1922 to Christian Church (General Convention of the Christian Church).

This church had no creed and derived all its doctrines from the Bible. Christian character is the one test of church fellowship. Baptism is generally by immersion and open communion is practised.

In 1931 the Congregational churches and the Christian churches merged as the Congregational Christian Churches.

ORGANIZATION:

Each church unit or congregation is free in its own life. It belongs to a group of churches which group is also free in its sphere. These groups again unite in state or district organizations which are self-determining. Over these is a national body which has no authority, but gives an opportunity to all for mutual counsel, inspiration, and a basis for united effort.

Church officers are the pastor, a board of deacons, a clerk and a treasurer. Admission to membership is generally based on the declared purpose to lead a Christian life. Infant baptism is customary, and the form optional, though sprinkling is generally practised. The Lord's Supper is open to all followers of Christ.

DOCTRINE:

The Congregational Christian Churches are founded on the church covenant through which "the members express their common convictions as to truth and duty and pledge unanimity of thought and purpose as to the best way of expressing that truth and discharging that duty."

An excellent example of such a covenant may be found on page 141 of the church manual: "The object of this church shall be to bind together followers of Jesus Christ for the purpose of sharing in the worship of God and in making his will dominant in the lives of men, individually and collectively, especially as that will is set forth in the life, teachings and death of Jesus Christ."

The broad statement of faith quoted on page 182 is accepted by the Congregational Christian Church and incorporated in the manual, as are also the following six principles:

1. The Holy Bible, our only rule of faith and practice.
2. The Lord Jesus Christ, the only bread of the church and our only Saviour.
3. Christian, a sufficient name for Christ's followers.
4. Christian character or life, the only test of fellowship.
5. Individual interpretation, the right and privilege of all Christians.
6. The union of all the followers of Christ, that they shall all be one even as Christ prayed.

FORM OF WORSHIP:

There is a *Book of Church Services* which contains forms of worship for every kind of gathering. The use of these liturgies and forms is not, however, obligatory, and many churches continue non-liturgical, emphasizing the sermon as the center of the service, and the pulpit as the center of the church. Here again the congregation is allowed perfect freedom to find what form of worship best suits the majority of its members.

The Church is active in many lines of missionary and educational work. It is interesting historically to note that Harvard, Yale, Williams, Dartmouth, Bowdoin, Amherst, Oberlin and other famous colleges, in all amounting to fifty or more, owe their origin to the Congregationalists.*

THE DISCIPLES OF CHRIST (PROGRESSIVES)—1,889,066
THE CHURCHES OF CHRIST (CONSERVATIVES)—309,551

These two groups grew out of one and the same movement, which started in western Pennsylvania early in the nineteenth century. It was in this region that the Scotch-Irish who came to this country in 1807 were largely settled. Thomas Campbell, an Irish seceder Presbyterian minister, filled with zeal to unite Christendom, was disciplined by the synod of his own church for divergence from its sectarian rules. Convinced that the use of creed and dogma was the underlying cause of division in the church as a whole, he proposed to return to the church of apostolic times, as it existed before fixed statements of faith had arisen. He felt that could the clock be set back eighteen hundred years and a new start made, the Christian church throughout the world might once more be united.

To attain this end it would be necessary to do away with

* At the biennial meeting of the General Council of the Congregational Christian Churches held in June 1948, official action was taken looking toward union with the Evangelical and Reformed Church, and it is anticipated that the union will be consummated in June, 1949.

formal creeds, with doctrine and dogma, and all the accumulation of tradition and man-made opinion which had grown up over the centuries. Resting upon the Bible for authority, and united by the love of Christ and the desire to do His will, the church could once more go forward as one body.

Campbell's idea was not to found a new church; his movement was intended to be interdenominational, a matter of personal relationship of man to man and of man to Christ. What he looked for was "a union of churches, visible and universal, yet without any external enforcement of unity." His position at all times was: "In essentials, unity; in opinions, liberty; in all things, charity."

In 1809 he published a statement of his views entitled *Declaration and Addresses,* confident that he would find a large public in agreement with him. The book did not even arouse comment, but was completely ignored. Sublime as the vision was, straightforward and simple in conception, the differences of eighteen centuries were too deeply rooted to be at once removed.

In this same year Campbell was joined by his family, and his eldest son Alexander began to work with him. Thomas Campbell had already gathered about him a group of like-minded people, mostly Presbyterians, whom he organized as the "Christian Association of Washington, Pennsylvania." This group he asked the Presbyterian synod to receive into its communion. When the request was rejected, there seemed nothing left but to found a new church.

The Christian Association accordingly became the Bush Run Church, and here Alexander Campbell was licensed to preach. Study of early church procedures convinced the group that baptism by immersion was the apostolic way, and since on this question they agreed with the Baptists, the Bush Run Church joined the Redstone Baptist Association, with whom they worshiped from 1813 to 1830, still holding their own distinctive views and rejecting creeds and dogma.

Campbell was convinced that "in conversion, the Holy Spirit acts only through the word," as opposed to the theory that the "mourner" must have some special inner experience of the Holy Spirit before he can have saving faith. As a result of his preaching, therefore, the followers of the Campbells broke away from the Baptists and together with a number of converts from other churches united themselves as Disciples of Christ. The local churches were called Christian Churches or Churches of Christ.

Three other movements with the same objective had been going on, one among the Methodists in North Carolina, another among the Baptists of New England, and the third among the Presbyterians in Kentucky. Many of these in 1832 united with the Pennsylvania group, and thousands of new converts were soon added.

As the church grew in numbers, some kind of organization was found necessary, and in 1849 the first national convention was held in Cincinnati. It was during the period of expansion after the Civil War that the division in the group arose. The conservative members were opposed to missionary societies and instrumental music in public worship as "unscriptural," and gradually withdrew and formed the "Churches of Christ." Until 1890 Conservatives and Progressives were reported together in the census as Disciples of Christ, but in 1906 the "Churches of Christ" had become a distinct sect.

The Disciples of Christ

The Disciples of Christ are the largest religious body purely American in origin. Their greatest strength is in the Middle West.

ORGANIZATION:

The churches are strictly congregational, each church managing its own affairs with no supervision or interference.

The officers of the church are elders and deacons and the pastor is considered one of the elders. Following the custom of the early church, the elders care for the spiritual interests of the church, the deacons for its financial affairs and charities. For purposes of conference there exists an International Convention of the Disciples of Christ of Canada and the U.S.A., which is composed of individual members of the Church and, again, has no authority.

MEMBERSHIP:

Persons are received for membership on profession of faith in Christ, and baptism.

DOCTRINE:

The Disciples of Christ accept the inspiration of the Bible and declare its adequacy as a revelation of God's will and a rule of faith and life. They acknowledge two sacraments, baptism and the Lord's Supper.

Besides these general beliefs, in which they agree with many other Protestant sects, they have certain distinctive emphases of their own:

1. They seek to restore Christianity as described in the New Testament.
2. They reject all creeds and confessions.
3. They consider "the divine sonship of Jesus" the fundamental fact of Holy Scriptures.
4. They do not consider the Old and New Testaments equally binding on believers. The New Testament is a perfect constitution for the worship, government and discipline of the New Testament Church.
5. They do not insist that the "Disciples" are the only Christians.
6. They accept the divine personality of the Holy Spirit,

and insist that men must hear, believe, repent and obey the Gospel to be saved.

7. They consider baptism by immersion essential.

8. They celebrate the Lord's Supper as a memorial feast from which no follower of Christ is excluded.

9. They look on the Lord's Day not as the Sabbath, but as a New Testament institution in memory of His resurrection.

10. They are opposed to sects and other divisions in the Church.

FORM OF WORSHIP:

The Church is nonliturgical and the form of worship varies according to the preference of the individual congregation. The Sunday service is centered about the Lord's Supper, which is celebrated every Sunday, as a memorial of the Last Supper of Biblical times.

ACTIVITIES:

The Disciples of Christ lay great stress on educational and missionary work. Among other activities in this country they support several colleges, six homes for the aged and six for children, besides many other teaching and benevolent organizations. Abroad their missionary activities are spread through Africa, China, India, Japan, the Philippines, Mexico and South America. Education and medical care are an important feature of all this work, and everywhere and in all that they do they emphasize the importance of religious unity rather than sectarianism.

The Churches of Christ

As has been said in the general article on the Disciples of Christ, the Churches of Christ were the conservative members of the group who began to split off from the main stem after the Civil War. Their ideals may be found in a quotation from the writings of Alexander Campbell in regard to the apostolic Christians.

"Their [the apostolic] churches were not fractured into missionary societies, Bible societies, and educational societies; nor did they dream of organizing such. . . . They knew nothing of the hobbies of modern times. In their church capacity alone they moved. . . . They viewed the Church of Jesus Christ as the scheme of salvation to ameliorate the world. As members of it they considered themselves bound to do all they could for the glory of God and the good of men. They dared not transfer to a missionary society a cent or a prayer, lest they should rob the Church of its glory and exalt the inventions of men above the wisdom of God."

To these principles the conservative element stuck, refusing to subscribe to missionary societies, unscriptural means of raising money, and "modern pastors." They also opposed any kind of instrumental music in the church services.

Today there is a clear distinction between the conservative and progressive elements and the Churches of Christ are listed as a separate group.

ORGANIZATION:

In their congregational organization they have the same officers as do the Disciples of Christ. Each local church is independent, no emphasis is laid on the ministerial office, and there are no ministerial associations.

DOCTRINE:

Their doctrine is again very like the doctrine of the Disciples. They reject creeds and confessions, emphasize "Jesus the divine Son," and the "divine personality of the Holy Spirit," accept the Lord's Supper as a memorial supper and observe it each Lord's Day, and teach baptism by immersion.

In general they preach the doctrine of nonresistance.

FORM OF WORSHIP:

Each congregation is free to use any form of worship which it finds satisfactory. As a rule, the Churches of Christ use no liturgy or ritual, however, preferring a simple form of worship.

In spite of their opposition to missionary societies, the Churches of Christ do active missionary work and maintain several educational institutions, seven orphanages, and two homes for the aged. They also publish thirteen journals devoted to religious instruction.

THE EVANGELICAL AND REFORMED CHURCH—695,971

America was settled by people from many lands in Western Europe, and many of its religious organizations still reflect the religious affiliations of the early colonists in the lands from which they came. A large number of settlers in Pennsylvania and Ohio were people of German stock who belonged to either the Lutheran or the Reformed Church and brought their religion with them. In the scattered communities of the New World they had perforce to organize their own congregations, although they frequently sent back to Europe for pastors; but in 1725 the Reformed Church in the United States celebrated its first communion at a place called Faulkner's Swamp, forty miles north of Philadelphia, without however severing its ties with the old country. In 1747, Michael Schlatter was sent over from Holland to organize a local governing body or coetus in Philadelphia, subject to the synod in Holland.

In 1793 after the Revolutionary War the coetus declared its independence of Holland and became the Synod of the German Reformed Church in the United States. As the members of the new church moved south and west a new synod was formed in Ohio and missionary and educational work started. In 1863 the Ohio and Pennsylvania synods united in a general synod which ceased to function only in 1934.

Another body, the Evangelical Synod of North America, had its origin in a group of six ministers who met in 1840 near St. Louis, Missouri, and formed the Evangelical Union of the West. At this time there were many independent congregations of German background and speech in Ohio and westward, and by 1872 these had joined the Union, which in 1877 became the Evangelical Synod.

In 1934, after some years of friendly negotiation, the Reformed Church and the Evangelical Synod united to form the Evangelical and Reformed Church.

MEMBERSHIP:

Membership comprises all persons who have been confirmed and enrolled as "communicant members."

ORGANIZATION:

The Evangelical and Reformed Church has a presbyterial form of government. Each congregation is governed by a consistory or church council elected by its members. A "charge" is composed of one or more congregations, and a group of charges forms a synod of which there are thirty-four in all. The synods are composed of the pastors and a lay member from each charge. Above the synod is the General Synod which represents the whole Church. It meets every three years, elects its own officers, and supervises and directs the work of the Church.

DOCTRINE:

Three standards of faith had to be recognized to form the union, the Augsburg Confession (1530), the Heidelberg Catechism (1563), and Luther's Catechism. In formulating the doctrinal statement of the combined churches, there were written into the constitution these words:

"The Holy Scriptures of the Old and New Testaments are recognized as the word of God and the ultimate rule of Christian faith and practice.

"The doctrinal standards of the Evangelical and Reformed Church are the Heidelberg Catechism, Luther's Catechism, and the Augsburg Confession. They are accepted as an authoritative interpretation of the essential truth taught in the Holy Scriptures.

"Wherever these doctrinal standards differ, ministers, members, and congregations, in accordance with the liberty of conscience inherent in the Gospel, are allowed to adhere to the interpretation of one of these confessions. However, in each case the final norm is the Word of God."

The Church accepts the two sacraments of Holy Baptism and the Lord's Supper. Baptism is usually administered to infants, but confirmation, which precedes attendance at the Lord's Supper, does not follow until the child is thirteen or fourteen. Adults also are baptized before reception into the Church.

FORM OF WORSHIP:

Congregations are allowed freedom of worship but a liturgy and hymnal have been formulated and in the interests of unity and harmony their use in common worship is advised.

WORK:

The Church carries on missionary work both at home and abroad. It combines education and medical care with the work of evangelization, and in connection with the work conducts publishing houses and educational institutions of which there are at least fourteen in the country. It has also ten hospitals, ten homes for orphans, two for epileptics and twelve for the aged.

On January 22, 1947, a basis of union was adopted by the Joint Committee of the Congregational Christian Churches and the Evangelical and Reformed Church. Whether or no this union is to take place will be decided in June, 1949.

THE EVANGELICAL UNITED BRETHREN—705,102

The name of this church represents a union of the Evangelical Church and the Church of the United Brethren in Christ, which was accomplished in 1946. Both denominations are distinctly American churches and were the outgrowth of the same period of spiritual awakening in the eighteenth century which gave rise to Methodism in America.

William Otterbein and Martin Boehm in Pennsylvania and George A. Guething in Maryland became convinced that only through "conscious salvation," a personal experience of God's grace, could religion be made a living force. As they gathered an increasing number of fellow believers they found that an organization was necessary and accordingly in 1800 united themselves in a society known as the Church of the United Brethren in Christ. In 1815 a conference was called to formulate a book of discipline which contained the doctrine and rules of the Church. This the membership was admonished to observe strictly.

In the year 1800 when the Church of the United Brethren in Christ was organized, another evangelical group in eastern Pennsylvania under the leadership of Jacob Albright united to pray with and for each other to be saved from sin and from the wrath to come. They agreed to spend each Sunday in prayer, to meet each Wednesday evening in prayer, to avoid evil and sinful things, and do all manner of good as God gave them strength. In thus ordering their lives according to a plan they were much like the early Wesleyans. The first classes were formed in 1803; the first conference was held in 1807; and in 1816 they formally adopted the name Evangelical Association. In 1891 there was a division in the Church which endured until in 1922 the two denominations again united as the Evangelical Church.

For many years the leaders of the United Brethren and those of the Evangelical Church made earnest efforts to unite the two churches, between whom there was always maintained a "friendly and brotherly fellowship."

At the General Conference of the Church of the United Brethren in Christ in 1933 the resolution to enter into negotiations leading to a merger was adopted. In 1945 the Plan and Basis of Union and the Book of Discipline in accord with the respective Constitutions and Disciplines of the two churches were accepted by the General Conference of this church. In 1942 the General Conference of the General Conferences adopted the plan and basis of union, and in 1946, after completing their individual business, the two conferences joined to form the Evangelical United Brethren Church.

ORGANIZATION:

The local church is the unit, and any minister of the Evangelical United Brethren Church, with the approval of the conference superintendent or the annual conference may organize a local church. He shall cause to be elected a class leader and an assistant class leader and such trustees as may be required and appoint one or more stewards.

The minister is the ranking officer and pastor of the congregation. A local church is a class, and the leaders are chosen to assist the minister. The stewards have practically the duties of the deacons in the early church, looking after alms and providing the elements for the sacrament of the Lord's Supper, securing unfermented wine.

The local churches hold annual congregational meetings to transact church business. A charge is a local church or number of churches. Over each charge there is a quarterly conference. Over the quarterly conference is an annual conference held in each annual conference territory. The general conference for the entire Church is held every four years. This, the supreme court of the Church, elects the bishops and other general church officers.

The order of ministry is elders and probationers, more or less corresponding to priests and deacons in their duties. Bishops are elected from among the itinerant elders.

DOCTRINE:

The Evangelical United Brethren Church accepts as doctrinal standards "The Confession of Faith" of the Church of the United Brethren in Christ and the "Doctrines of the Church" as contained in the Discipline of the Evangelical Church. These they have officially declared are in agreement with each other and with the Christian doctrines as contained in Holy Scripture. These are combined in a confession of faith in two parts, the first of thirteen, the second of nineteen articles. As a result each article of belief is twice stated and the close resemblance between the two original confessions is very clear.

The Evangelical United Brethren believe in the Trinity; they accept Holy Scriptures, Old and New Testaments, as the Word of God. They celebrate two sacraments, baptism and the Lord's Supper, but leave to the individual the mode of baptism and the manner of observing the Lord's Supper, also whether or not the practice of foot washing shall be observed. Some of their basic tenets are: man is naturally depraved, and penitent sinners may be justified by faith only; good works are acceptable to God and prove man's faith. They keep the Christian Sabbath, believe in the resurrection of the dead, eternal punishment for the wicked, and eternal bliss for the righteous.

FORM OF WORSHIP:

The Church is semiliturgical. No ritual is provided for the regular forms of public worship, the choice being left to the congregations. But for the administration of the sacraments, rites, and ordinances, rituals have been provided and ministers are expected to use them.

In the older churches the pulpit is the central feature, but many churches more recently built have put up altars in the chancel and moved the pulpit to a less prominent position. Vestments are worn by the ministers in some congregations, but this again is left to individual preference.

THE LUTHERAN CHURCHES—over 5,000,000

There were Lutherans among the first settlers in the colonies, and two of the oldest churches in this country, Holy Trinity (Old Swedes), in Wilmington, Delaware, and Gloria Dei, in Philadelphia, both built by Swedish Lutherans about 250 years ago, are still standing, though no longer Lutheran. As early as 1648 a Lutheran congregation was formed on Manhattan Island. The chief source of Lutheranism in America, however, was German immigration in the eighteenth century, and German and Scandinavian in the nineteenth. Of the earlier German immigration, some was to New York, some to Georgia and some to the Carolinas, but the main current flowed into Pennsylvania, until by the middle of the eighteenth century there were about 60,000 Lutherans in the colony.

It was some time before the Lutherans in America were

able to set up any kind of organization wider than the individual congregation, and they were further hampered by a dearth of pastors, who were still recruited in the old country. In 1748 Henry Melchior Mühlenberg established the Ministerium of Pennsylvania, which was followed by a synod in New York in 1786, in North Carolina in 1803, in Maryland and Virginia in 1820, and in Tennessee in the same year. In this year also the General Synod of these groups was formed and the link with Europe broken. Hartwick Seminary had been founded in 1797 to train the ministry, and the Lutheran Church in America took over its own missionary work.

As the Lutheran immigrants began to settle in the West and Northwest in the nineteenth century, however, a new set of conditions arose. The development of Lutheranism in Scandinavia had differed from its development in Germany. In Sweden, for example, the Reformation did not sweep away the entire structure of the earlier church. Bishops and clergy were retained, and because the break with the past was less violent, the new church could preserve an unbroken apostolic succession for its bishops. Elsewhere in the Lutheran world the older structure was discarded; and to this distinction was added the difference in language. There was no central authority. In America, when the frontiersmen who were carving their homes out of the wilderness called for pastors, their call was answered by independent preachers of the Church, many of whom were from the Ministerium of Pennsylvania, but some belonged to no synod whatever.

Gradually, however, congregations formed and new groupings began to arise. In 1818 the Synod of Ohio and Adjacent States was established, today a part of the American Lutheran Church; in 1847 the Synod of Missouri and Other States came into existence; 1854 saw the birth of the Norwegian Church and the German Iowa Synod; and in 1860 the Augustana Synod (Swedish) was set up.

In 1863 there was a breach in the General Synod, due

to the violent differences engendered by the Civil War, and the Southern Synods organized the United Synod of the South. In 1866 a second break occurred, led by the Ministerium of Pennsylvania, which resulted in the separate formation of the General Council. Between 1870 and 1910 the Lutheran Church spread widely and membership increased in all the synods. This period of expansion was followed by a period of consolidation. In 1917 three bodies of Norwegian Lutherans united to form the Norwegian Lutheran Church of America, now known as the Evangelical Lutheran Church; the next year four German synods united as the Joint Synod of Wisconsin; in 1930 the Iowa, Ohio and Buffalo synods combined as the American Lutheran Church. The largest merger occurred in the East, where the three great eastern bodies joined as the United Lutheran Church in America. There is ever-increasing co-operation among the many Lutheran churches in the land, and an international organization which gives hope that in time the Lutheran, the largest of the Protestant bodies, may be closely united in a world-wide organization.

ORGANIZATION:

The congregation is the unit and together with the pastor has all authority except such as is specially delegated to the larger body. The synod, which is composed of the ministers and chosen lay representatives of a group of congregations, is in some cases merely an advisory or consultative body, in others has a wider degree of authority. The general bodies representing the synods, and variously designated within the different Lutheran organizations, are national in scope and growing more widely inclusive of all the branches of Lutheranism.

DOCTRINE:

Since the whole Reformation may be said to be based on a "Return to Scripture," it is but natural that the basis of

Lutheranism is the canonical books of the Old and New Testaments. The three ecumenical or general creeds, the Apostles', the Nicene and the Athanasian, are accepted as in accord with Bible teaching. All Lutheran churches acknowledge the Unaltered Augsburg Confession and the Small Catechism as the official statement of faith. The Confession is the oldest Protestant statement of faith. There are also the Apology, the Smalcald Articles and the Formula of Concord, which are generally listed as statements of faith, and which are elaborations or expositions of the creeds and the Confession. The Confessions and the Apology set forth and in part explain the differences between Lutheranism and Catholicism. The Formula of Concord tries to harmonize the conflicting views within Lutheranism itself. Luther wrote two catechisms for use in religious training, the Large and the Small, which put into question and answer form the basic teachings of the Church. The Small Catechism, for example, discusses the Ten Commandments, the Apostles' Creed, the Lord's Prayer and the sacraments in terms comprehensible to the catechumen.

The Ten Commandments are here divided in the Augustinian manner, the first two included in one, and the last divided into two. In many ways Luther followed very closely the teaching of the early church, and in all the centuries since it was written, the Lutheran Church has never found it necessary to change the Small Catechism in any way.

Justification by faith alone in Jesus Christ is the central doctrine of the Church. Two sacraments are acknowledged, baptism and the Lord's Supper. These are regarded, not simply as memorials, but as means of grace. The Lutheran Church believes in the real presence of the body and blood of Jesus Christ in the Lord's Supper. The doctrine of transsubstantiation, consubstantiation and impanation, however, are denied, though the Church declares that the body and blood are "given in, with and under the bread and wine."

FORM OF WORSHIP:

The church services are liturgical and for the most part are those contained in the Common Service Book, which is most widely used among Lutheran groups in America. The basis of the forms, as in the Anglican Church, is the Roman Catholic liturgy. Certain of the Lutheran groups have made variations according to their traditions and preferences.

Since the Church in the United States is gathered from all parts of northwestern Europe, where separate Lutheran churches have been in existence for four hundred years, it is surprising, not that there should be local differences, but that there is such general agreement. Some of the Lutheran distinctions are caused by doctrinal emphases, but most of them by language and national background, coupled with variant modes of life in widely separated communities. With succeeding generations brought up in the United States and learning a common language, many of the separate groups have joined, and for all practical purposes the six main divisions of the earlier part of the century have been reduced to three, of which two have taken the further step of joining a common Council. The three main divisions are the United Lutheran Church in America, the American Lutheran Conference, and the Lutheran Church, Missouri Synod, the last named having been known prior to May 1, 1948, as the Synodical Conference. "Of these, the American Lutheran Conference (comprising the American Lutheran Church, the Augustana Synod, the Evangelical Lutheran Church, the Lutheran Free Church and United Evangelical Lutheran Church) joined with the United Lutheran Church, the Danish Lutheran Church and the Finnish Suomi Church to form the National Lutheran Council, which was created in 1918 for co-operative effort in emergency work arising out of World War I." The Second World War has carried the co-operative movement even further, and today the only important Lutheran group which does not take part in the Council is the Lutheran Church, Missouri Synod.

THE UNITED LUTHERAN CHURCH IN AMERICA— about 1,700,000

This body represents the original Ministerium of Pennsylvania, organized in 1748 but existing even in early colonial days. During the latter part of the nineteenth century it split into three sections, but in 1918 the breaches were healed and the separate parts reunited. Today it is the largest Lutheran body in America, comprising thirty-two constituent synods.

ORGANIZATION:

Though primarily congregational like all Lutheran churches, the United Lutheran Church confers large powers on the synods and the general organization. The biennial convention, composed of delegates from the various synods, has power to adjust the external relations of the synods and to control organizations affecting the United Church. It also decides matters of doctrine, interprets laws and publishes books of devotion and instruction. Between conventions an Executive Board of fifteen members meets quarterly. The executive officers are a president, secretary and treasurer, elected biennially.

DOCTRINE:

The Church receives the Bible as the inspired Word of God and the only infallible rule of faith and practice. It accepts the three ecumenical creeds and holds that the Augsburg Confession is the correct interpretation of them.

WORK:

The Church is organized nationally in boards and commissions covering every field of its activity. Educational work is carried on by thirteen senior colleges and one junior college, ten seminaries, more than 200 student centers and more than 2,000 schools. The Church also maintains about 5,100 Sunday schools. Missionary activities include 574 pastoral charges in North America served by home missionaries, and foreign missions in India (founded in 1842), China, Japan, Liberia, Argentina and British Guiana. Provision is made for retired and disabled pastors and families of pastors, and much work is done in the fields of evangelism, welfare and emergency relief.

The United Lutheran Publication House in Philadelphia carries on the publishing activities of the Church.

The American Lutheran Conference—1,636,900

The American Lutheran Conference represents a free association of the American Lutheran Church, the Augustana Synod (Swedish), the Evangelical Lutheran Church (Norwegian), the Lutheran Free Church (Norwegian), and the United Evangelical Lutheran Church of America (Danish), all of them generally representing settlements in the Middle West. Some of the roots of Swedish Lutheranism reach far down into American colonial life, for it established a small settlement in Delaware early in the history of the colony, and the first book to be translated into an American Indian tongue was Luther's Small Catechism, the translation of which was due to the Reverend Johan Campanius. However, these early settlers in Delaware gave way to the English, and have left few traces in the scene of their first settlement, other than two old church buildings, still standing.

As I have said before, there were differences in organization and variations in doctrinal emphasis between the Scandinavian Lutherans and the German. These, together with differences in background and language, were largely responsible for the separate establishment of their own churches and synods by the Scandinavians who settled so much of the Middle West in the nineteenth century. In 1930 the five groups formed a federation for two purposes, as stated in its constitution, first, "mutual counsel concerning the faith, life and work of the Church," and second, "co-operation in matters of common interest and responsibility."

The churches thus united in a common purpose keep their individual independence of organization and action, and the Conference is chiefly advisory.

The Lutheran Church: Missouri Synod—1,366,072

The cult of "rationalism," introduced by the French philosophers and spread over Europe by the French Revolution and the Napoleonic Wars, had a profound effect on German Lutherans. In the German states religion was controlled by the ruler, and most of the kings and princes accepted the new French viewpoint and tried to introduce it into the Church. The Prussian king finally went so far as to try to force the Lutheran and Reformed Churches of his kingdom into union, with utter disregard for the convictions of the congregations involved. Everywhere new prayers, new hymns and even changes in doctrine were prescribed by the state authorities. The old confessional standards were modernized and rationalized, sermons became lectures, and to many who were opposed to the new views spiritual values seemed to be disappearing.

Emigration from Germany to America became a constantly swelling stream during the first half of the nineteenth century. Some left their homes because of economic conditions, others for political reasons, and many because of an increasing dissatisfaction with the Church in the form which it had then assumed. Among these "exiles for faith" was a congregation of "Confessional Lutherans" from Saxony who settled in Missouri, and a congregation from Bavaria, also "confessional," who settled in Michigan on the Saginaw River. Life in these frontier regions was hard and the new settlers were poor, too poor to build churches, schools and seminaries, or even to import pastors from overseas. There were many Lutheran congregations already established in America and some had built churches even in the newly opened West, but the newcomers steadfastly refused to join or even attend any church which did not accept in their completeness the confessional writings of the Lutheran Church.

Little by little they organized congregations of their own, served at first by devoted men who came from Germany. In time they were able to build churches, start schools, publish a newspaper and establish seminaries to train their ministers. In 1847 they organized their own synod, in which were included groups as widely separated from each other as the Bavarian settlers on the Saginaw and the Saxons in St. Louis. The synod took its name from the Missouri settlement and was called the Synod of Missouri and Other States, and to this day has remained separate from the other Lutheran bodies in the country, representing the conservative element in the Church.

ORGANIZATION:

The Synod is pronouncedly congregational in polity. Pastors are called directly by congregations, and it is only after a call by a Christian congregation that a minister is ordained and installed in his sacred office. At all conventions, both district and general, congregations are represented by equal numbers of ministerial and lay members, and all resolutions of the Synod are subject to approval or disapproval by the congregations. The Synod has therefore only an advisory function.

DOCTRINE:

The Missouri Synod recognizes but one standard, the Bible as the infallible and inspired Word of God. They do not accept the readings of "higher criticism" and reject the theory of evolution. They accept the three ecumenical creeds, the Apostles', Nicene and Athanasian; and the six Lutheran Confessions, namely, the Augsburg Confession, the Apology of the Augsburg Confession, the Smalcald Articles, the Large and Small Catechisms of Luther, and the Formula of Concord, not "in so far as" but "because" they agree with Scripture. Those desiring to be admitted to the public ministry must pledge themselves to teach in accordance with these standards.

FORM OF WORSHIP:

The services in the Church are liturgical, and in general follow the Common Service Book used by most Lutheran churches in America. However, the congregations of the Missouri Synod have their own hymnbook, which contains hymns drawn from ancient and modern sources and in agreement with the Confessions of the Church. They practice close communion, admitting to the Lord's Supper only those in confessional unity with the standards of the Missouri Synod.

WORK:

The Synod is very active in educational and missionary work. It has colleges, seminaries and schools in St. Louis, Missouri; Springfield, Illinois; Fort Wayne, Indiana; St. Paul, Minnesota, and many other parts of the country. It also has its own publishing house, Concordia Publishing Company, and supports missions in India, China, Africa and other foreign lands.

THE MENNONITES—over 100,000

The Mennonites are one of the Christian bodies which stem from the so-called Anabaptists of Reformation times. The Anabaptists, founded by Conrad Grebel in Zurich in 1525, were the left-wing or radical group of the period who sought more sweeping changes in the church than either Luther or Zwingli advocated. The Mennonites, for example, wished to abolish sacerdotalism, or priestly rule, in any form, which was, of course, contrary to the whole tradition of the church.

The Anabaptists received their name from their insistence on adult baptism, and the consequent need for rebaptism of converts who had been baptized in infancy.

As a result of persecution many of Grebel's followers left Switzerland and carried with them the Anabaptist teachings, which spread widely in Europe. The organization of the new faith was a loose confederation, approaching as nearly as possible that of the early church, and imposing no rigid conformity on the congregations. Several of the groups went to Holland and were joined in 1536 by a former priest, Menno Simons, from whom that portion of the new faith known as Mennonites took its name. From this group in Holland and from the Dutch Mennonites of Crefeld in Germany came the first members of the sect to seek religious freedom in America. They settled in Pennsylvania and were soon followed by other groups, until an extensive colony had grown up in Lancaster County, where they engaged in farming, making the region famous for its fertility and productiveness.

Originating in different parts of Europe and coming to America at different times, the Mennonites are not a homogeneous and united church, nor do their beliefs permit a centralized church organization or government. There are a dozen or more separate bodies, many of them very small, and ranging from liberal through moderate to conservative in doctrine and tradition.

DOCTRINE:

All Mennonites agree on the following articles of faith:

1. The divine authority and sufficiency of the Word of God.
2. The necessity of a holy life in obedience to the Word of God.
3. The separation of church from state.
4. The separation between the church and the world.
5. Abandonment of war and the use of force. In its stead must be placed the gospel of peace.
6. The baptism of converts upon confession of faith. (Infants are regarded as saved without baptism.)
7. Opposition to secret orders.

There is no fixed creed to which they subscribe, but several confessions of faith have been drawn up which express to some extent the doctrines of the different groups. The strict conservatives and most of the moderates favor the Dordrecht Confession of 1632, the liberals and progressives favor the broader Cornelis Ris Confession of 1766, which agrees with the Dordrecht Confession on fundamentals but differs from it in detail.

1. The Mennonite Church is the largest single body of Mennonites in the United States. Its first general conference was held in 1898, and since then (1916-1926) a number of Amish (conservative Mennonite) congregations have merged with the original group, bringing the membership up to some 52,000 souls.

MEMBERSHIP:

Consists of those who accept Christ as their personal Saviour and are baptized. Baptism is by pouring.

DOCTRINE:

The Church accepts the Dordrecht Confession as the official statement of belief. The ordinances of the Church are baptism; the Lord's Supper; feet washing, which is based on John 13:4-10 and is observed at the close of the Communion service; the holy kiss (Romans 16:16); and anointing with oil for the healing of the body (Mark 6:13, James 5:14). During worship the sisters wear a "prayer veil," in America usually a white net cap. Close communion is practised, that is, only those who are in full fellowship in the congregation can receive the emblems of the Lord's Supper.

The Church not only holds to nonresistance, but refuses even to help in the manufacture of munitions. Litigation, swearing oaths, and membership in labor unions or secret societies are forbidden. One of the cardinal rules is simplicity. The ministers and some of the laity wear coats without "collars or lapels," the women wear bonnets or hoods. All jewelry, including the wedding ring, is forbidden.

Marriage with members of other faiths is prohibited, and divorce is recognized only for unfaithfulness. Emphasis is also laid on total abstinence from alcohol and tobacco; and theaters and moving pictures are frowned upon.

FORM OF WORSHIP:

The meetinghouses are very plain, having neither steeple, bell, organ, altar nor works of art. The minister is addressed as "brother," frequently has no special training, and is unpaid, earning his living by farming or some other occupation. There is, however, a growing conviction that the ministry should be both trained and paid, and the Mennonite Church now maintains two senior colleges, a junior college and many academies to train its ministry.

The service is simple and dignified. The congregations sing four-part music, unaccompanied; and the worshipers kneel for prayer.

2. The General Conference of the Mennonite Church of North America is the name of a separate sect, and is entirely distinct from the general conference of the Mennonite Church mentioned above. It was organized in 1860, as an effort to unite all Mennonite groups. Another body, the Central Conference, merged with them in 1946, and today there are about 44,000 baptized members. The effort toward amalgamation in 1860 largely failed, and the sect remains today a separate body, progressive in doctrine and polity. Their stand may be epitomized in the phrase "In essentials unity, in nonessentials, liberty." They adhere to the traditional doctrines: believers' baptism; opposition to the oath; the stand against membership in secret orders; and nonresistance. They are not absolutely and universally opposed to lawsuits, do not object to "mixed marriages," do not insist on close communion, have discarded the worship veil, given up plain clothing forms, support an educated and salaried ministry, and have introduced musical instruments and choirs into the church services.

3. Mennonite Brethren Church of North America. Some of the Mennonites early moved to Russia from Germany and from there many migrated to America. Among these were the Mennonite Brethren who came here in 1874. There are now about 17,000 of them in this country. They are moderates, and one of their distinctive features is baptism by immersion. They are an active missionary body, and keenly interested in the personal conversion and salvation of their associates. They baptize by immersion backwards.

4. Old Order Amish Mennonite Church. "The Amish" as they are generally called, are the very conservative Mennonites, and cling to the customs and traditions of the past, even using German in their preaching, Bible reading and hymn singing. They settled originally in southeastern Pennsylvania and Johnstown was named after one of the members, Joseph

Schantz (Anglicized as Johns), in 1800. They carry simplicity into every detail of life, the way of cutting the hair, clothing which must be fastened only with hooks and eyes, vehicles drawn by horses and painted only one color. The men wear dark clothes, broad-brimmed hats and full beards, the women large bonnets and long, full dresses, of solid colors. The houses have no modern plumbing or telephones.

They are strict congregationalists, and have no church buildings. Every two weeks they meet for service in the home of a member. The service lasts for some hours, and is followed by a meal given by the family in whose house the service is held. They have no missionary activities, no Sunday schools, and are not opposed to the use of alcohol and tobacco. The mode of baptism continues to be pouring. Their membership, which is growing, is about 13,600.

The Amish are especially famous for their farming methods and husbandry.

5. Mennonite Brethren in Christ. This is a "holiness" group. Their confession of faith is substantially the Dordrecht Confession accepted by most Mennonites, but they are evangelistic in practice, believe in sudden conversions followed by instantaneous and complete sanctification. They accept immersion as the mode of baptism. Their membership is 12,800.

6. Old Order Mennonites. This is a conservative group but by no means as strict as the Amish. They number about 4,600.

7. Conservative Amish Mennonites. In some districts these are nearly as strict as the Amish, except that they permit the use of the automobile. In others they are very like the Mennonite Church, and moderate.

8. Church of God in Christ Mennonites, or "Holdemans." This sect was organized in Ohio in 1859, in an effort

to re-establish the order and discipline of the Church. They have adopted as far as possible the life and faith of their fathers.

9. Evangelical Mennonite Brethren. This was a group from Russia which settled in the Middle West. The Brethren are conservative and actively evangelistic. They observe foot washing at the Communion Service and baptize by either pouring or immersion.

10. Evangelical Mennonite Church. This group separated from the Old Order Amish because of a new emphasis on conversion and revivalism. They teach that the "Baptism with the Holy Ghost" is an experience separate from regeneration. They also believe in divine healing.

11. The Krimmer (Crimean) Mennonite Brethren resemble the Mennonite Brethren (3) except that they immerse converts forwards while the Mennonite Brethren immerse them backwards.

12. Kleine Gemeinde. This is another group that came from Russia. In many ways it is like the Amish, but does have Sunday schools and Bible meetings for young people.

13. Reformed Mennonites. This is a small reformation group within the Mennonite faith. It has tried in every way to return and conform to the Biblical teachings of Menno Simons (1492-1559).

All so-called "Russian" Mennonites are really Dutch ethnic groups, German in language and culture, who for various reasons lived in Russia before coming to America.

One of the Mennonite practices frequently mentioned is "shunning" or "avoidance" of those who are expelled from the Church. By this is meant shutting out from all intercourse with the faithful those excommunicated from the congregation. The faithful may not eat, drink, visit, buy or sell with any excommunicated person. "Shunning" is practised by most of the strict conservative groups, such as the Amish, Church of God in Christ, and Reformed Mennonites.

In most congregations the Lord's Supper is celebrated twice a year, and is accompanied by foot washing, which is regarded as a holy ordinance. There is no liturgy or prescribed form of worship, since each congregation is free to choose its own way of conducting services. Most Mennonite churches are country churches, since the congregations are composed chiefly of farmers. Though pacifists in creed, the Mennonites are very active in alleviating the ravages of war. The united relief agency of the various Mennonite bodies, the Mennonite Central Committee of Akron, Pennsylvania, is carrying on an enormous relief program in France, Poland, Germany, Austria, China, the Philippines, etc.

METHODISM—about 10,000,000

By the beginning of the eighteenth century the religious conflict which had been troubling England for well over a hundred years was finally ended. Anglicanism had won the day and the Established, or state, Church of England was henceforth the moderate middle line of faith between Roman Catholicism and Separatism. For many years to come, indeed up to this very day, there would be a continuing difference between "high" and "low" church, but no real effort to change either doctrine or polity. The most ardent dissenters of both right and left wings of religion had found asylum in America. For the rest, nonconformist meetinghouses and Roman Catholic chapels were tolerated, but their members were disregarded both socially and politically and were obliged to pay taxes to support the state church.

As religious discussion decreased and active opposition to Anglicanism was suppressed, the Established Church began to grow lax. The ministerial profession frequently became a means to social or political advancement; livings were secured by questionable means and were frequently so poorly paid that one man had to hold several in order to support life for himself and family. Many of the clergy were quite ignorant, and could not have afforded books even had they wanted them. In the crowded city slums no provision whatever was made for the poor, and unless a nonconformist meetinghouse cared for them, they lived and died without benefit of clergy.

In 1701 the War of the Spanish Succession began between France and England—a war waged on sea and land for thirteen years, which absorbed all the country's energies. As in recent wars, profiteers grew rich; the poor migrated in increasing numbers to the cities, where there was work; manufacture and invention were stimulated, morals were relaxed. Then came the postwar recession, with unemployment, crowded living conditions and general lawlessness. Hard liquor began to take the place of ale, which had been the general beverage of everyone at a time when tea and coffee were still unknown. In George II's reign (1727-1760) gin was introduced and at so low a price that even the poor could afford it. There ensued a period of looseness and corruption under the Hanoverian kings which has never been equaled in English history.

It is a strange anomaly that even at so low an ebb of private morals England's public conscience was awake and active. The early eighteenth century was the age of Jonathan Swift's scathing satires, of Addison and Steele's *Spectator* papers, full of ironical commentary on the life of the times, of Hogarth's pictures of contemporary abuses, such as Gin Lane and the Rake's Progress. New churches were built in London to look after the displaced population crowding the slums; foundling homes, hospitals, charity schools were set up; poor laws were improved; and in the Church itself there grew up religious societies of earnest seekers for spiritual life.

It was into this world that John and Charles Wesley were born, John in 1703, Charles in 1707. The Wesley family had for a hundred years been professional men, for the most part in the ministry or in medicine. The grandfather of these two was a nonconformist minister; their father, Samuel Wesley, took orders in the Anglican Church. Both he and his wife seem to have been people of rare spiritual quality, bringing up their children in the fear of God and fulfilling their duties in a world where an assured church living was too often an excuse for neglect of duty.

Reared in such an atmosphere, it is not surprising to find John Wesley showing its effects even when he was a student at Oxford. He drew up a timetable for studies, carefully limited his expenditures and avoided the gay social life of his fellow students. Charles spent a year in "diversions" before he settled down, and then seems to have had a change of heart which led him also to follow a schedule, more especially in religious matters. He persuaded some of his friends to attend Holy Communion every week, which led one of his fellow students to speak of the group as Methodists. The name spread in Oxford and so the new movement started.

At first it was, as the name implies, only an effort to revitalize religion and bring it back into every day life. Both John and Charles felt that they could not be saved without holiness, an inner conviction of God's presence, and an urge to spread His gospel, but none of this necessitated founding a new church. The Holy Club which met in Wesley's room at Oxford every Sunday evening was orthodox, and Wesley was himself a High-Churchman as late as 1735. It was then that he and Charles came across the ocean to Savannah at the invitation of some prominent Georgians to preach the gospel. On the ship were a group of Moravians, whose sincere faith deeply impressed John Wesley, although he was too much of a High-Church Anglican to have much immediate sympathy with their simple piety, much as the lesson was to bear fruit later.

The visit to America was a failure. The vision had not yet come to Wesley, and his High-Church views offended many of the people, who looked upon them and upon him as narrow-minded. When after two years of fruitless effort he sailed for home, he was in a state of profound depression: he found that he feared death, that he had no joy in faith, and that dread of the unknown future life shadowed his life on earth. For it must be remembered that at this time the doctrine of the established Church of England was still strongly Calvinistic; some were elected to be saved, some to be damned, and no man, however good, could be sure of salvation.

It was in this state of mind that in May, 1738, rather unwillingly, he attended a meeting at Aldersgate, where he heard Luther's preface to the Epistle to the Romans, emphasizing as it does the conception of salvation by faith in Christ. This meeting was the turning point in Wesley's life. The old punctilious observance of church rules, the external theology and the unsatisfied doubts of his earlier days gave way to a new sense of personal relationship with God. No longer did he struggle over his own salvation. Through a vivid personal experience he had become assured of it, and set out to bring salvation to others. He had become an accepted fellow worker with God Himself.

Before beginning active work, he visited the Moravians at Herrnhut in Saxony, harking back to his meeting with them on the ship. In September he was back in England, preaching and speaking in churches and prisons. As friend and fellow worker he had the assistance of George Whitefield, one of the great preachers of all time. Their enthusiasm and religious fervor, together with the hymns which both John and Charles Wesley wrote, offended the conservative English clergy, and the young men soon found themselves excluded from one pulpit after another. Nothing daunted, they began to preach in barns and fields; once in Epworth, when Wesley was denied the pulpit which his father had occupied, he preached from his father's grave, and preached to hundreds. His audiences were drawn chiefly from the poorer classes. To many of these the Word of God was something quite new, and must have come as a blinding revelation of hope in a drab and degraded existence.

It took great courage to make this break with the past, for John Wesley found himself excluded and ostracized by his own kind. The division between the new movement and the church within which it had grown up became wider, and Methodism finally became a separate denomination, organized in 1739 as the United Societies. Charles Wesley remained in the Church of England, and that the separation from his church was hard for John may be gathered from the fact that during his whole career he always set the hour for the Methodists' meeting so as not to interfere with the service of the English Church, of which he still felt himself a member. In 1745 he issued the rules for the new organization, which may be found today in the Methodist Book of Discipline.

It will be remembered that when the Wesleys first visited America, they were still members of the Church of England, with no thought of separation. The Methodism that later arose from their preaching was introduced into the colonies in 1766, when Philip Embury began to preach in New York; but the great missionary who established the church here was Francis Asbury, who landed in Philadelphia in 1771. By the close of the Revolutionary War the new society had become firmly rooted, but its preachers were men who had been specially sent out from England, and who returned home with the war, leaving the new church without spiritual leadership. In this emergency Wesley, responding to an appeal, ordained two elders and consecrated a presbyter, or bishop, to "preside over the flock of Christ" in America. On Christmas Eve, 1784, the Methodist Episcopal Church in this country was organized, and the Articles of Religion and form of worship provided by Mr. Wesley were accepted.

I

METHODIST EPISCOPAL CHURCH METHODIST PROTESTANT CHURCH METHODIST EPISCOPAL CHURCH, SOUTH	} 1939, the Methodist Church

In 1828 a disagreement arose in the Methodist Episcopal Church on matters of polity. A division resulted, and a new body was set up which called itself the Methodist Protestant Church. The doctrine of the two churches was identical, but the Methodist Protestant Church had no bishops and gave laymen a greater power in church affairs. In 1844, as a result of the slavery issue, there was another split in the parent body which resulted in the Methodist Episcopal Church, South.

In 1939 the three churches were once more united, and became the Methodist Church with a membership of nearly 8,000,000 souls, about 1,000,000 of whom are Negro.

MEMBERSHIP:

Is open to all "who desire to flee from the wrath to come and to be saved from their sins," granted to those who have been baptized and, after preliminary instruction, are received into a congregation according to a prescribed ritual.

ORGANIZATION:

The ministry is a threefold order consisting of bishops, elders and deacons. The organizational unit is the single parish, or if a minister has charge of more than one parish, then the circuit. Since the union in 1939 of the three Methodist churches, the local church chooses between a "Board of Stewards" and an "Official Board" to manage the administrative and financial matters of the parish. The governing body of the charge, that is, the parish or circuit, is the quarterly conference, which in turn is under the jurisdiction of the General Conference, which meets every four years.

DOCTRINE:

There are twenty-five articles of religion, taken from the Thirty-nine Articles of the Church of England out of which the Methodist Church sprang. The archaisms of language have been changed, and passages which are no longer applicable deleted. One new section concerning the Ruler of the United States has been inserted.

Besides the articles there are certain rules for church members which have been taken over from the rules Wesley drew up for the United Societies. These rules are all concerned with one's duty toward God and toward one's neighbor, and with attendance upon the divine ordinances which are:

1. Public worship of God.
2. The ministry of the Word, either read or expounded.
3. The Supper of the Lord.
4. Family and private prayer.
5. Searching the Scriptures.
6. Fasting or abstinence.

In general the Methodist doctrine is Arminian, in that it accepts free will and denies the Calvinist teachings on election and predestination. Appended to the twenty-five articles there is one short paragraph on sanctification, which is a distinctively Methodist doctrine:

"Sanctification is that renewall of our fallen nature by the Holy Ghost, received through faith in Jesus Christ, whose blood of atonement cleanseth from all sin; whereby we are not only delivered from the guilt of sin, but are washed from its pollution, saved from its power, and are enabled, through grace, to love God with all our hearts and to walk in his holy commandments blameless."

This doctrine does not imply a sinless perfection, but "a freedom from sin, from evil desires and evil tempers, and from pride." This state can be attained by faith only.

Two sacraments are recognized—baptism and the Lord's Supper.

FORM OF WORSHIP:

The liturgy contained in the Book of Worship is based on Cranmer's liturgy as contained in the Book of Common Prayer used by the Anglican Church. Its use is optional except in the case of the sacraments, where it is prescribed. There are a number of variations in the orders of worship for general and for occasional use, and many collections of prayers and suggested services for all manner of occasions. The Psalter and the collections from the Epistles and Gospels are not included, but otherwise the book is more comprehensive than the Episcopal prayer book.

WORK:

The Methodist Church carries on wide and numerous activities both at home and abroad. These include the Methodist Youth Fellowship (which has replaced the Epworth League); the American Bible Society; large publishing houses, missions and hospitals together with educational institutions extending from primary schools through training in technology.

II

African Methodist Episcopal Church—868,735
African Methodist Episcopal Zion Church—520,157
Colored Methodist Episcopal Church—381,000

The Methodist Church has a large Negro membership both in the Methodist Church described above and in separate organizations. The three largest independent colored Methodist groups are the African Methodist Episcopal Church, the African Methodist Episcopal Zion Church, and the Colored Methodist Episcopal Church. All of these were organized to give the colored people freedom of expression and self-government in their religious life.

The African Methodist Episcopal Church was organized in 1816 in Philadelphia, the African Methodist Episcopal Zion Church in New York in 1796; the Colored Methodist Episcopal Church in Jackson, Tennessee, in 1870, when it separated from the Methodist Episcopal Church, South, by mutual consent.

With a few minor variations the doctrine, organization and government of these churches agree with those of the Methodist Church.

WORK:

All three churches carry on active missionary work. The African Methodist Episcopal Zion Church, which is the oldest, is also doing educational work through a number of colleges and industrial schools, chief of which is Livingstone College, at Salisbury, North Carolina.

There are a great number of smaller Methodist bodies varying in either doctrine or polity from those listed above. Some are congregational in government, some stress holiness, some seek to return to the simplicity of the early church, and still others are frankly revivalist and work entirely through camp meetings.

THE MORAVIAN CHURCH IN AMERICA—43,809
(*Unitas Fratrum*)

In this account of the religious denominations in the United States, I have made it a general rule to confine the discussion to those with a membership of 50,000 or more. In one case, however, I have made an exception, that of the Moravians, of whose origin and growth a short outline is given below. My reasons for the exception are that they constitute the oldest Protestant sect which has had a continuous history from its inception in the fifteenth century until now, and that they had a profound influence on John Wesley, the founder of Methodism.

John Hus (1369-1415) was a student at the University of Prague, in Bohemia, where he became acquainted with the writings of the English reformer, John Wycliffe. After his ordination as priest in the Roman Catholic Church he became preacher at Bethlehem Chapel and there began to put some of the reform teachings of Wycliffe into his sermons. As a result he was summoned before the Council of Constance, and in spite of a safe-conduct which had been promised him he was burned at the stake for heresy in 1415. A year later his associate, Jerome of Prague, was also martyred.

The death of these leaders did not stamp out the fire of the movement, but drove it underground, where it spread secretly until in 1457 it again flared up, and an association was formed to foster pure Scriptural teaching and apostolic discipline. By the time of Luther's Reformation there were already from a hundred and fifty to two hundred thousand Protestants practicing and preaching their reformed faith in Europe; and in this statement the term "Protestant" is used in its literal meaning of one who *protests* against certain practices in his own mother church.

During the Thirty Years' War (1618-1648), which had its rise in Bohemia and ravaged all of Western Europe, the association was decimated by persecution and the few who remained again went underground, so ending the first phase of their existence.

The leaders of the Unitas Fratrum, as they called themselves, had long been prepared for this contingency. Before his death in 1670, their last bishop, John Amos Comenius, provided for the perpetuation of the episcopacy by instituting two bishops to carry on the secret work. He also wrote the *Ratio Disciplinae,* giving the history, discipline and doctrine of the association; and commended the care of the church to the Church of England.

It was not until 1722 that the Unitas Fratrum again arose, under the leadership and guidance of Count Zinzendorf of Saxony. At Herrnhut, on his estate in Saxony, he established a Moravian settlement which became the pattern for other like settlements which he set up elsewhere in Europe, Great Britain and America. Himself a bishop of the Brethren's Church, he remained in communion with the state church, which was Lutheran, and in this way disarmed persecution. The communities which he established were self-contained and in their isolation from the world permitted undisturbed to develop their special religious and spiritual ways of life. It was not long after this (1735) that John Wesley, on his way to Georgia, met a group of Moravians who by their fearlessness in face of danger, and their deep religious faith, made him feel the inadequacy of his own approach to God. After his own awakening at Aldersgate, Wesley spent a summer at the Herrnhut settlement before setting out on the spiritual adventure that led to the founding of Methodism.

Though the Moravians, unlike other churches, were not permitted to expand outside of their centers, they soon began to send out missionaries to foreign countries, and even at home they found work to do in what they looked upon as their "Inner Mission," revivifying faith in members of other communions. Their interest has always been, not in converting people to their own way of thinking, but in stirring up faith and reviving spiritual and religious interest in any form.

In the United States their chief settlements were in Bethlehem, Pennsylvania, and in Winston-Salem, North Carolina. The separate way of life of these towns ended in 1856, and in 1899 the Moravian system throughout the world was remodeled. Today the church is expanding widely and rapidly and for administrative purposes is divided into four provinces, British, Continental, Czecho-Slovakian (1946) and American, North and South. The four provinces form one body, but each is free to develop in its own way.

ORGANIZATION:

A general synod, held every ten years, is the supreme governing body. Under this are five provincial synods in which clergy and laity are about equally represented. These meet at regular intervals and between the meetings each is represented by an executive board, the Provincial Elders' Conference.

There are three orders of the ministry, bishops, presbyters and deacons. Deacons may preach and administer the sacraments, and after a certain period of service are ordained presbyters or priests. Only bishops may perform the rite of ordination.

DOCTRINE:

The Moravians have no new doctrinal system, but are in agreement with the teachings held in common by most evangelical churches. They consider "but one thing needful, to love our Lord Jesus Christ in sincerity and live to His glory." In general their doctrine is in accordance with the Apostles' Creed. They are Trinitarians; hold that the Scriptures are inspired and the sole rule of faith and conduct; that man was created perfect and fell by Adam's transgression; and that Jesus was sent to the world to redeem and save him. Prayer they regard as an all-important means of grace. They accept two sacraments, baptism and the Lord's Supper.

FORM OF WORSHIP:

The Church is liturgical, but allows free prayer in public worship. The Moravian hymnbook is very old, but many of the modern hymns have been added to it. Their great annual festival is Easter Day, when in a long service they make a complete statement of belief.

It was in the Moravian settlement at Bethlehem that the great annual Bach Festival was instituted, which takes place every spring. One of the most interesting of their many publications is a book of Daily Texts which is published every year. This book was first put out by Count Zinzendorf when he organized the first Moravian settlement. For each day there is a passage from the Old and one from the New Testament, each followed by a verse from a hymn.

In missionary work the Church is active in all parts of the world. The aim of the Moravian Church is unity of faith for all the world, whatever the denominational variations.

PENTECOSTAL SECTS

There are many religious sects in the United States which may be grouped together under the general heading of "Pentecostal." In Chapter 2 of the Acts of the Apostles, St. Luke has given a vivid description of the feast of Pentecost not long after Christ's death, at which the Holy Ghost appeared to His followers. "And when the day of Pentecost was fully come, they were all with one accord in one place. And suddenly there came a sound from heaven as of a rushing mighty wind, and it filled all the house where they were sitting. And there appeared unto them cloven tongues like as of fire, and it sat upon each of them. And they were all filled with the Holy Ghost, and began to speak with other tongues, as the Spirit gave them utterance."

It is on this and other like passages in the Bible that the Pentecostal sects base their faith, insisting that "speaking with other tongues as the Spirit gives utterance" is a proof that the Holy Spirit has entered the new member, or, in other words, is the "initial physical evidence" of baptism of believers in the Holy Ghost. The movement arose at about the turn of the century, seeming to spring up simultaneously in many widely separated parts of the world. It was not owing to the preaching or guidance of any individual man or group of men, but was rather in the nature of the spontaneous and world-wide outburst of an idea.

For the first fourteen years the movement had no standard of doctrine, because its membership was drawn from varying religious backgrounds, held together only by faith in "speaking with tongues." It was during these years that the various groups formed small nuclei from which later grew the numerous Pentecostal churches in existence today.

The three largest Pentecostal sects in the United States are:

The Assemblies of God
The Church of God
The Church of God in Christ (Colored)

The Assemblies of God—241,782

In 1914 a group of pastors of independent Pentecostal churches throughout the country met at Hot Springs, Arkansas, where "they agreed upon an organization primarily cooperative in religious effort." The organization was incorporated in Arkansas in 1914 and in Missouri in 1916 as "The General Council of the Assemblies of God."

MEMBERSHIP:

Membership consists of those who profess rebirth, live Christian lives, believe in the inspiration of the Holy Spirit, and assume personal responsibility for the conduct of the Church.

ORGANIZATION:

The Church is organized in part on congregational and in part on presbyterian lines. The local churches are congregational, but act under the advice and suggestion of the district and general presbyters. The work is divided into forty districts, largely along state lines. Each district has a presbytery chosen by the members of the district churches. The presbytery attends to the examination, licensing and ordaining of the ministers.

A General Council composed of all ordained ministers of the denomination meets every two years. Here general officers are chosen, doctrinal standards decided upon, and church extension planned. Heads of departments are also chosen who serve as executive presbyters. A general presbytery composed of three members from each district council acts in an advisory capacity to the executive presbyters.

DOCTRINE:

The Assemblies of God are largely an evangelistic and missionary body. The chief tenets of their faith are:

1. That the Holy Scriptures are divinely inspired.
2. That man fell and is to be redeemed.
3. That baptism in the Holy Ghost is necessary, accompanied by the speaking in other tongues.
4. That sanctification is the goal of all believers.

5. That the church is a living organism.
6. That the ministry is divinely called and Scripturally ordained.
7. That divine healing is a reality.
8. That Jesus will return to reign on earth for a thousand years before the last judgment.
9. That there will be everlasting punishment for the wicked and a new heaven and earth for believers.

The Assemblies of God are opposed to war, and although many of their members entered the armed services during the recent conflict, many others requested noncombatant service in deference to the tenets of the denomination.

WORK:

The Church is actively engaged in missionary work both at home and abroad. Among the home missionary projects are Alaska, the American Indians, and deaf-mutes. Their work in the foreign field is greatly aided by the Youth Department, organized as "Christ's Ambassadors." They have recently organized a "Speed-the-Light" campaign and have raised the money for over two hundred vehicles, including airplanes, jeeps, motorboats, motorcycles and station wagons to carry the gospel to the ends of the earth.

The Assemblies of God further support a large printing plant and are now moving in the direction of social service and special advanced education for their Bible Institutes.

The Church of God—135,000

In Eastern Tennessee in the year 1884 a Baptist missionary minister named Richard G. Spurling found himself more and more out of sympathy with his church. For an ordained minister a change in faith is an extremely serious matter, and a man must be very sure of his ground before he acts. Spurling spent two years studying the Bible and church history before he found what seemed to him the flaw in the church as he knew it. In 1886 he called a conference of those who, like himself, were dissatisfied with existing conditions, and gave the results of his prayer and studies. His conviction was that at the time of the Protestant Reformation the reformers laid too much stress on the break with Rome and too little on a break with outworn creeds; that they stressed faith instead of love; and failed to accept the power of the Holy Ghost and conscience.

Later in the same year a meeting was held for the organization of the new group and the name Christian Union was adopted. The platform preached by Spurling was very simple: "As many Christians as are here present, that are desirous to be free from all man-made creeds and traditions, and are willing to take the New Testament or law of Christ as your only rule of faith and practice; giving each other equal rights and privileges to read and interpret for yourselves as your conscience may dictate, and are willing to sit together as the Church of God to transact business as the same, come forward."

The Church grew very slowly at first. After the death of the founder, his son, Richard G. Spurling, Jr., took over the work, but for ten years his preaching and exhortation sounded on deaf ears. In 1896 three members of the little parish organized a meeting in a schoolhouse in the nearby section of North Carolina. At the revival quite a number of converts were made, but the antagonism of community churches was aroused. In spite of this, however, the new converts began a Sunday school and held regular prayer meetings. The result was a tremendous spiritual awakening which grew and spread, until the effect was that of the Pentecostal miracle, worshipers fell prostrate, and rose filled with a new and fervent faith.

The enemies of the revival actively persecuted the believers, breaking up meetings and burning their places of meeting. Furthermore, fanaticism and factions crept into the new church itself. In 1902 a better organization was set up, and by 1905 the first Annual Assembly of the Holiness Church, as it had then come to be called, was held in Cherokee County, North Carolina.

At this time basic doctrines were discussed, and communion and foot washing were accepted since they were New Testament teachings. In 1907 the church was named Church of God and an order of ministry called "evangelist" was provided for. Later in the year a revival was held in Cleveland, Tennessee, where, according to the records, "hundreds of people were converted and many were sanctified and filled with the Holy Ghost."

Persecutions continued wherever the new gospel was preached, but the missionary spirit of the little band was undaunted and the Church grew and spread, surviving even a major schism when the general overseer, A. J. Tomlinson, broke with the parent church and set up a new church of his own, which came to be known as the (Tomlinson) Church of God. Today the Church of God numbers over 135,000 members and is still growing.

MEMBERSHIP:

The conditions of membership are a profession of faith in Christ and the experience of being born again.

ORGANIZATION:

The Church itself describes its organization as a "blending of congregational and episcopal, ending in theocratic" government. By "theocratic" they mean that in the last analysis the Word of God is decisive.

Each local church is governed by a pastor and a board of deacons or councilors. After the pastor has announced a decision made by the board and himself, a vote is taken to find out the feeling of the congregation. Officers of the Church are bishops, deacons, evangelists and exhorters. Bishops and deacons must be at least twenty-five years old, have experienced sanctification and the baptism of the Holy Ghost (as displayed by speaking in unfamiliar tongues), and must have lived what they profess. There is no age limit for evangelists and exhorters. All alike must have a good general education, wisdom, judgment and the ability to speak. Women may be evangelists, but may not administer the sacraments.

DOCTRINE:

In general the doctrine of the Church of God is Arminian and in accord with Methodist doctrine. No creed is recognized as authoritative, and all decisions are made according to the Bible. Together with repentance and regeneration, sanctification is essential, by which is meant a personal experience of God subsequent to regeneration. Baptism, which is evidenced by speaking in unfamiliar tongues, is administered after sanctification. Three sacraments are recognized: water baptism by immersion, the Lord's Supper, and foot washing. Divine healing, the dedication of one's talents to the service of the Church, the Second Coming of Jesus and the millennium, eternal life for the righteous and eternal punishment for the wicked are other elements of doctrine. These teachings are set forth under twenty-nine headings, each including the Bible texts which authorize the particular tenet. Total abstinence from liquor, tobacco and narcotics; an ordinance against the wearing of jewelry, and objection to war are important elements of faith.

FORM OF WORSHIP:

There is no liturgy, regular form of worship or ritual in the Church of God. Many of the meetings are revival, or camp, meetings, which are conducted according to the guidings of the Holy Spirit. Congregational singing is an important element in worship.

The Church is very active in missionary and uplift work and has missions in all parts of the world. There is also an active branch of Negro members within the church organization.

The Church of God in Christ (Colored)—300,000

The founder of the church was Elder C. H. Mason, who had been brought up in the Baptist Church. Finding himself at variance with some of the Baptist doctrines, he joined Elder C. P. Jones and a group of like belief in founding a body known as the Church of God. In 1897, while seeking a name which would distinguish the church from others and be Scriptural, the name "Church of God in Christ" was revealed to Elder Mason. In 1907 Elder Jones split off from the founding church. Later in the same year Elder Mason founded the first general assembly of the Church of God in Christ.

ORGANIZATION:

The form of organization is based directly on the Scriptures. It includes the chief apostle (general overseer), apostles, prophets, evangelists, pastors, elders, overseers, teachers, deacons, deaconesses and missionaries.

Each church has its overseer. A state overseer is at the head of a group of churches and holds annual state convocations. A general convocation meets annually and takes up questions referred to it by state overseers and elders of the state convocations.

DOCTRINE:

The doctrine is Trinitarian. The Bible is accepted as the Word of God. Repentance, regeneration, justification and sanctification are required of each member. The Church believes in the power of speaking with tongues through the Holy Ghost in baptism. Three ordinances or sacraments are recognized: baptism of believers by immersion, the Lord's Supper, and foot washing.

THE POLISH NATIONAL CATHOLIC CHURCH—250,000

The career of Poland has always been stormy, and her fortunes during the history of Europe have ranged from great power to complete obliteration. On account of her proximity to Russia, and the long struggle for power between the two nations, her eyes early turned westward rather than eastward, and she joined the Roman Church and not the Greek, of which most of the neighboring states to the south and east were members.

In the time of John Hus the same wave of reformation which swept over Bohemia touched Poland, but the power of the nobles was too great for the masses, and the fire of revolt was soon stamped out and Catholicism continued to be the state religion through all the vicissitudes that followed.

Toward the end of the nineteenth century immigration from Central Europe increased in the United States and great numbers of Poles, fleeing from the poverty and oppression of their native land, found haven in the cities and countryside of the northeastern states. It was now that the fires so long smoldering broke out again. Wherever Polish Roman Catholic churches were set up, trouble arose. Sometimes it was because of dissatisfaction on the part of the laymen with the "absolute religious, political and social power over the parishioners" claimed by the Roman Catholic priesthood, sometimes with the priests appointed to the churches. There were disturbances in Buffalo, Chicago, Scranton and several other church centers.

In 1904 a convention of independent congregations was held in Scranton, Pennsylvania, which resulted in repudiation of the papacy by parishes in five states—Pennsylvania, Massachusetts, Connecticut. New Jersey and Maryland—and the formation of a Polish National Church. The Reverend Francis Hodur was elected as its head with the title of bishop, and was later consecrated by the National Catholic Bishops of the Netherlands, so maintaining unbroken the apostolic succession in the new Church. A constitution was adopted, and the Latin books of church rites were ordered translated into the Polish language, which was henceforward to be used in the Church.

In 1906, at a special session of the synod, and at the synod following, five new feasts were added to the church calendar: the Feast of Brotherly Love and Union of the Polish People in America, the Feast of the Poor Shepherds, the Feast of the Institution of the Polish National Church, the Feast of the Memory of the Martyrs of the Polish Nation, and the Feast of the Christian Family. There were also instituted memorial days, three of them very significantly dedicated to the early reformers, Peter Waldo, John Hus and Hieronim Savonarola.

In the second plenary synod of 1908, "hearing the word of God as preached by the Church" was declared a sacrament. In 1921 the rule of celibacy of the clergy was abrogated. The Church grew rapidly and in 1928 its constitution and creed, ceremonies and symbols were accepted by the reformed church in Poland, where thirty-eight congregations were founded.

Though similar in doctrine to the Old Catholic Church in the United States, the Polish National Catholic Church has no ecclesiastical relation with it. It is, however, in direct union with the Swiss, Dutch and Polish Old Catholic churches of Europe. None of these is related to or connected with the Eastern Orthodox Church, which cannot accept their orders or permit their peculiarities of worship. This group of churches really represents an effort to return to the church of the period of the first great ecumenical councils, the last of which was the Council of Chalcedon in A.D. 451.

ORGANIZATION:

Each congregation is governed by a board of trustees who are elected by the members. The rector is appointed by the bishop according to the wishes of the congregation. Bishops are elected by the synod, which is composed of clerical and lay members. It meets every ten years and is the highest power in the Church. Its administrative power is vested in the bishops and the grand council, the latter composed of three clerical and three lay members. Three orders of ministry are recognized, bishops, priests and deacons.

DOCTRINE:

The Polish National Catholic Church not only broke away from papal supremacy, but also reverted to an early form of Christian faith, basing its doctrine on the Bible and more especially on the New Testament as expounded by the Apostles, the first four ecumenical councils, and the Niceo-Constantinopolitan Creed. In this creed the filioque clause is omitted and the Holy Ghost is declared to proceed from the Father only, not from the Son. This is the creed used by the Eastern Orthodox Church. The Polish Catholic Church also accepts further interpretations of doctrine as pronounced by the church synods.

Those desiring to join the Church must assent to a profession of faith in eleven articles which discuss in detail the essence of God the Creator, Jesus the Guide and Redeemer, and the Holy Spirit which is the spirit of God, controlling the universe in a natural and moral order. From the Holy Spirit flows a grace which aids man in his effort to find union with God in eternity, unending happiness and the fulfillment of his being. The profession also discusses the purpose of the

Church, the duty of man, the equality of men and the right of all men to life, happiness and the means of livelihood. The last two articles follow in full, since it is impossible to summarize them briefly:

"10. I believe in the ultimate righteousness of God; in future eternal life, which will be a continuation of our mortal struggle and pilgrimage on this earth; and which, as to its condition and degree of perfection and happiness, is dependent upon our present life, and above all upon the state of our soul in the last few moments of this life.

"11. I believe in immortality and happiness in the life to come; in the union of people with God, all generations, and at all times; because I firmly believe in the omnipotence of God's love, mercy, justice, and nothing else do I desire, but that it might be so. Amen."

The Church rejects the infallibility of the Pope and reserves to all men the right to interpret the Word of God. It does not accept the doctrine of eternal punishment, for it believes that "even sinful man, after undergoing an intrinsic regeneration through contrition, penance and noble deeds, may have a chance to regain the grace of God." As man approaches God more nearly, sin will grow less until "Man will become the true image and child of God, and the Kingdom of God will prevail upon earth."

The Church accepts the sacraments of baptism, confirmation, penance, communion, unction, matrimony and ordination, with which it includes the sacrament of the Word of God heard and preached.

FORM OF WORSHIP:

The liturgy and ritual are a modified form of those used in the Roman Catholic Church. Services are read, however, not in Latin, but in Polish. As in the Roman Church, the Mass is the important feature of church worship. The Church maintains a theological seminary, Savonarola Seminary, at Scranton, Pennsylvania.

PRESBYTERIANISM

The Presbyterian Church claims for its authority the tradition of the earliest Christian Church as it was founded by the Apostles at a time when Christianity was still a Jewish sect. The founder of the Church was John Calvin (1509-1564) who, unlike Luther, sought not only to reform the abuses in the Roman Church, but to re-establish the primitive Christian church.

Calvin was French, with a clear and logical mind, and in his preaching and writing appealed to a highly intellectual group. He was convinced that the church should be the controlling factor in the state, and the government which he set up in Geneva was a theocracy, ruled by Calvin as vicegerent of God for the ordering of every phase of the community life. John Knox, a Scottish divine who studied under Calvin, carried the great reformer's teachings and practice back to Scotland, and from there Presbyterianism spread to England and for a long time struggled with the Anglican Church for supremacy.

Some of the earliest settlers in colonial America were Presbyterians, and there was a Presbyterian church in Wethersfield, Connecticut, as early as 1630. But it was not until the Scotch-Irish from Ulster, in Ireland, began to pour into the country in about 1680 that the faith may be said really to have become established in the colonies. In 1682 Francis Makemie was sent over here at the request of the Scotch-Irish settlers in Maryland, where he founded five Presbyterian churches, although no general presbytery was organized on this side of the water until 1706. The northernmost churches at this time were in Philadelphia, New Jersey and Long Island, with the main body in Delaware and Maryland, so that for many years one presbytery sufficed for all.

At first the Church was slow in spreading because it insisted on adequate ministerial training, and for many years no schools or colleges in the colonies were equipped to train Presbyterian ministers. The pulpits had therefore to be filled from England, and there were not enough men in the mother country willing to enter what was essentially a mission field, to fill the needs even of existing congregations, let alone found new ones. The religious revival known as the Great Awakening, which swept the colonies from about 1725 to the time of the Revolutionary War, galvanized all the Protestant denominations into action, and during these years the Presbyterians founded first "Log College" near Philadelphia in the 1730's, and later the College of New Jersey (now Princeton University) in 1746. The latter was intended to serve the Presbyterians of the Middle States as Harvard and Yale served the Congregationalists in New England.

As a group the Presbyterians were very active patriots in the Revolutionary War, and John Witherspoon, the president of Princeton, was the only signer of the Declaration of Independence who was a minister of a church. The Church claims that certain features of the new government embodied in the Constitution are based on their system of organization.

After the confusion following the war, the Presbyterian Church spread rapidly. In New Jersey and New York it found itself in competition with Congregationalism, which was creeping south and west from New England. In 1801 the two churches formed a union, within which the Congregationalists were left to work without Presbyterian competition in New England, and in turn refrained from competing elsewhere. In 1837 those who objected to this plan of union split from the Presbyterian Church, and the Civil War caused another split, which brought into existence the Presbyterian Church in the United States (Southern).

ORGANIZATION:

One of the distinguishing features of the Church is its form of government, which is really a representative democracy, and as like the early church as possible. In early New Testament times the presbyters or elders were the officers who constituted the ruling body of the new faith, and in this modern church there is no order of ministry higher than the presbyters from which the denomination derives its name. All presbyters are of equal rank, but are differentiated by their several functions.

In each congregation there is a minister (presbyter) and several elders, all of whom are elected by the body of communicants, although the choice of minister must be confirmed by the presbytery, noted hereafter. Once confirmed and pending good behavior, his tenure is for life, so that the independence of his position is assured. Together these elective officers form the "session," with the minister as moderator, and the session is the governing body of the congregation.

The ministers and certain elders from congregations within a prescribed area form a presbytery, one of them being chosen as moderator. The presbytery oversees and guides the congregations within its area and is the body which must confirm the election of their ministers.

Representatives from a group of presbyteries form a synod, of less administrative importance, but serving as a kind of preparatory council for the General Assembly.

The General Assembly, formed of representatives from the whole church, is its supreme governing body. One of the presbyter members is chosen as moderator, and during his term of office is recognized as the official head of the Church. The Assembly meets annually to make laws governing the course of the denomination as a whole, and also to direct missionary work, appoint theological professors and settle complaints referred from the lesser bodies. Its decisions are implemented and co-ordinated by a smaller General Council, which supervises the four boards of National Missions, Foreign Missions, Christian Education and Pensions, and thus performs an important function in administrative mechanism.

Each congregation is made up of enrolled communicants and their children. Besides its minister and elders, it is served by trustees who attend to its secular work and deacons who care for the poor.

DOCTRINE:

The only condition of membership in the Church is a sincere profession of faith in Christ, but the Church is none the less doctrinal and requires ministers and elders to subscribe to certain definite doctrinal standards. The formal statement of faith is found in the Westminster Confession of Faith and the Larger and Shorter Catechisms, which are not three separate creeds, but three expressions (of varying length and purpose) of a single creed.

The Westminster Standards, as these three statements are called, were drawn up and adopted by the Westminster Assembly during sessions from 1643 to 1648. This assembly was called together by Parliament at the time when Presbyterianism was predominent in England, for the purpose of settling doctrinal dispute. It was composed of an extraordinary body of outstanding men, 152 in all, who met at Westminster Abbey and in almost continuous session over a period of five and a half years discussed, wrote and rewrote every phrase and paragraph of the documents which they eventually gave to the world as the standards of faith for the Presbyterian Church. All types of men, orators, statesmen, preachers, theologians, rich and poor alike and from all parts of the country worked ceaselessly to produce a creed which might withstand the wear of criticism and of time. One of the rules of the Assembly was: "What any man undertakes to prove as necessary, he shall make good out of Scripture." As a result the Standards are based firmly on the Bible, in the pure Calvinistic tradition.

How well the Assembly succeeded in its purpose is evidenced by the fact that three hundred years later, though there have been minor changes made in the Confession at various times, the two catechisms have remained as they were originally written.

According to Calvin and to the Shorter Catechism, the chief end of man is "to glorify God, and to enjoy Him forever." This statement is the epitome of Presbyterianism. The definition of God, also in the Shorter Catechism, is peculiarly adequate and beautiful, and according to tradition was literally an answer to prayer: "God is a spirit, infinite, eternal and unchangeable, in His being, wisdom, power, holiness, justice, goodness and truth."

In general the Church has continued to accept the five points of Calvinism which were originally the distinctive tenets of Presbyterianism:

1. Unconditional election which means that God determines from the outset who is to be saved, and man is unable by the exercise of free will to change the ultimate verdict. This is the theory of predestination preached by St. Augustine.

2. Atonement is limited to the elect.

3. Man's depravity is total as to ability and merit.

4. Grace is irresistible. By divine power the will is impelled to believe.

5. Perseverance of the saints. (Those elected by God are sustained by Him in a state of grace, and so, in spite of weakness and falls are assured of final salvation.)

Modern Presbyterianism has to some extent modified these statements of faith. Free will is generally accepted as valid within the omniscience of God, though there is no attempt to explain its workings. The doctrine of infant damnation has been omitted and it is agreed that all persons dying in infancy are elect and therefore saved.

The four main divisions of the church in America are:

1. The Presbyterian Church in the United States of America—2,234,789

This is the parent organization and most widely spread in the country. Its standards are the Westminster Confession and the Larger and Shorter Catechisms, as adopted in 1729. After the Revolutionary War in 1788 certain amendments were made in accordance with the Constitution, expressing the independence of the Church and of religious opinion from state control. In 1886 the clause forbidding marriage with a deceased wife's sister was omitted, and in 1903 the statement was inserted declaring that persons dying in infancy were elect and therefore saved.

Besides the standards of faith the Church accepts certain standards of government, discipline and worship, contained in the documents known as *The Form of Government, The Book of Discipline,* and the *Directory for Worship*. These form the constitution of the Church. Two sacraments are recognized, baptism and the Lord's Supper.

FORM OF WORSHIP:

This varies according to the inclination of ministers and people. There exists a Book of Common Worship for optional use, which is very generally accepted and which provides a great variety of liturgies. In some churches the clergy wear Geneva gowns, the choir is vested, and there is an altar; in others the clergy wear no vestments and there is a communion table in the center of the chancel. Baptism is by sprinkling or pouring and is administered to both infants and adults. The

Lord's Supper is brought to the congregation sitting in the pews. Only ministers may administer the sacraments, but the material elements are distributed by the elders.

WORK:

The Presbyterian Church in the United States of America is more "famous for colleges than cathedrals" and has always led in educational work. In the field of higher education it reports 44 colleges and 10 theological seminaries. It carries on wide missionary activities in which education is combined with Christian teaching.

2. The Presbyterian Church in the United States (Southern)—616,337

This group was organized in Augusta, Georgia, at the outbreak of the Civil War (1861) and has retained its separate identity ever since. In doctrine and polity it is basically in agreement with the Presbyterian Church in the United States of America, from which it split. It does not, however, permit women to be ordained as ruling elders or deacons, and is less inclined to use any liturgy in the church services. Those congregations who do use a prescribed form of worship generally use the Book of Common Worship approved by the parent church, but in all cases the Presbyterian Church in the United States (Southern) uses its own hymnbook in preference to those used by the other groups.

The Church is strongly missionary both at home and abroad, and does fine educational work among the Negroes, Indians and "poor whites."

There is at this time a very definite movement on foot toward reunion of the Southern Church and the Presbyterian Church in the United States of America. A plan of reunion is at present being studied, but when and whether it will be accepted, it is too early to know.

3. United Presbyterian Church of North America—198,815

This church represents the union in Pittsburgh in 1858 of two Scottish Presbyterian churches, one Covenanters and one Secession, which were known in America as the Associate Reformed Synod and the Associate Synod.

DOCTRINE:

Besides the Westminster Confession and the catechisms they accept a Confessional Statement of forty-four articles which contains not only the substance of the Confession but also certain convictions of a later date. Cause for divorce is restricted to unfaithfulness, universal infant salvation is affirmed, communion is administered to all professed Christians, membership in secret societies is permitted, et cetera.

The Church takes a conservative stand on theological issues and affirms the plenary verbal inspiration of Scripture as the rule of faith and practice.

WORK:

The Church does wide educational work and is especially active in the mission field.

4. Cumberland Presbyterian Church—75,427

In the early years of the nineteenth century a strong revivalist movement occurred in the Presbyterian Church in Cumberland County of Kentucky and in Tennessee. To the main body of the Church it was distasteful and when, as a result of a need for preachers, the "revivalists" introduced into the ministry men without the usual academic and theological training, the feeling against the new movement was intensified. In October, 1813, the "revivalist" group split off and became a separate denomination with its own presbyteries and synod.

Since that time there have been various attempts at union with other churches, and in 1906 some of the membership returned to the parent body, but the Cumberland Church has continued, and maintains its separate identity today.

The organization of the Church is thoroughly presbyterian. In doctrine it is moderately Calvinistic, but has substituted for the Westminster Confession a revision of its own which emphasizes human responsibility as opposed to "election." In worship it is nonliturgical, and the sermon is the chief feature of the church service.

WORK:

The Cumberland Presbyterian Church has founded Bethel College and a theological seminary at McKenzie, Tennessee. It carries on both home and foreign missionary work, the former chiefly in the South and Southwest, the latter in Japan, China and Mexico.

THE REFORMED CHURCH IN AMERICA—176,244 (DUTCH REFORMED CHURCH)

The Reformed Church in America is a daughter organization to the Reformed Church in Holland, which was founded before 1560. It came to New Netherlands with the first Dutch settlers, and in 1628 was recognized as part of the church organization of Holland. The Collegiate Church in New York City, the oldest in the Middle Atlantic States, was formally organized in that year. At first the church was in charge of the classis of Amsterdam and the ministers were sent from Holland. This proved a very unsatisfactory arrangement, and furthermore, by the end of the eighteenth century the Dutch language was passing out of use and the

Church had become definitely American. At this time, therefore, after fifty years of effort, it broke away from the Dutch and became an independent organization. The final name, The Reformed Church in America, was adopted in 1867.

MEMBERSHIP:

All baptized persons who have made confession of faith before the elders and ministers.

ORGANIZATION:

The church organization is presbyterian. Each local church is controlled by a consistory composed of minister, elders and deacons, elected by the church members over eighteen years old.

The classis supervises the churches and ministry of a district in which are several churches. It consists of all the ministers in the district and an elder from each consistory.

Above the classis ranks the Particular Synod, which acts as an intermediary board between the classes and the General Synod, which is the highest court of the Church. It is made up of ministers and elders from each classis who were nominated to the Particular Synod and appointed by it to the General Synod.

The Reformed Church in America also recognizes a special kind of church organization called the Collegiate Church (college of churches), which is a collection of worshiping congregations controlled by a single consistory.

DOCTRINE:

The Church is Calvinistic in doctrine and accepts the faith as summarized in the Apostles' Creed. Its doctrinal standards are the Belgic Confession (1561), the Heidelberg Catechism (1562), and the Canons of the Synod of Dordrecht (1618-19). These teachings, according to the Reformed

Church, are substantially the same as those of the Church of England, the Presbyterian Churches and the Reformed Churches of Scotland, Switzerland, France and Germany. The basic tenet of faith is the substitutionary death of the Son of God, Jesus Christ.

FORM OF WORSHIP:

This is semiliturgical, and especially rich in its forms for the administration of the sacraments. The liturgy for ordinary services is optional, but is growing in favor and being more widely used than formerly. The liturgy for the sacraments is obligatory.

WORK:

The Reformed Church is very active along educational lines, believing in an educated people and ministry. Rutgers University, New Brunswick, New Jersey, now designated the State University, was founded by ministers and elders of the Church in 1766 with royal charter as Queens College. The New Brunswick Theological Seminary in New Jersey, the oldest theological seminary in the country (1784); Hope College, Holland, Michigan; Central College, Pella, Iowa; Northwestern Junior College and Academy, Orange City, Iowa; Pleasant Prairie Academy, German Valley, Illinois, and Western Theological Seminary are all Dutch Reformed institutions.

The Church was one of the pioneers in missionary work. It opened a mission in Amoy, China, in 1842, a mission in South India in 1853, and sent out the first mission set up in Japan under Guido F. Verbeck, known as Verbeck of Japan, in 1859.

THE RELIGIOUS SOCIETY OF FRIENDS —113,465 (THE QUAKERS)

There are many denominations which have based their faith on the need of a personal experience of God before the human spirit can be fully alive to religion. The Anabaptists of Luther's time, who were the spiritual ancestors of the Baptists, the Mennonites, Congregationalists, Methodists, Unitarians and the Disciples of Christ, all required their special personal revelation as a prerequisite of grace; and in the Pentecostal and Holiness sects of today, a very real and personal demonstration of God's grace is a fundamental tenet of belief.

To only a few is this revelation a continuous occurrence. To the great mystics like St. Francis of Assisi, Catherine of Siena, Tauler and Eckhart it was granted many times, and their lives were expressions of the intimate revelation of God. On this inner knowledge of God's will they could rest and be at peace.

It is generally during periods of stress and strain in world events that mystics appear as leaders. Some inner conviction seems to stir them up and some secret strength sustains them. It is not surprising, therefore, that one of the world's great mystics should have carried on his ministry in the troubled times of seventeenth-century England. The Reformation was still not complete, and the factions of Protestantism as well as the remnants of Catholicism were struggling for mastery in the land. Religious discussion, secret meetings and even open warfare were the order of the day. Into this confusion was born George Fox (1624-1691), son of a weaver in Leicestershire. From childhood he was sensitive and conscientious beyond his years, and his family thought at one time of educating him as a clergyman. Eventually, however, he was apprenticed to a shoemaker, and so was denied the opportunity of formal education.

None the less he read the Bible thoroughly and reflected on its teachings, finally leaving his home and family to seek spiritual guidance. He got little satisfaction from either churchmen or dissenters. At last, quite apart from the Church and its ministries, he had a transforming experience of the spirit of Christ and the overcoming power of God's love.

In 1647 he began a lifelong ministry, traveling widely and directing men to the Christ within for salvation. Fox was opposed to the empty formalism of current religion and preached the gospel of universal brotherhood and obedience to the inner light granted each man by the Holy Spirit. He made converts, especially in the north of England, and under his teaching the movement grew so fast as to alarm the authorities of church and state alike. In all, six of the first twenty-eight years of Fox's ministry were spent in prison, but in his free intervals he continued to travel and preach, not only in England, but on the Continent, in Ireland, in the West Indies and in North America. As he went he enlisted a large number of enthusiastic young men and women, who helped spread his message.

By 1660, what Fox had started as a purifying movement in the Church had become another Christian sect. At first the organization called itself "Children of Truth," "Children of Light," or "Friends of Truth." The name which they finally adopted and by which they are known today is "The Religious Society of Friends." The name "Quaker" seems to have been given them by a justice before whom Fox was being tried, and whom he admonished to "tremble at the Word of the Lord."

From the outset the Quakers refused to conform to those current social and religious customs which they thought unchristian or meaningless. They retained simplicity in dress at a time when color and richness of fabric distinguished social classes, and they spoke simply and directly in a society where manner was of more importance than matter. As testimony to the equality of men, they used the second person singular in addressing all classes, refusing the usual "you" to nobles and clergy. These practices and their refusal to attend the established church, pay tithes, take oaths or engage in war brought them into conflict with the ruling powers and subjected them to persecution both in England and in all the English colonies except Rhode Island. It was not until the Toleration Act of 1689 that they were relieved of persecution and of most of their civil disabilities.

In 1681 the colony of Pennsylvania was established by William Penn as a refuge for the Friends, and here they were finally free to live and worship in their own fashion. Penn seems to have been a man of amazingly high and pure principles, with faith in the essential goodness of mankind. He made an elaborate system of laws for the colony, all on the highest ethical level, laying special stress on religious freedom and tolerance for all who believed in God. The punishment of offenses against God and society were severe.

The opposition of the Quakers to war or any kind of violence raised difficulties for them from the beginning. They refused war "for the kingdoms of this world or for the kingdom of Heaven." While adhering to their principles they have done much to lessen the horrors of war by their donations of money and of personal service in every kind of relief work, both during and in the intervals between conflicts.

ORGANIZATION:

Their organization is very loose, existing chiefly for business in connection with the Church. There are monthly, quarterly and yearly meetings in all parts of the Society, the monthly meetings being grouped into the quarterly and the quarterly into the yearly, each with higher authority. The monthly meeting is the executive body. There is no ordained ministry. Those who manifest a gift in public ministry are simply "recorded" or "recognized" as having this special talent to supervise the spiritual and moral life of the members. Women are on terms of absolute equality with men.

(In 1827-1828 there was a local split among the Quakers in the Baltimore, Philadelphia and New York area, caused by social, organizational and theological forces. The group which broke away is called Hicksite, after its original leader, Elias Hicks. Since 1917 all branches of the Friends have been working together, essentially as one denomination.)

DOCTRINE:

The Friends have no formal creed as a condition of membership, nor do they practise any outward ordinances such as baptism or the Lord's Supper. Their central tenet is obedience to the personal teaching and guidance of the Holy Spirit, which they call the "Light Within" or the "Inner Light." In everything they seek the guidance of the "Spirit of Christ which moves them." They believe that in matters of church policy spiritual guidance is corporate, through common seeking, meditation and discussion.

FORM OF WORSHIP:

Their services, or, as they are usually called, Friends' Meetings, are nonliturgical and follow no set order of worship. In Philadelphia the old customs are observed and there is no ritual, no music, not even congregational singing, on the theory that the Spirit of God moves the worshipers to prayer or preaching, and that unless and until it does so, they all sit in silent prayer and meditation. Elsewhere the traditional form of worship has been modified. Paid pastors are employed and preach regularly, music has been introduced, and although there is no fixed liturgy, the order of worship tends to follow the usual Protestant pattern.

Distinctive ways of dress and speech have generally been replaced throughout the Society by conformity to modern usage, which no longer follows class distinctions. The ideals set up by their founder continue, however, and led by these they carry on their work of alleviating the horrors of war. The American Friends Service Committee is known to the ends of the earth, and together with the British Friends Committee was awarded the Nobel Peace Prize in 1947. While straining every nerve to restore war-wracked areas, they also labor through legislation and education, not only to alleviate, but to do away with war itself. They have established missions and good-will centers in many parts of the globe, and are active in educational work, as well as in humanitarian and social reform movements. They visualize a world in which co-operation will take the place of competition, and where the antagonism of warring interests will be replaced by a genuine love and fellowship among men, guided by the spirit within. For, with the Friends, religion is an integral part of daily life, actuating all that they say and do.

THE REORGANIZED CHURCH OF JESUS CHRIST OF LATTER DAY SAINTS—116,888

The sudden and tragic death of Joseph Smith in 1844 was followed by a period of confusion and panic among his followers. Many were forever scattered, all were bewildered and uncertain about the future which had looked so rosy a few short months before. The organization founded in such hope, and which had shown such intrepid courage in the face of repeated disaster, seemed about to be blotted out.

After the first shock had worn off, however, courage revived, and the remnant which remained of the once flourishing community rallied to new leaders who sprang up from among them. A large number under Brigham Young moved west to Utah, where they founded the Mormon State. A somewhat smaller group remained true to the prophet's family and followed his son, Joseph Smith III. This group finally settled in Independence, Missouri, where it still has its headquarters.

MEMBERSHIP:

Consists of persons over eight years of age who have declared their faith in God, repented of past sins, and received baptism by immersion and the laying on of hands.

ORGANIZATION:

The church unit is a branch (corresponding to a parish) and is under the care of an elder. Several branches compose a stake or, in the case of outlying regions, a district. Zion, located at Independence, Missouri, is a stake made up of a central branch and fourteen outlying congregations. The Stake of Zion is directed by the president of the general church. There are four other stakes, each consisting of a large branch and several smaller neighboring congregations. A general conference of representatives from these stakes meets every two years.

Each stake has bishops, elders, priests, teachers and deacons, each order performing different functions.

DOCTRINE:

The official statement of belief of the Reorganized Church of Jesus Christ of Latter Day Saints is given briefly as follows:

"We believe in God the Eternal Father, and in his Son Jesus Christ, and in the Holy Ghost.

"We believe that men will be punished for their own sins and not for Adam's transgression.

"We believe that through the atonement of Christ, all men may be saved by obedience to the laws and ordinances of the gospel.

"We believe that these laws and ordinances are: (1st) Faith in God and in the Lord Jesus Christ; (2d) Repentance; (3rd) Baptism by immersion for the remission of sins; (4th) Laying on of hands for the gift of the Holy Ghost.

"We believe in the resurrection of the body: that the dead in Christ will rise first at his second coming when he appears to usher in the millennial reign, and the rest of the dead will not live again until the thousand years are ended.

"We believe in the doctrine of eternal judgment, which provides that man shall be judged and rewarded or punished, according to the degree of good or evil he shall have done.

"We believe that a man must be called of God and ordained by the laying on of hands of those who are in authority, to entitle him to preach the gospel and administer in the ordinances thereof.

"We believe in the same kind of organization that existed in the primitive church, viz.: apostles, prophets, evangelists, pastors, teachers, and all other officers provided for in the Scriptures.

"We believe that in the Bible is contained the word of God. We believe that the canon of Scripture is not full, but that God, by his Spirit, will continue to reveal his word to man until the end of time.

"We believe in the powers and gifts of the everlasting gospel, viz.: wisdom, knowledge, faith, healing, miracles, prophecy, discerning of spirits, tongues, interpretation of tongues.

"We believe that marriage is ordained of God; and that the law of God provides for but one companion in wedlock for either man or woman. In cases where the contract of marriage is broken by death the remaining one is free to marry again, and in case of breach of the marriage covenant the innocent one may also remarry.

"We believe that the doctrines of a plurality and a community of wives are heresies, and are opposed to the law of God. . . .

"We believe that in all matters of controversy upon the duty of man towards God, and in reference to preparation and fitness for the world to come, the word of God should be decisive and the end of dispute; and that when God directs, man should obey.

"We believe that men should worship God in "spirit and in truth"; and we claim the privilege for ourselves and all men of worshiping Almighty God according to the dictates of conscience, providing that such worship does not require a violation of the constitutional law of the land.

"We believe that all men are bound to sustain and uphold the respective governments in which they reside while protected in their inherent rights by the constitutional laws of such governments, and that sedition and rebellion are unbecoming every citizen thus protected.

"We believe in being honest, true, chaste, benevolent, virtuous, and in doing good to all men . . ."

The Reorganized Church accepts as the Word of God the inspired version of the Bible—i.e., the Bible as corrected and explained by Joseph Smith—and the *Book of Mormon.* It does not accept the Mormon doctrine of a progressive God, for it feels that the essence of divinity lies in its unchangeable and eternal quality.

The Church has a twofold aim, to evangelize the world and to build the kingdom of God on earth. Special emphasis is laid on the principle of stewardship, the brotherhood of man, the building of Zion. Property they claim is held in trust for God and the group, and both property and industry should be used for social ends.

WORK:

Missionary work, both home and foreign, is carried on by the "seventies" (Luke 10:1), directed by a quorum of twelve. Among other activities the Church maintains a junior college at Lamoni, Iowa, and a nurses' training school hospital at Independence, Missouri.

Several other churches grew out of the original Latter Day Saint movement:—

The Church of Christ (Temple Lot) were a group that returned to Independence, Missouri, in 1867, where they bought the Temple Lot which contains the "spot" indicated by the Lord for a site for His temple. In 1891 the Reorganized Church brought suit against them to recover the site and obtained judgment, which was reversed on appeal on the ground of laches.

Church of Jesus Christ (Bickertonites)—This group was organized in Greenock, Pennsylvania, in 1862, by William Bickerton, as a result of revelation. It is an effort to return to a more primitive form of the church and emphasizes the gift of tongues and divine healing. The Bickertonites are opposed to war.

Church of Christ (Cutlerites)—Alpheus Cutler claimed that he was one of the six elders in the original church body who with Joseph Smith himself had the authority to organize a church. By revelation he was to await a sign from God, in the form of two half-moons back to back in the sky, and upon fulfillment of the revelation he founded a church in 1853. The Cutlerites believe in an early apostolic form of church organization and teaching; they are monogamous, opposed to war, and diverge in several respects from later Mormon doctrines.

Church of Jesus Christ (Strangites)—regards itself as the one and only original Church of Jesus Christ of Latter

Day Saints, on the ground that James J. Strang claimed to have been ordained as leader according to God's revelations to Joseph Smith. It denies the virgin birth of Christ and the infinite atonement; it believes that Adam, by breaking the law, was rendered unfit to enter God's presence, and his corruption could only be removed by a resurrection. Jesus kept a perfect law, wherefore God raised Him from the dead.

THE SEVENTH-DAY ADVENTISTS—208,030

In the early years of the nineteenth century there arose in widely separate parts of the world a strange religious unrest. It was a time of breathless expectancy and anxious waiting for the Second Coming of Christ and the end of the world. The preacher of this doctrine in the United States was William Miller, a farmer-preacher of the Baptist Church from a small town in eastern New York. In his youth he had fought as a captain in the War of 1812, and on his return home, like many war-weary young men of all times, had become interested in religion and was led first to deism and the denial of God.

This influence was, however, not lasting, for a conviction of God and of Christ's saving grace came to him and he turned to the Bible for confirmation of his experience. After two years of careful study he was convinced that the prophetic portions of the Bible have significance for us, and testify to the early coming of the days of the Lord, and that the prophecies of Daniel and of the Book of Revelation must be pregnant with meaning not yet disclosed. With great care, testing every verse and comparing and collating them, he found that to date all the apocalyptic visions had been fulfilled. This being so, it seemed to him that there must be prophecies of things still to come in these books, and these he set himself to unravel.

In Daniel 8:14 occurred the words "Unto two thousand

and three hundred days; then shall the sanctuary be cleansed." This seemed to Miller a clear measurement of the period which must elapse before the last day. Twenty-three hundred days he could translate into twenty-three hundred years, but the question was "from when." By comparison with other prophetic passages in the Bible he finally worked out that the date to reckon from was 457 B.C. when, under the decree of Artaxerxes, Ezra started to rebuild the Temple in Jerusalem. Twenty-three hundred years later than 457 B.C. brought the date to 1843 or at the outside 1844—after the 2300 years had elapsed.

Basing his belief on the imminence of the last day, Miller set out on a preaching tour to carry the message and warn the people to repent and prepare for the coming of Christ and the last judgment. Inspired by his preaching men, women and children were converted and made ready for the end of the world. But 1843, and October, 1844, the last possible date according to reckoning, passed uneventfully. Greatly discouraged and shaken in faith, many of the Millerites fell away and the group was pretty well scattered.

In western New York, however, a few faithful followers continued to search the Scriptures, sure that the answer lay there, and that only an error in calculation was to blame for the discrepancy. After much study they felt themselves justified, for they found that their basic fault was not knowing what was meant by the "cleansing of the sanctuary."

In the Hebrew ritual as ordained by God in the Old Testament there was appointed a time each year when the High Priest went into the holy place or sanctuary where the Ark was kept and sacrificed for the sins of the people (Leviticus 16). Just such a ritual was the "cleansing of the sanctuary" in heaven. As the great high priest, Jesus went into the sanctuary in heaven and there instituted an "investigative judgment" of the sins of the world. The year 1844, then, was valid, but not for the Second Coming. It was at this time that

Jesus went into the holy place to look over the records, blotting out sins repented, and evaluating the righteous and the wicked. This over, He would come again in glory and the wicked would be destroyed by the same cleansing fire that purified the good.

As they read and studied, another group of the Adventists, in Washington, New Hampshire, became convinced that for years they had been wrong in celebrating the Sabbath on the first day of the week. In Matthew 5:17-18 Jesus said, "Think not that I am come to destroy the law, or the prophets: I am not come to destroy, but to fulfil. For verily I say unto you, Till heaven and earth pass, one jot or one tittle shall in no wise pass from the law, till all be fulfilled." Certainly the fourth commandment prescribed the seventh day as the Sabbath, and there was nothing in the Bible anywhere to authorize a change to the first. "All scripture language is to be taken literally unless there exists some good reason for regarding it as figurative. All that is figurative is to be interpreted by that which is literal" (*Daniel and the Revelation,* Uriah Smith). This is a fundamental belief of the Adventists, and when, therefore, this new reading of the prophecies was made and the new church arose, it accepted the doctrine of the seventh day as Sunday, and in time called itself "Seventh-day Adventists."

The new church was peculiarly fortunate in having in its membership a young girl of extraordinary spiritual gifts. Ellen G. Harmon, later Mrs. Ellen G. White, was barely seventeen when she began to have visions which instructed her in many matters concerned with the faith. It was largely through her efforts that the new findings of the Adventists were published to the world, where they at once roused a broad and lively interest. From then on to the end of a long life (she lived to be nearly eighty-eight) she gave herself to the cause of spreading the gospel and was acknowledged by her fellow believers as a prophet.

With her help and encouragement, and guided by her visions, her husband issued the first publications of the Seventh-day Adventists. From that time on she gave the main patterns to the growing movement, and it was largely through her clearsighted efforts that no hint of fanaticism was permitted to invade it. She was an indefatigable worker and, inspired by her revelations, wrote literally scores of books and pamphlets covering every phase of belief and activity in the organization. When she died in 1915 the tiny group of her youth had already grown to such proportions that they had carried the gospel to the remotest corners of the earth.

MEMBERSHIP:

Is composed of those who have been baptized by immersion and received into a local church after confession of faith.

ORGANIZATION:

The local church is congregational in government. Its officers, elected annually by the congregation, include one or more elders, deacons and deaconesses; treasurer, clerk and department leaders.

Church elders may conduct the regular services and sacraments. They assist in these services where a pastor is in charge of the church.

A number of churches form a conference or mission, of which a selected body meets every two years, composed of delegates elected by the member congregations. The conferences on missions are united in groups to form union conferences, which hold meetings every four years, and every four years also delegates from the union conferences and missions throughout the world assemble in General Conference.

All ordained and licensed ministers in a local conference serve under its direction and pay. The ministry is supported out of tithes, which are distributed, not by congregations, but by the conference. A licensed minister is given ordination after a period of service in which he has proved his calling, and given evidence of successful ministry.

DOCTRINE:

The Seventh-day Adventists believe in:

1. The supernatural and plenary authority of the Scriptures.

2. God, and the Trinity of the Godhead.

3. The substitutionary death of Jesus Christ. The salvation thus provided is freely offered to all men, and is sufficient for all, but becomes efficacious only in those who believe in Jesus Christ. In the final accounting, He will formally blot out the sins of men and they will be remembered no more forever.

4. The Holy Spirit.

5. God as Creator and Sustainer of our world.

6. The inherent sinfulness of the human race.

7. The reality and personality of Satan. He was originally Lucifer, full of wisdom and perfect in beauty until the day that iniquity was found in him. At the close of the millennium he and the evil angels will be destroyed in the lake of fire.

8. The second coming of Christ in this generation.

9. The millennium. There will be a period of a thousand years between the end of the Christian era and the beginning of the new earth state.

10. The immortality of man. Immortality will be conferred upon the righteous at the second coming of Christ.

11. The unconscious state of the dead, who are "asleep" until the first resurrection if they are righteous, or until the second if they are numbered among the wicked.

12. The punishment of sinners. Eternal death, total extinction by fire will be meted out to them.

13. The judgment. This is divided into two phases, the investigative and executive. The former is now in progress, the latter will come at the close of the millennium.

14. The earth renewed—after the millennium.

15. The moral law, the Decalogue.

16. The seventh day Sabbath as ordained in the Old Testament.

17. The rite of baptism by immersion once in water. Only those who have come to the age of accountability shall be baptized.

18. The tithing system.

19. The gift of prophecy.

20. Liberty of conscience and religion.

21. The maintenance of bodily health. No alcoholic liquor, tobacco, or narcotic is permitted and the use of tea and coffee or other food or beverage containing a harmful element is discouraged.

The religion by no means stops with doctrine, but enters every phase of life. The Seventh-day Adventists, like the Jews, look upon themselves as people marked out by God to do His work in these last hours of the earth's history. For, though they set no date for the Second Coming, they believe that events now taking place were foretold in the Books of Daniel, Revelation, and other prophetical books of the Bible, and are leading inexorably to the appointed hour. It is their responsibility to carry the message everywhere according to the commands of Jesus.

Men must be prepared for the coming, and not only in soul, but also in body, for man is one whole—body, soul and spirit—and must be perfected in all three aspects. The bodies are the temples of the Holy Spirit, and therefore attention to the laws of health is essential. One main subdivision of the church work is medical, and Mrs. White devoted a volume to the laws of health. The Church has no occult views on healing, and its practice is in line with the best medical science of the day. It does, however, lay special stress on physical therapy, mental hygiene and diet, which is largely vegetarian. Members abstain from alcohol and tobacco and are educated against the use of tea and coffee.

Education too is stressed, and the Church, feeling that its members should be separate, runs educational institutions which start with elementary schools and go through college and even technical schools. The Seventh-day Adventists do not believe in the theory of evolution and accept the Bible as true as it is written. It is, therefore, important not to let the children come into contact with modern theories on these matters until they are old enough not to be led astray. In physical and experimental science they teach the most modern practices in their educational institutions. Separation is the price of holiness, and though they are in the world, they are not of it.

FORM OF WORSHIP:

There is no church liturgy. The Sabbath begins at sundown on Friday and lasts until sundown on Saturday. The Friday evening service is frequently for young people, and rather informal. The main services are on the Sabbath morning, and it is often then that the baptisms take place. Generally the pool is either under or back of the pulpit. The elder lays the candidate down backwards in the water and then raises him saying the words appointed for the service as he does so. The ceremony is very dignified and impressive and in many of the churches very beautiful.

The Seventh-day Adventists have been and still are working very hard and fast, for they feel themselves crowded for time in the work of evangelization. They have schools, hospitals and publication centers everywhere in the world, and during the war converts to the faith in the South Sea Islands helped our fighting men and in many cases saved their lives.

Their hospitals and sanitariums accept people of all denominations and give not only efficient but also happy treatment to all they care for. One of their publications is an excellent magazine called *Life and Health.* It is a book of practical medical help and instruction to the layman. It is largely by means of the printing press that the Church does its work, and for that reason its presses are scattered far and wide and working at top speed in every language known to man today.

THE AMERICAN UNITARIAN ASSOCIATION—74,789

The distinguishing feature of the Unitarian faith is freedom—freedom from creed and external authority. The only authority Unitarians recognize is that of Truth and Right as they commend themselves to the individual soul. They deny the divinity, or rather the deity, of Jesus Christ. Though respecting him as man, and believing that he, like other men, is endowed with divine attributes, they do not accept him as God. Almost at the dawn of Christianity this difference of belief began to show itself and the Arian heresy which split Christendom for so many centuries was Unitarian. The Unitarians assert that theirs was the original faith of early Christianity and that Trinitarianism was a later development instituted by the church fathers.

As soon as the Protestant Reformation released thought and discussion on the continent of Western Europe, Unitarian views, for many centuries suppressed under the dominance of the Roman Church, found expression in Arianism under Michael Servetus in Switzerland; Socinianism, led by Faustus Socinius in Poland; and Unitarianism according to Francis David in Transylvania. The movement did not develop in England until the eighteenth century, when it was organized under Theophilus Lindsey who in 1774 opened the first Unitarian chapel in England. Joseph Priestley, discoverer of oxygen, a little later, by his preaching and writing did much to spread its influence in both England and America.

In this country Unitarianism developed from New England Congregationalism, since the Congregationalists, insisting on the freedom of the individual congregation, left the way open to great divergence of belief. The churches who gave up the Trinitarian belief at first called themselves Liberal Christians, and accepted the name Unitarian very reluctantly. The first church to take the name was the First Unitarian Church in Philadelphia (1796), founded by Joseph Priestley, who had been driven out of England.

In 1819 William Ellery Channing of Boston, in an ordination service in Baltimore, defined and defended the Unitarian views. This "Baltimore Sermon," as it is called, led to the development of a separate movement and the formation in 1825 of the American Unitarian Association.

The real period of the Church's growth did not come until after the Civil War, but since then there has been steady development. Though it is still not a large body, its influence upon Protestantism and its contribution to the development of American democracy has been out of all proportion to its size.

ORGANIZATION:

The Unitarians are strictly congregational and each congregation is independent of all others. For purposes of fellowship and the promotion of common ends, they have formed a national organization and hold regional and national conferences. They have, besides, an international organization, the International Association for Liberal Christianity and Religious Freedom. Their ministry is highly trained and educated.

DOCTRINE:

The Unitarians have no creed and do not require of either members or ministers the profession of any doctrine. It is a very personal religion, laying more emphasis on the fruits of faith, such as moral advancement, ethical position and social reform, than on doctrine. They accept in general the religious teachings of Jesus and look upon him as an inspired religious leader but they do not regard him as the Son of God. They do not accept the Bible as directly inspired by God nor as an adequate authority for present-day living, though they use its teaching where it seems to them valid. They insist that an enlightened reason and an open mind are better than blind faith. Truth, not authority, is the criterion of all faith. Man possesses within himself the possibility of growing in character and, having divinity within his soul, becomes increasingly a son of God. Their view of God is impersonal and cannot be exactly defined, since individuals vary in their conception of Deity. For the most part he is regarded as a moral and spiritual force. The future life they do not emphasize, feeling that for man in his present state right living here and now is of paramount importance. They feel very strongly that religion must grow, must be open to new ideas, new thoughts, and must keep abreast of the social and scientific development of the world. For that reason no creed can ever be adequate or truly represent the position of the Church. A recent statement lists individual freedom of belief, discipleship to advancing truth, the democratic process in human relations, universal brotherhood, undivided by nation, race or creed, and allegiance to the cause of a united world community as the basis upon which Unitarian churches are organized.

FORM OF WORSHIP:

The form of church worship is again congregational and therefore variable. There is generally an order of service with the Lord's Prayer, hymns, Scripture readings—which may be ancient or modern—and a benediction. The sermon is the important feature of the service and is very apt to be concerned with burning questions of the hour and their relation to religion.

There are many social activities connected with the parishes and much social service work is carried on, particularly at the present time by the Unitarian Service Committee abroad.

THE PRINCIPAL FEASTS AND FASTS OF THE WESTERN CHRISTIAN CHURCH

The Church Year begins with the First Sunday in Advent, which falls about a month before Christmas and looks forward to that feast. All of the principal feasts that commemorate and stem from the Nativity fall on fixed calendar dates. On the other hand, the feasts and fasts which lead up to or look back upon the Easter season are movable, since they are reckoned from the date of Easter itself, which is determined by astronomical considerations. In addition to the principal feasts and fasts, many saints' days are observed, their importance varying in the several denominations and varying also in the same denomination from country to country. Because Easter and its attendant feasts and fasts are movable and the saints' days are fixed by the calendar, it may happen that two observances would normally fall upon the same day; and in this case the greater observance takes precedence over the less.

The First Sunday in Advent, determined as the Sunday nearest the Feast of St. Andrew on November 30.
December 8: The Immaculate Conception of the Blessed Virgin Mary.
December 25: Christmas Day.
January 1: The Feast of Circumcision.

January 6: Epiphany (Twelfth Night).
February 2: The Purification of the Blessed Virgin Mary.
March 25: The Annunciation of the Blessed Virgin Mary.

Feasts and fasts of which the dates depend on the date of Easter	Ash Wednesday, a fast day falling on the 46th day before Easter; the first day of Lent. The Lenten Season, ending on Easter Sunday. Palm Sunday, the Sunday before Easter (and like all Sundays in Lent, a feast day). Maundy Thursday, the Thursday before Easter; a fast. Good Friday, the Friday before Easter; a fast.

Easter Sunday, the first Sunday after the first full moon following the spring equinox (March 21st); if the full moon falls on a Sunday, Easter is celebrated on the Sunday following. This determination of the date makes Easter a movable feast, which may vary in calendar date by more than a month. The same variation applies to all the feasts and fasts which are reckoned from the date of Easter.

Feasts and observances of which the dates depend upon the date of Easter	Ascension Day, falling on the Thursday forty days after Easter; a feast. Pentecost, or Whitsunday, the seventh Sunday after Easter; a feast commemorating the descent of the Holy Ghost upon the Apostles, and the gift of tongues. Trinity Sunday, the eighth Sunday after Easter.

August 6: The Feast of the Transfiguration of Christ.
August 15: The Assumption of the Blessed Virgin Mary.
November 1: All Saints' Day.

CHAPTER FIVE

In My Father's House Are Many Mansions

SINCE RELIGION is largely a matter of personal experience, it is probable that there are as many variations of religion as there are individuals. Where the variations are not too great and some common central thought can serve as a bond of union, there is a joining of forces in a denomination or sect, wherein people can organize and work and worship together on the basis of agreement in essentials and the overlooking of minor differences. Besides the thirty groups which I have listed in the fourth chapter of this book, there are scores of smaller sects and denominations which have broken off from the larger organizations, together with others which have sprung up independently. Furthermore, there are a number of large and growing groups, ethical and religious in purpose, which the world scarcely classifies as sects, and upon a few of which I touch in this last chapter because of the number of inquiries constantly made about their origins and beliefs.

The oldest and largest of these associations is the Free and Accepted Masons, more generally referred to as the Masons. This is a secret society of ancient origin, so ancient that it is impossible to date it accurately. Its rise has been found in the trade guilds of the Middle Ages, but has also been ascribed to the builders of Solomon's Temple in the early part of the tenth century B.C. While the Masons are distinctly a religious organization, they are nonsectarian and their membership is of all creeds and all walks of life, held together by a vow of secrecy and the great body of ritual which has grown up through the ages. It is, therefore, not a church, but an extraecclesiastical society of men who are striving to attain one of the great ideals of Christianity—brotherhood.

Another group is the Salvation Army, founded in England by William Booth, a member of the Methodist Church. It is really a tremendous missionary organization, drawn up on a military basis with army ranks and regulations. Every soldier in it is pledged not to use intoxicating drinks and harmful drugs, and this pledge is called the "Articles of War." The Army sets as its goal the spiritual regeneration of mankind. Its members enter the worst slums and deal with the most degraded and hopeless sections of the human race in the course of their soul-saving work. It conducts all kinds of missions, vacation homes, lodging houses, clothing bureaus, soup kitchens and hospitals. In no case is there any personal profit from these enterprises, nor are distinctions made of race or creed. All the Salvation Army institutions are run at very low cost and are therefore available to those who would otherwise be unable to afford the services offered. The Salvation Army, like the Masons, is working for the brotherhood of man.

Besides these well-known and established organizations, there are other less conforming groups which have seized on the God-hunger of men and grown with phenomenal rapidity, though it is still too early to prophesy what their future development will be. Standing on street corners, canvassing from house to house, Jehovah's Witnesses may be seen every day, earnest, shabby men and women who persistently continue their work of saving the world in spite of rebuffs and discouragement. They are Adventists who are convinced that the final battle of Armageddon is at hand, after which will follow the Second Coming of Christ. The date set for the Advent is somewhere before 1972. They have been preaching and working since 1874, but as the critical date approaches they feel the need of increasing their effort so that everyone may have a chance for salvation. There is nothing in it for themselves. All that they seek is to save others from eternal destruction. The tremendous work of printing and distributing their literature, which they offer to all who will accept it, is financed solely by voluntary contributions.

The Four Square Gospel was organized by Aimee Semple McPherson during the restless years after the First World War. The name was based on Ezekiel's vision of beings each with four faces, those of a man, a lion, an ox and an eagle (Ezekiel 1:10), symbols which the Church accepted as meaning the four Evangelists. Mrs. McPherson translated the vision into different aspects of Christ. The man was Jesus the Saviour; the lion, Jesus the Baptizer with the Holy Ghost; the ox, Jesus the Great Healer; the eagle, Jesus the Coming King. The Four Square Gospel might be called the apotheosis of the revival spirit, and tuned into the spectacular quality of life in the 1920's. Mrs. McPherson used every means known to the promoter and high-pressure salesman to popularize and advertize her teachings. It was generally believed that only the force of her personality drew together the great crowds of believers who thronged to hear her, and that after her death they would melt away. But, although she died in 1944, the movement according to statistics is still growing, and in California alone there is an average Sunday-school attendance in the group of 15,000. Into thousands of drab lives the Four Square Gospel has brought life, color and drama, and who can say that it does not also have a function in raising the thoughts of its believers to higher things?

Nearly everyone at some time has experimented with

spiritualism. The wish to know beyond peradventure that there is a future life where one will meet one's loved ones again, the need to be assured that they are well and happy, the desire for one more reassuring contact with them, becomes almost overpowering, and few are able to withstand it. As a result of this mass need there have arisen hosts of "mediums" and a large number of organized "Spiritual Associations" and "Churches." Most of these have no tenets of faith, no body of dogma; they consist merely of people united by the wish to penetrate into the unknown, and in the certainty of a future life to find courage for this one.

The Oxford Group or Buchmanites, now generally known as M R A or Moral Rearmament, originated in the 1930's under the leadership of Frank N. Buchman, an American Lutheran minister. During the Second World War it suffered a partial eclipse, but is now on the upswing again. It advocates confession of and reparation for past errors, and reliance on prayer: not the usual prayer of thanksgiving and petition, but an inner communion with God, listening for His orders and obeying them. The Buchmanites lay great stress on a quiet fifteen minutes each morning, during which the believer sits with pencil and paper jotting down God's suggestions as they come. In its publicity work M R A has many of the earmarks of revivalism, but seems to satisfy many who have found help nowhere else.

The Peace Mission Movement claims to be ruled by God Himself incarnate among us. Father Divine says that he "visibilates God." Wherever the movement spreads, prosperity is believed to spring up. Its aim is to break down the barriers between men and nations and establish the rule of love and peace.

Unity was started by Charles and Myrtle Fillmore in 1891, and has been adding to its membership slowly but steadily ever since. It is less spectacular than the Four Square Gospel or M R A, and less evangelistic than Jehovah's Witnesses, and appeals to a smaller and more eclectic group. It is an effort to tap the hidden forces that are latent in men, forces which the Fillmores claim are cosmic and able to heal, to bring prosperity and peace of mind, in short, to meet every situation. It is an affirmation of positive thought, which is constructive, as opposed to negative thought, which is destructive.

To members of established and recognized religious denominations these bypaths of religion, as they might be called, often seem suspect. The Masons have been severely attacked by many of the sects, largely because of their oath of secrecy. Do these critics ever remember, or do they know, that in its earliest days Christianity was in many regions a secret cult, partly for safety's sake but partly also because all "mysteries" were secret? Some of the groups are derided and despised for their peculiarities of dress, their unconventional advertising, or their religious exuberance. Three hundred years ago John Fox and his followers, the Quakers, were being laughed at and even persecuted for the same differences, and Wesley and the Methodists were forced out of the Church of England for their unbecoming and excessive religious fervor. The Mormons, who claim that man can become as God and who recognized Joseph Smith as a prophet, were driven into the wilderness by an enraged public, partly because of their faith and partly because of their prosperity. The Christian Scientists endured sneers and laughter seventy years ago. The great attraction of Christianity to many during its early years was its promise of life to come and the certainty of meeting again those whom death had taken. It was, furthermore, an Adventist sect, and expected the Second Coming momentarily.

The musician seeks the infinite in music, the scientist in an impartial search for truth. Not surprisingly, many of the greatest of these finally come to mysticism—a belief in the unknowable. They all have sought a faith and entered one of the many mansions in their Father's house. Each of us can but seek the truth according to our lights, and that truth shall make us free.

The world and customs change, but not human nature. Like children coming from darkness into a lighted room and knowing that shortly they must pass into darkness again, men seek for help to face the unknown to come. If they cannot find it, whose is the fault? They are to be pitied, not censured, for theirs is the loss. If the help they find seems to others inadequate or absurd, who is to blame? Surely not the seeker, who seizes on what offers him most support and hope. Any faith which makes for love, charitableness and joy deserves recognition, respect and tolerance, as one more link between man and the unseen and inscrutable power which makes for righteousness.

Glossary

The symbol (O) indicates that the term is used in the Eastern Orthodox Church; (J) that it is used in Judaism.

ABBEY. The church connected with a monastery.

ABBOT. The head or superior of a monastery.

ABSOLUTION. A formal forgiveness or remission of sin; given in certain churches, notably the Roman Catholic, by a priest in virtue of authority derived from Christ.

ACOLYTE. In the Roman Catholic Church, the highest of the four minor orders, being ordained to carry the wine and water and the lights at Mass. In the Episcopal Church, a boy who serves at the altar or performs other duties in the church service.

ADVENT. The first season of the Church Year, beginning on the fourth Sunday before Christmas. It is a season of preparation for Christ's coming.

AGAPE. In the early Christian Church, a communal meal taken in connection with the Holy Communion.

AGNOSTIC. One who takes the position that he does not know positively of God's existence.

AIR, THE (O). A large linen cloth with which both paten and chalice are covered.

ALB. The linen vestment worn in Roman Catholic and Anglican Churches by the priest officiating at the Eucharist.

ALL SAINTS' DAY. The last great festival of the Church Year, held on November 1st.

ALTAR. Originally a stone or heap of stones on which a sacrifice was made. In the Christian Church, the Communion Table.

ALTAR CANDLES. The candles used during Holy Communion, typifying the two natures of Christ, human and divine. They are lighted just before the Communion service, and are put out before the congregation leaves its seats.

AMBO. A pulpit for reading selections from the Bible.

AMBULLA OR AMPULLAE. The cruets for wine and water in the Communion service.

AMEN. "So be it"; used at the end of a prayer, hymn or confession of faith as a ratification.

AMICTUS or AMICE. A piece of embroidered linen worn by the priest around the neck or fastened at the breast.

'AMIDAH (J). A week-day public prayer. See SHEMONEH 'ESREH.

ANABAPTISTS. In Reformation times, the extreme leftists of the Reformation movement. The name was given them by their opponents, and referred to their denial of the validity of infant baptism. Anabaptism is Reform doctrine carried to its extreme limit, and is a way of thought, not a sect. Many of the modern sects are descended from the original so-called Anabaptists.

ANAPHORA. The part of the liturgy which begins at the Sursum Corda ("Lift up your hearts").

ANGEL. A supernatural messenger of God.

ANGLICAN CHURCH. The Church of England or one of the churches in communion therewith. These are the Church of Ireland, the Scottish Episcopal Church, the churches in the various British dominions, and the Protestant Episcopal Church in the United States.

ANNUNCIATION. The announcement to Mary by the Archangel Gabriel of the Incarnation of Christ; commemorated by a feast held on March 25.

ANTEPENDIUM. Also called *frontal,* is the vestment hung in front of the altar.

ANTHEM. A selection from the psalms, or other hymn of praise, set to music.

ANTIDORON (O). The bread which has been offered for the service of the altar but which has not been required for consecration.

ANTIPHONAL. Alternate singing by two choir groups. Often used in the responses of the church service.

APOCALYPSE. This is a Greek word meaning *revelation* and is applied to the Book of Daniel and the Revelation of St. John.

APOCRYPHA. Certain writings of doubtful or uncertain authority which are not included in the Old or the New Testament and not generally accepted as inspired. The apocryphal books of the Old Testament are sometimes inserted between the Old and New Testaments and excerpts from them are appointed as "lessons" or regular Bible readings in the Episcopal Church. The New Testament Apocrypha is used only by the Roman Catholic Church.

APOSTLE. One of the twelve original disciples of Christ. Later Paul and others were added.

ARCHANGEL. An angel of the highest rank (SS. Michael, Gabriel, Rafael and Uriel).

ARCHBISHOP. Chief bishop.

ARCHDEACON. A chief deacon; the ecclesiastical dignitary next in rank below a bishop.

ARIAN. Member of an early heretical group who did not believe that Christ was of the same substance as God. They therefore denied the Trinity.

ARMINIAN. Arminian theology is named from a Dutch theologian, James Arminius (1560-1609). It is a revolt against the Calvinistic doctrines of predestination, or unconditional election, and irresistible grace. It grants a certain degree of free choice in man, and asserts that those who "are ready for the conflict and desire Christ's help, and are not inactive" will be kept from falling.

ASCENSION DAY. The Thursday falling on the fortieth day after Easter (counting Easter Sunday itself), and commemorating Christ's ascent into Heaven.

ASCETIC. One who practises extreme self-denial and mortification of the flesh.

ASH WEDNESDAY. The first day of Lent.

ASPERGIL. A brush for sprinkling Holy Water. It is sometimes made of hyssop.

ASHKENAZIM (J). Jews of Central and Northern Europe and their descendants.

ASPERSION. Baptism by sprinkling.

ASTERISK (O). Two large thin pieces of metal in the form of an arch and crossing each other in the middle. It supports the veil above the paten so that it may not touch the Holy Body. Its mystical meaning is the star which led the Wise Men.

Atheist. One who disbelieves or denies the existence of God.

Aumbrey. A recess in the chancel in which are kept the sacred vessels.

Ave. Literally, "Hail!"; the first word of the Ave Maria, which has been used as a hymn or prayer in the Roman Catholic Church since before 1200.

Baptism. A symbolic pouring on or sprinkling with water, or immersion of the candidate, whereby he is made a member of the church.

Baptistry. In the early church, a separate building used for the rite of baptism. In modern times, the tank used for baptismal immersion.

Benediction. A blessing, especially the blessing pronounced by a priest in the course of the service.

Bishop. A spiritual overseer or director. The cleric of the highest order in the Christian churches.

Breviary. A book containing the daily or canonical prayers of the Roman Catholic or of the Eastern Church for the canonical hours.

Bull. A papal letter. Its name is derived from the *bulla,* a two-sided seal with the representation of St. Peter or St. Paul on one side and the name of the pope who uses it on the other.

Burse. A case in which the corporal and pall are kept when not in use.

Cabbala (J). A system of mystical thought which began to be current among the Jews during the Middle Ages.

Canon. 1. A law or rule of doctrine or discipline enacted by the council and confirmed by the pope. The canon, the canonical law of the Church.

2. A collection or list of books accepted as genuine and inspired Holy Scriptures.
3. The section of the Mass between the Sanctus and the Paternoster.
4. An ecclesiastic residing in the chapter house of a cathedral; in modern times one of a number of dignitaries who form a sort of council to the bishop.

Canonical Hours.

1. Matins—service before daybreak.
2. Lauds—at daybreak.
3. Prime—later morning service.
4. Tierce—service between six and nine o'clock.

5. Sexts—between nine o'clock and noon.
6. Nones—service soon after noon.
7. Vespers—evening service at four or later.
8. Compline—service before bedtime.

CANTICLE. A little song, not metrical. The Benedicite, the Magnificat and the Nunc Dimittis are canticles.

CANTORIS. The side of the choir upon which the cantor, precentor or choir leader sits.

CARDINAL. An ecclesiastical prince of the group which constitutes the pope's council, or the sacred college. They are appointed by the pope and there can never be more than seventy. It is the College of Cardinals which elects the pope.

CAROL. A festival hymn sung at Christmas or Easter.

CASSOCK. The long, close-fitting garment reaching to the feet worn by the clergy of certain churches.

CATECHISM. A summary of religious doctrine in question and answer form.

CATECHUMEN. One who is receiving instruction in Christian doctrine.

CATHEDRAL. The principal church of the diocese, where the bishop has his throne.

CATHOLIC. Universal.

CELEBRANT. The officiating priest in the celebration of the Mass or Communion service.

CELEBRATION. The sacred performance of the Holy Communion.

CENSER. A vessel in which incense is burned.

CHALICE. The cup used for wine in the sacrament of the Eucharist.

CHALICE VEIL. Made of lace or cambric and used for covering the chalice.

CHANCEL. That part of the church from which the service is read and in which the altar is placed.

CHAPLAIN. One who conducts religious exercises for an organization such as, for example, the Army or the Senate.

CHAPTER. 1. Meetings of the members of a religious group or order, such as canons, monks, etc.
2. The body or members of a religious group or order.

CHASUBLE. Sacrificial vestment worn by the celebrant at the Holy Communion. It is oval, generally open at the sides, and with a hole for the head.

CHIMERE. A loose upper robe to which are attached long lawn sleeves caught in at the wrist. It is worn by the bishop.

CHRISM. Oil, mixed with balm and spices, consecrated by the bishop, and used for anointing as in extreme unction.

CHRIST. The Anointed One.

CIBORIUM. A container with a lid to hold consecrated bread.

CLERGYMAN. An ordained minister.

COADJUTOR. A bishop coadjutor is an assistant to a bishop and has the right eventually to succeed him.

COLLECT. A brief and comprehensive prayer suited to a special occasion.

COMMUNICANT. One who partakes of the Lord's Supper after admission to the church.

COMMUNION. The celebration of the Lord's Supper, usually as a sacrament. It commemorates the supper of Christ and His disciples on the night wherein He was betrayed and brought to trial and death.

COMPLINE. The seventh, or last, canonical hour of the day. The last prayer of the day to be said after sunset.

CONFESSION. The act of disclosing one's sins to a priest to obtain absolution. Confession may be public, as in the general confession of some Protestant liturgies, or may be made in private. In the Roman Church confession is a prescribed part of the sacrament of penance.

CONFIRMATION. A rite in which the candidate for church membership confirms his baptismal vows. In some churches it is regarded as a sacrament.

CONGREGATION. The lay membership of an individual parish or church.

CONSUBSTANTIATION. The presence of the actual body and blood of Christ in and with the material elements of bread and wine.

CONVENTION. A meeting of clerical and lay delegates.

COPE. A long cape or cloak worn by some ecclesiastics in religious processions.

CORPORAL. The white linen cloth on which the Blessed Sacrament is laid.

COTTA. A short surplice. It is frequently worn by members of a choir.

CREDENCE. A small table near the altar on which the bread and wine are placed before they are consecrated.

CREED. A summary of belief.

CROSIER or CROZIER. The official staff of the archbishop.

CRUCIFER. The one who carries the cross at the head of a religious procession.

CRUCIFIX. The representation of Christ on the cross, or loosely, the cross.

CURATE. An assistant of a rector or vicar of a church or chapel.

DALMATIC (O). Worn by the bishop in place of a chasuble.

DEACON. An official in the Christian Church appointed to subordinate duties; in the Episcopal Church, he is ordained and graduates to the priesthood; in the Presbyterian, his position is more like that of a deacon in the early church, with duties in the communion and the care of the poor; in the Congregational, he is a layman with duties like those of a Presbyterian elder; in the Lutheran, a layman subordinate to the pastor and elders, or an assistant minister.

DEACONESS. In the Anglican Church, a woman set apart by the bishop for church work. In other Protestant sects, a chosen helper in church work.

DECALOGUE. The Ten Commandments.

DECANI. The side of the choir opposite to the cantoris (q.v.).

DEIST. One who believes in God, but not necessarily in Christian revelation.

DISCIPLE. A follower who has learned to believe in the truth of his master's teaching.

DOCTRINE. A teaching.

DOGMA. A doctrine formally stated and authoritatively pronounced.

DOXOLOGY. A hymn or formula expressing praise to God. Generally used as an ending to a hymn or psalm or even to a service.

EAGLE (O). The circular rug on which the bishop stands during divine service.

EASTER. The first Sunday after the first full moon after the spring equinox (March 21st); reckoned in the Western Churches by the Gregorian, in the Eastern Church by the older Julian calendar, which in 1948 is thirteen days behind the Gregorian. This is the great feast day of the Christian world, celebrated in memory of Christ's rising from the dead.

ECCLESIASTIC. Of or pertaining to a church.

ECUMENICAL or ŒCUMENICAL. General.

ELDER. A church official whose position and duties vary according to the denomination.

1. Among Presbyterians a layman or laymen who assist the minister in regulating church matters.
2. In some churches, including the Methodist, the elder is a fully ordained minister.
3. In the Mormon Church he is a high officer.

ELEMENTS. The bread, wine and water used for Holy Communion, also water for Holy Baptism.

ELEVATION. The lifting up of the Blessed Sacrament after consecration.

EMBER DAYS. Days set apart for fasting and prayer in each of the four seasons of the year. They were appointed in 1095, to be the Wednesday, Friday and Saturday after the First Sunday in Lent, after Whitsunday, after September 14 and December 13.

EPIPHANY. A church festival celebrated on the 6th of January, twelve days after Christmas, hence also called Twelfth Night. It commemorates the appearance of the star to the Magi, or Wise Men, symbolizing the making known of Christ to the Gentiles.

EPISCOPAL. Governed by bishops.

EPISTLE. Literally, a letter; specifically applied to letters written by certain Apostles and leaders of the early church and incorporated in the New Testament; applied also to a selection from these letters appointed to be read in the church service.

ESCHATOLOGY. The study of knowledge of last things, such as death, judgment and life hereafter.

EUCHARIST. The sacrament of the Lord's Supper.

EVANGELICAL. Basing one's faith and teaching directly on the Gospels rather than on creeds or church dogma.

EXCOMMUNICATION. The exclusion of a person from the church and its rites and benefits.

EXEGESIS. Critical explanation of the text and portions of the Scriptures.

EXTREME UNCTION. In the Roman Catholic Church, the sacrament of anointing the dying. The consecrated oil is applied to eyes, ears, nostrils and mouth of the dying person for the remission of sins.

FAIR WHITE LINEN CLOTH. The cloth covering the top of the altar, generally embroidered with five crosses to symbolize the five Sacred Wounds.

Fasting Communion. The reception of the Sacrament before any food has been taken as was the practice of the early church.

Fathers or Church Fathers. The Christian expounders of the faith of the first five centuries after the Apostolic Age.

Filioque Clause. The Latin phrase in the Nicene Creed which declares that the Holy Ghost proceeds "from the Father *and the Son* (*Filioque*)." In the Eastern Church, the Holy Ghost is regarded as proceeding from the Father alone.

Five Points of Arminianism.

1. Election and condemnation depend upon the faith or unbelief of man.
2. Atonement is for everyone, but only believers enjoy its benefits.
3. Man is unable to come to God unless aided by the Holy Spirit.
4. Grace is not irresistible.
5. The perseverance of saints is a doctrine open to inquiry.

Five Points of Calvinism.

1. Unconditional election.
2. Atonement is limited to the elect.
3. Man's depravity is total as to ability and merit.
4. Grace is irresistible. By divine power the will is impelled to believe.
5. Perseverance of the saints. (Those elected by God are sustained by Him in a state of grace, and so, in spite of weaknesses and falls, they are assured of final salvation.)

Flagon. A large vessel in which the Communion wine is placed before consecration.

Font. The vessel in which the water for baptism is contained.

Fountains (O). The red and white buttons sewn on the bishop's mantle.

Free Will. The power to choose one's course of action without divine restraint.

Friar. A brother of one of the begging orders, Franciscan, Dominican, etc.

Gauntlets (O). These are worn on the wrists by priests serving at the altar.

Gedaliah (J). The day following Rosh ha-Shanah and commemorating the slaying in 586 B.C. of the governor of Judah appointed by Nebuchadnezzar.

GENEVA GOWN. Loose, large-sleeved black academic gown used by many Protestant clergy when they are officiating in the church.

GET (J). The decree of religious divorce.

GLORIA IN EXCELSIS. "Glory (to God) in the Highest." An old hymn of praise, used by many churches in the Communion service.

GLORIA PATRI. "Glory be to the Father." The beginning of the doxology.

GLORIA TIBI. "Glory be to Thee," said or sung after the announcement of the Gospel in the Communion Office.

GOOD FRIDAY. The Friday before Easter, kept as a fast in memory of Christ's crucifixion.

GOSPEL. Glad tidings—the story or record of Christ's life as contained in the first four books of the New Testament.

GOSPEL LIGHTS. These are the candles lighted by the acolytes during the reading of the Gospel.

GRACE. The mercy and help of God. To be in a state of grace is to be acceptable to God.

GRADINE. The ledge at the back of the altar on which to put flowers, lights, etc.

GRADUAL. A sentence or hymn sung after the reading of the Epistle.

GRATIAS TIBI. "Thanks be to Thee," said or sung after the reading of the Gospel in the Communion Office.

HABDALAH (J). The ceremony concluding the Sabbath day.

HAFTARAH (J). Selection from the Books of Prophets read on Sabbath, festival and fast days, supplementary to the reading of the Torah.

HANUKKAH (J). The festival week commemorating the rededication of the Temple by Judah Maccabeus after it had been defiled in 164 B.C.

HAZZAN (J). The reader or cantor of prayers in public service.

HENOTHEISM. The belief in one god, but not to the exclusion of other gods for other people.

HERESY. Dissent from a previously or generally accepted creed; frequently dissent from one or more articles of a creed without its complete denial.

HEXATEUCH. The Pentateuch and the Book of Joshua.

HIERARCHY. Rule in sacred matters.

HIGH CHURCH. Those churches which attach importance to ceremony and symbols and express themselves in an elaborate ritual.

HIGH MASS. The principal mass on a feast day.

HILLUL HA-SHEM (J). The profanation of the name of God in times of persecution.

HOLY WATER. Water with salt in it, exorcised and blessed every Sunday. It is usually placed in a basin in the church vestibule, and worshipers dip their fingers in it and cross themselves as they enter or leave the church.

HOMILETICS. The art of preaching.

HOST. The consecrated wafer or bread in the sacrament of the Eucharist.

HUPPAH (J). The canopy used in the marriage ceremony.

HYMN. A sacred lyric or song of praise or adoration.

HYMN TERSANCTUS. "Holy, Holy, Holy"—as in the Communion service.

ICONOSTASIS (O). A screen separating the sanctuary from the main body of the church. On it are hung the sacred icons.

ICONS (O). Religious pictures.

I.H.S. The first three Greek letters of Jesus' name.

IMMERSION. A form of baptism wherein the candidate is dipped in water while the words of consecration are said. It is used in several of the churches, notably the Baptist and Eastern Orthodox, and may symbolize death and rebirth, or a cleansing from sin.

IMMACULATE CONCEPTION. A doctrine held by the Roman Church that the Blessed Virgin Mary was conceived and born without sin.

IMPANATION. The theory that under the sacramental elements of bread and wine there is the substance of the body and blood of Christ.

INCARNATION. Being clothed in flesh, hence the union of Godhead with manhood.

INCENSE. Its use in church services is very old. Where it is used it is offered:

1. In Holy Communion three times, at the Introit, at the Gospel, and at the Offertory.

2. At funeral celebrations—at the Introit, the Gospel, and oblations.
3. At Solemn Vespers the altar is censed at the Magnificat.

INDEX. A list of books the reading of which is prohibited or restricted by the church authorities in the Roman Catholic Church.

INDULGENCE. Remission of punishment for sins.

I.N.R.I. The initials of "Iesus Nazarenus, Rex Iudaeorum," Jesus of Nazareth, King of the Jews; the mocking inscription placed by the Romans over the head of Jesus when they crucified Him.

INTROIT.

1. In the Roman Catholic Church, the words said in Mass after the Confiteor.
2. In the Anglican Church, an anthem or hymn sung as the priests enter the sanctuary to celebrate the Eucharist.

INVESTITURE. A giving possession. So the pope in feudal times assumed the right to give the possession of certain benefices to men he specified, and in return received certain payments.

INVOCATION. Solemn prayer to a divine being.

JEWISH CALENDAR. The months of Tishri, Marchesvan or Heshvan, Kislev, Tebet, Shebat, Adar, Nisan, Iyyar, Sivan, Tammuz, Ab, Ellul. The Jewish calendar is lunar and seven times in nineteen years an additional month called Second Adar is intercalated before Nisan.

JUSTIFICATION. The forgiveness of a sinner and his restoration to a right relationship with God.

KADDISH (J). An Aramaic prayer glorifying God. It is now used in the Reform Temples as a memorial for the departed.

KETUBAH (J). A document detailing the obligations of husband and wife. A marriage certificate.

KIDDUSH (J). The festival ceremony at the beginning of the Sabbath meal. It asks blessings on the day, on the lighting of the candles and on the wine and bread.

KITTEL (J). White linen garment traditionally worn on New Year's and Atonement.

KOL NIDRE (J). The opening prayer and service on the eve of Yom Kippur.

KOSHER (J). Fit to eat according to the dietary laws.

KYRIE ELEISON. The Greek words for the phrase, "Lord have mercy upon us," used in the Communion service or Mass of the Eastern, Roman and Anglican Churches. Frequently called the "Kyrie."

LAITY, LAY, LAYMAN. Not pertaining to or a member of the clergy.

LAUDS. A religious service which with matins is the first of the canonical hours. Usually comes at daybreak and ends with Psalms 148-150.

LAY READER. A layman licensed by the bishop to read the parts of the church service which do not require a priest.

LECTERN. Desk from which the Scriptures are read.

LENT. The annual period of fasting in the spring, in preparation for the Easter festival. The period embraces about forty fast days, Sundays being excepted because they are always feast days.

LITANY. A solemn form of supplication, usually penitential.

LITURGICAL COLOR.

White, color for happiness or joy used in vestments, altarcloths, etc., for Christmas and Easter and other feasts.

Violet is used for penitential seasons such as Advent or Lent.

Black is used for mourning on Good Friday.

Red, which symbolizes blood or fire, is used for anniversaries of martyrs and for Whitsunday.

Green, the great ground color of Nature, used for the remainder of the Church year.

LITURGY. The form of public worship; a ritual.

LITURGY OF CATECHUMENS (O). Second part of the liturgy, consisting of prayers, reading and singing in preparation for the Holy Sacrifice.

LITURGY OF THE FAITHFUL (O). Third part of the liturgy. The celebration of the Holy Mysteries.

LOW CHURCH. Those churches which lay little stress on ritual.

LOW SUNDAY. The first Sunday after Easter.

LULAB (J). A cluster of palm branches which with sprays of myrtle and willow and one citrus fruit is used on the feast of Sukkoth (Leviticus 23:40).

MA' ARIB (J). Evening prayer.

MAFTIR (J). Reader of the Haftarah (q.v.).

Mass. The Sacrament of the Holy Communion.

Massah (Matzah) (J). Unleavened bread used during Passover.

Massebah (J). Monument at grave set up a year after death.

Matins. A service or office for morning. Usually said at midnight or at daybreak, sometimes even the evening before the celebration of Mass.

Maundy Thursday. Thursday before Easter.

Messiah. The Anointed One.

Mezuzah. A piece of parchment on which is written part of the Law. In Jewish homes the parchment is then placed in a small wooden, metal or glass container and fastened to the doorpost.

Minister. Literally a servant. In church usage one who is authorized to serve at the altar, conduct Christian worship, preach, etc.

Minyan (J). An assembly of ten males forming a quorum for public service.

Mishnah (J). The traditional doctrine of the Jewish church as developed chiefly by the rabbis before the third century A.D.

Missal. The book containing the service of Mass for the entire year.

Miter. The official headdress of a bishop since about A.D. 1000.

Mizrachi (J). Those Zionists most interested in establishing Palestine as the center of Jewish religious life.

Mohel (J). The person who performs circumcision.

Monk. One of a religious community living under a rule.

Monotheism. Belief in one god only.

Monstrance. A transparent receptacle in which the Host is shown to the congregation.

Nave. That part of the church between the main entrance and the chancel steps, excluding the transepts and the side aisles. Ship of God.

Navicula. The incense boat.

Ne 'ilah (J). The fifth and concluding prayer on the Day of Atonement.

Nones. An office meant to be recited at the ninth hour—3:00 P.M. In the Roman Catholic Church it is now usually recited somewhat earlier.

Novena. A nine days' devotion for any religious purpose.

NUN. A woman devoted to the religious life under vows of poverty, chastity and obedience.

OFFICE OF OBLATION. The first part of the liturgy, during which the priest prepares the sacred bread and wine.

OLD CATHOLICS. Those members of the Roman Catholic Church who refused to accept the dogma of the infallibility of the pope, promulgated by the Vatican Council of 1870. They represent a tendency of long standing in the Church, and in the beginning, at least, aimed at restoration of the earlier Catholic system of local diocesan responsibility and authority.

OMOPHORION (O). The bishop's stole.

ONEG SHABBAT (J). A community gathering of a joyful character in observance of the Sabbath. Usually refreshments are served.

ORARIUM (O). The deacon's stole.

ORDINANCE. A religious usage authoritatively enjoined by the Church.

ORIENTATION. Originally, facing eastward in certain acts of worship, because to many of the early Christians, Jerusalem lay to the east, and consequently a church was built with its altar at the eastern end. In many modern churches, architectural considerations have prevented the east-west alignment, and altars are no longer always so placed. The custom has accordingly become one of facing toward the altar, rather than toward the east.

ORPHREY. The band of embroidery fixed to the vestment.

ORTHODOX.

1. Sound in religious doctrine.
2. Belonging to the Eastern Church.
3. Belonging to the traditional wing of Judaism.

PALL.

1. A cloth spread over a casket.
2. A square card covered with silk on one side and fine linen on the other, used to cover the chalice.

PALLIUM. An altarcloth.

PANTHEISM. The belief that the whole universe is God.

PANTHEON. A temple dedicated to all the gods. The word is used collectively to designate the gods of a people.

PARACLETE. The Comforter; a term used for the Holy Spirit.

PARISH. The jurisdiction of a church.

PAROCHIAL. Pertaining to a parish.

PASCHAL. Pertaining to the Passover or Easter.

PASSING BELL. A bell tolled in the church when a soul is passing away, to obtain prayers for the departing spirit.

PASSOVER HAGGADAH (J). The book containing the order of prayers and songs for the home celebration at the beginning of the Passover.

PASTOR. The minister of a church or parish.

PATEN. The plate from which bread is given in Communion.

PATERNOSTER. The Lord's Prayer.

PATRIARCH. In the early church a bishop, later the bishop of a country. The Patriarch of Constantinople is the highest dignitary in the Greek Orthodox Church.

PAX. The kiss of peace.

PEDE CLOTH. A carpet for the altar steps.

PEDOBAPTISM. Infant baptism.

PENANCE. One of the seven sacraments of the Roman Catholic Church. Its three necessary parts are Contrition, Confession and Satisfaction, which are followed by Absolution.

PENTATEUCH. The first five books of the Old Testament: Genesis, Exodus, Leviticus, Numbers, Deuteronomy.

PENTECOST. A great Jewish festival, celebrated on the fiftieth day after the second day of Passover. In the Christian Church it commemorates the descent of the Holy Spirit on the Apostles, which occurred on the day of Pentecost. This feast is also called Whitsunday by the Christians.

PESACH (J). Jewish feast of the Passover. It occurs on the full moon of the first month of spring. It is the great festival of the rebirth of nature and commemorates the exodus from Egypt.

PHARISEES. The liberal and learned middle-class group of Jews in Bible times. They preached the value of conduct as against the value of ritual observance, and accepted the Persian belief in a resurrection.

PHYLACTERY (J). A small leather box in which are slips of parchment inscribed with parts of the Law. These are worn, one on the head and one on the left arm, during weekday times of morning prayer.

PLACEBO. The vespers for the office for the dead.

POLYTHEISM. Belief in many gods.

PRAYER. The act of addressing the Deity.

PRAYER SHAWL (J). A tasseled shawl worn over the head or round the shoulders while at prayer. See TALLIT.

PRECENTOR. The leader of the singing in a choir.

PREDELLA or FOOT PACE. The platform in front of the altar.

PRELATE. A dignitary of the Church.

PRESBYTER. An elder in the early Christian church. In the Presbyterian Church today a member of the presbytery, the governing body of the Church, whether lay or clerical.

PRIEST. One authorized by formal ordination to perform religious duties.

PRIMATE. A ranking bishop in the Roman Catholic and Anglican Churches.

PRIME. The first canonical hour after lauds in the Roman Catholic Church.

PRIOR. The head of a priory.

PRIORY. A religious house ranking next below an abbey.

PROCESSIONAL. A hymn or anthem sung as the choir and clergy enter the church.

PROSELYTE. A convert to a faith.

PROTESTANT. Any Christian not of the Roman Catholic, Old Catholic, or Eastern Church.

PROTHESIS (O). Table on which the Eucharistic bread and wine are prepared.

PSALTER. The Book of Psalms as used in the Church.

PULPIT. The elevated place in which the preacher stands.

PURIFICATOR. A linen cloth used for wiping the sacred vessels at the end of the service.

PURIM (J). The festival prescribed in the Book of Esther.

PYX. The container in which the Host is reserved.

RABAT. A clerical collar, or a scarf fitted to a collar.

RABBI (J). Teacher. A title used by Jews as a sign of respect for a teacher or doctor of *The Law.*

RECESSIONAL. A hymn or anthem sung as the choir and clergy leave the church.

RECTOR. A priest who is in charge of a parish.

REFORMATION. The Reformation was the sixteenth-century movement which resulted in the formation of the various Protestant churches.

REQUIEM. The Mass for the dead.

REREDOS. The screen behind the altar.

RESERVATION. Retaining part of the bread and wine of the Eucharist after a celebration of Mass to be used for the Communion of the sick.

RITUAL. Form of conducting worship.

ROCHET. A vestment like the surplice, but with close sleeves reaching to the hands.

ROGATION DAYS. The three days next before Ascension Day. They are days of fasting and special supplication.

ROOD. In ecclesiastical usage a cross or crucifix.

ROOD SCREEN. A screen at the entrance of the chancel on which the rood or crucifix is supported.

ROSARY. A series of prayers to be recited in order. The word is also used to designate the string of beads used in counting the prayers.

ROSH HA-SHANAH (J). Religious New Year's Day.

RUBRIC. A direction for the conduct of a service. These directions were formerly printed in red.

SACRAMENT. The word means *oath*. Today it is used in the Church to denote an outward and visible sign of an inward and spiritual grace. The Roman Catholic and Eastern Churches recognize seven—baptism, confirmation, Eucharist, penance, holy orders, marriage, and extreme unction. The Protestant churches for the most part accept baptism and Holy Communion, or the Eucharist.

SACRAMENTAL FANS (O). Represent the six-winged seraphim. With them the Holy Elements are fanned to keep off insects. They are made of silver.

SACRISTAN. An officer of the church in charge of the sacristy, utensils, etc.

SACRISTY. The room in a church where the vestments and sacred utensils are kept.

SADDUCEES (J). The conservative, aristocratic and priestly group of Jews in late Bible times. They denied the validity of real tradition and the doctrine of the resurrection.

SAINT. A holy or godly person. One of the spirits of the blessed departed to heaven. One who is canonized by the Church. The spirits of the dead cannot become angels, but may be saints.

SANCTUARY. That part of the chancel which contains the altar, commencing at the rail before which communicants kneel. The most sacred section of any religious building.

SANCTUS BELL. Rung at the elevation of the Host in the Mass. The elevation of the Host takes place immediately after the consecration.

SANHEDRIN (J). The governing body and supreme court of the Jews before A.D. 70.

SCAPULAR. Two small squares of cloth connected by cords and worn around the neck and under the clothing as an act of devotion.

SCRIBE (J). A doctor or teacher of the Law in the Jewish faith in Bible times.

SECULAR. Concerned with things not spiritual or religious.

SEDER (J). The service celebrated on the first or second nights of Passover. See PASSOVER HAGGADAH.

SEE. The official seat or throne of a bishop; the jurisdiction of a bishop.

SELAH. In the psalms probably a liturgical sign to denote a doxology.

SEPHARDIM (J). The descendants of the Jews of Spain and Portugal.

SEPTUAGINT. The Greek translation of the Old Testament made by the Jews in Alexandria in about the third century B.C.

SEXTON. An underofficer of the church who takes care of the building and its contents, waits on the clergy, rings the bell, attends to funerals, etc.

SHABAT or SABBATH. The seventh day of the week. The day of rest ordained of God in the Decalogue.

SHABUOT (J). The feast of Pentecost. It occurs fifty days after the Passover and is primarily the festival of the wheat harvest. It also commemorates the acceptance of the Ten Commandments.

SHAHARITH (J). Morning prayer.

SHAMMASH (J). Sexton in Jewish temples and synagogues.

SHEMA (J). A statement of the Jewish faith. It begins, "Hear, O Israel: the Lord our God, the Lord is one" (Deuteronomy 6:4-9).

SHEMINI AZERETH (J). The eighth day of Sukkoth.

SHEMONEH ESREH (J). A frequently used name for weekday public prayer. See 'AMIDAH.

SHIVA (J). The week of mourning for the dead.

SHOFAR (J). The ram's horn sounded at the morning prayer of Rosh ha-Shanah and at the conclusion of Yom Kippur.

SHOHET (J). A person trained for ritual slaughtering.

SIMHAT TORAH (J). The ninth, or final, day of Sukkoth. The annual reading of the Torah concludes and begins on this day and it is therefore the day of rejoicing in the Law.

SIN. Transgression of the law of God; a wrongdoing.

SOFER (J). In Bible days a scribe, today one who writes a Torah scroll.

THE SPEAR (O). The implement with which the particles are taken from the altar breads.

SPONSORS. Godfathers and godmothers. They become responsible for the child's religious training until the child is confirmed.

THE SPOON (O). All persons are communicated with the Holy Body and Blood by the sacred spoon.

STOLE. The narrow silk band, often richly embroidered, which the clergy wear around the neck and hanging down in front. The deacon wears his over his left shoulder and fastened on the right side.

In the Eastern Orthodox Church it is much wider and has a hole for the head to pass through.

SUFFRAGAN BISHOP. An assistant bishop who does not automatically succeed his superior upon the latter's death or retirement.

SUFFRAGE. An intercessory prayer or petition, such as the response in the Litany, "We beseech Thee to hear us, good Lord."

SUKKOTH (J). Feast of Tabernacles. It marks the autumn and late harvests (October).

SURPLICE. The outer vestment of white linen worn over the cassock by the clergy.

SURSUM CORDA. "Lift up your hearts"—a phrase from the Communion service.

SYNOD. A formal meeting to consult and decide upon church matters. It is composed of ministers and delegates from congregations of the same faith, and may be advisory or governing.

TALLIT (J). A prayer shawl.

TALMUD (J). The body of Jewish civil and canonical law. It consists of the Mishna (text) and Gemara (commentary).

TEMPORAL. Limited by time; therefore of this present world and not eternal.

TENEBRAE. Service on the last three days of Holy Week.

TEPHILLIM (J). Phylacteries.

THEISM. Belief in the existence of one god, who both transcends the universe and is at the same time present in it.

THEOCRACY. The government of a state by God.

THEOPHANY. A physical appearance of God or some material expression of His presence.

THURIBLE. The censer or vessel for incense.

THURIFER. The acolyte who carries the censer.

TIPPET. A black cape worn over the surplice, like an academic hood.

TISHA B'AB (J). The anniversary of the burning of the first and second Temples.

TITHE. The tenth part of one's income, or of what one makes over living expenses, to be paid to the Church.

TONSURE. Cutting the hair of one who is initiated into the clerical state. The custom is very old, and symbolizes renunciation of the world.

TRANSEPT. The transverse part of a cruciform church.

TRANSUBSTANTIATION. The changing of the substance of bread and wine into the body and blood of Christ.

TRINE. Threefold. Trine immersion means baptism thrice repeated as a sign of the Trinity.

TRINITY. The union of Father, Son and Holy Ghost in one Godhead.

TRINITY SUNDAY. The Sunday next after Whitsunday or Pentecost, observed as a feast in honor of the Holy Trinity.

TSEDAKAH (J). Acts of charity.

TSITSITH (J). The fringes on a prayer shawl.

UNITARIAN. One who denies the Trinity and believes in God in only one person.

VESPERS. Evening prayer or evensong.

VESTMENTS. Garments worn especially when performing divine service.

VESTRY. 1. The room connected with the church where the vestments, altar linen, etc., are kept.

2. In the Anglican or Episcopal Church, the body of laymen who look after parochial affairs.

VIATICUM. The Eucharist when administered to the dying.

VICAR. A deputy or substitute. In the Anglican or Episcopal Church, generally the rector of a chapel belonging to a parish church.

WAFER. A thin cake or piece of bread used in the Eucharist to represent the Body of Christ.

YESHIVAH (J). Jewish academies.

YOM KIPPUR (J). Day of Atonement.

ZONE or GIRDLE (O). Worn by the priest when serving at the altar above the cassock and stole.

Bibliography

ADENEY, WALTER F., *The Greek and Eastern Churches.* New York: Charles Scribner's Sons, 1928.

ANGUS, S., *The Mystery Religions and Christianity.* New York: Charles Scribner's Sons, 1925.

ANGUS, S., *The Religious Quest of the Graeco-Roman World.* New York: Charles Scribner's Sons, 1929.

BACH, MARCUS, *They Have Found a Faith.* New York: The Bobbs-Merrill Company, 1946.

BACON, BENJAMIN F., *Jesus and Paul.* New York: The Macmillan Company, 1921.

BOISSONADE, P., *Life and Work in Mediaeval Europe.* New York: Alfred A. Knopf, 1927.

COULTON, G. G., *Mediaeval Panorama.* London: Cambridge University Press, 1939.

DOBSCHÜTZ, ERNST VON, *Christian Life in the Primitive Church.* New York: G. P. Putnam's Sons, 1904.

HULME, EDWARD MASLIN, *The Renaissance, the Protestant Revolution and the Catholic Reformation of Continental Europe.* New York: The Century Company, 1914.

KLAUSNER, JOSEPH, *Jesus of Nazareth.* New York: The Macmillan Company, 1925.

PARRINGTON, VERNON LOUIS, *Main Currents in American Thought.* New York: Harcourt, Brace & Company, 1930.

PICKMAN, EDWARD MOTLEY, *The Mind of Latin Christendom.* London: Oxford University Press, 1937.

RAMSAY, W. M., *The Church in the Roman Empire.* New York: G. P. Putnam's Sons, 1893.

SMITH, PRESERVED, *The Age of the Reformation.* New York: Henry Holt and Company, 1920.

STEPHENSON, CARL, *Mediaeval History.* New York: Harper & Brothers, 1935.

STRAWLEY, J. H., *The Early History of the Liturgy.* London: Cambridge University Press, 1913.

TYLER, ALICE FELT, *Freedom's Ferment.* Minneapolis: The University of Minnesota Press, 1944.

Religious Bodies, 1936. U. S. Dept. of Commerce, Bureau of the Census.

A Yearbook of American Churches, 1947. Edited by Benson Y. Landis and George F. Ketcham. Lebanon, Pa.: The Sowers Printing Company.

Encyclopaedia of Religion. Edited by Vergilius Ferm. New York: The Philosophical Library, 1945.

Encyclopaedia Britannica, 1941.

Bibliographies of the Individual Denominations.

JUDAISM

FINKELSTEIN, LOUIS, *The Beliefs and Practices of Judaism.* New York: The Devin-Adair Company, 1941.

GRAYZEL, SOLOMON, *A History of the Jews.* Philadelphia: The Jewish Publication Society of America, 1947.

The Legacy of Israel. Oxford: The Clarendon Press, 1927.

MARGOLIES, MAX L., and ALEXANDER, MARX, *A History of the Jewish People.* Philadelphia: The Jewish Publication Society of America, 1927.

Popular Studies in Judaism. Published by the Union of American Hebrew Congregations.

STEINBERG, MILTON, *Basic Judaism.* New York: Harcourt, Brace & Company, 1947.

Union Prayer Book. Published in Cincinnati by the Central Conference of American Rabbis, 1944.

THE EASTERN ORTHODOX CHURCH
THE RUSSIAN ORTHODOX CHURCH

DEMETRY, REV. C. H., D.D., *The Christian Comparative and Apologetic Catechism* (1935).

The Divine Liturgy of the Holy Orthodox Catholic Apostolic Graeco-Russian Church. Translated by P. Kuvochinsky. London: Cope and Fenwick, 1909.

THE ANGLICAN (PROTESTANT EPISCOPAL) CHURCH IN THE UNITED STATES OF AMERICA

BERNARDIN, JOSEPH B., *An Introduction to the Episcopal Church.* New York: The Morehouse-Gorham Company, 1947.

The Book of Common Prayer. New York: Thomas Nelson Sons, 1944.

CRUM, ROLFE POMEROY, *A Dictionary of the Episcopal Church.* Baltimore, Md.: The Trefoil Publishing Company, 1942.

LOWRY, CHARLES W., "The Anglican Tradition, Part III," in the *Anglican Theological Review,* January, 1944.

PROCTOR, FRANCIS, *A History of the Book of Common Prayer.* New York: The Macmillan Company, 1881.

THE BAPTIST CHURCH

BENEDICT, DAVID, *A General History of the Baptist Denomination.* New York: L. Colby & Co., 1848.

HISCOX, EDWARD J., *The Standard Manual of the Baptist Churches.* American Baptist Publication Society, 1945.

NEWMAN, ALBERT H., *A History of the Baptists in the United States.* New York: Charles Scribner's Sons, 1915.

PENDLETON, J. M., *The Church Manual.* Philadelphia: Judson Press, 1945.

STRATON, HILLYER H., *Baptists—Their Message and Mission.* Philadelphia: Judson Press, 1941.

WALLACE, O. C. S., *What Baptists Believe.* Nashville, Tenn.: The Sunday School Board of the Southern Baptist Convention, 1934.

THE CHRISTIAN REFORMED CHURCH

BEETS, HENRY, *The Christian Reformed Church.* Grand Rapids, Mich., 1923.

THE CHURCH OF THE BRETHREN

KURTZ, D. W., "Ideals of the Church of the Brethren," from *The Gospel Messenger* for November 18, 1933.

THE CHURCH OF CHRIST, SCIENTIST

EDDY, MARY BAKER, *Manual of the Mother Church*. Boston, 1936.
——— *Science and Health, with Key to the Scriptures*. Boston, 1934.
Complete Concordance to Science and Health, with Key to the Scriptures. Boston, 1933.
A Few Questions and Answers about Christian Science. Boston, 1946.

THE CHURCH OF JESUS CHRIST OF LATTER-DAY SAINTS

The Book of Mormon. Salt Lake City, 1947.
MURDOCK, O. A., *The Succession of Joseph III*. Salt Lake City, 1913.

THE CONGREGATIONAL CHRISTIAN CHURCHES

The Book of Church Services. Boston: The Pilgrim Press.
Manual of the Congregational Christian Churches. Boston: The Pilgrim Press, 1947.
Year Book of the Congregational Christian Churches (1947).

THE DISCIPLES OF CHRIST

ENGLAND, STEPHEN J., *We Disciples*. St. Louis, Mo., 1946.
Year Book of the Disciples of Christ (1947).

THE EVANGELICAL AND REFORMED CHURCH

The Basis of Union of the Congregational Christian Churches and the Evangelical and Reformed Church (1947).
Mergers in the Evangelical and Reformed Church (1939).
STONESIFER, PAUL T., *Know Your Church*. Philadelphia: Department of United Promotion, Evangelical and Reformed Church.

THE EVANGELICAL UNITED BRETHREN

ALBRIGHT, R. W., *History of the Evangelical Church*. Harrisburg, Pa.: The Evangelical Press, 1942.

Discipline of the Evangelical United Brethren.
OWEN, JOHN WILSON, *A Short History of the United Brethren Church.* Dayton, Ohio: The Otterbein Press, 1944.
Year Book of the Evangelical United Brethren. 1947.

THE CHURCH OF THE NAZARENE

The Church of the Nazarene. Kansas City, Mo.: The Nazarene Publishing House. 1947.
Manual of the Church of the Nazarene. Kansas City, Mo.: The Nazarene Publishing House. 1944.

THE LUTHERAN CHURCHES

BAEPLER, WALTER C., *A Century of Grace.* St. Louis, Mo.: The Concordia Publishing House, 1947.
Common Service Book.
Luther's Small Catechism. Philadelphia: United Lutheran Publication House, 1932.
NOLDE, O. FRED, *Truth and Life.* Philadelphia: United Lutheran Publication House, 1937.
TRAVER, AMOS JOHN, *A Lutheran Handbook.* Philadelphia: United Lutheran Publication House, 1936.
WENTZ, ABDEL ROSS, *The Lutheran Church in American History.* Philadelphia: United Lutheran Publication House, 1933.

THE MENNONITE CHURCHES

BENDER, HAROLD S., *Mennonites and Their Heritage.* Akron, Ohio, 1942.
The Mennonite Quarterly Review. Goshen, Ind.
SMITH, C. HENRY, *The Story of the Mennonites.* Scottdale, Pa.: The Herald Press, 1941.
WENGER, JOHN C., *Glimpses of Mennonite History and Doctrine.* Scottdale, Pa.: The Herald Press, 1947.
YODER, JOSEPH W., *Rosanna of the Amish.* Scottdale, Pa.: The Herald Press, 1941.

THE METHODIST CHURCHES

The Book of Worship for Church and Home. New York: Methodist Publishing House, 1944-45.

Miller, Basil, *John Wesley.* Grand Rapids, Mich.: The Zondervan Publishing House, 1943.

The Journals of John Wesley. New York: The Methodist Book Concern.

Seleman, Charles C., *The Methodist Primer.* "Tidings," Medical Arts Building, Nashville, Tenn., 1945.

THE MORAVIAN CHURCH (UNITAS FRATRUM)

The Text Book of the Moravian Church (1948). Obtainable at the Headquarters of the Church, 67 West Church Street, Bethlehem, Pa.

The Moravian Church. A pamphlet published by the Inter-Provincial Board of Christian Education of the Moravian Church in America, and obtainable as above.

The Moravians and Their Faith. Bethlehem, Pa., 1946.

De Schweinitz, Edmund, *The History of the Unitas Fratrum.* Bethlehem, Pa., 1898.

The Moravian Manual. Bethlehem, Pa., 1901.

THE ASSEMBLIES OF GOD

The Origin and Development of the Assemblies of God (revised September, 1947). Obtainable from the Gospel Publishing House, 336 West Pacific Street, Springfield, Mo.

THE CHURCH OF GOD

Simmons, E. L., *The History of the Church of God.* Cleveland, Tenn., 1937.

Minutes of the 41st Annual Assembly. Cleveland, Tenn.

THE PRESBYTERIAN CHURCH

CARRUTHERS, S. W., *The Everyday Work of the Westminster Assembly*. Philadelphia: The Presbyterian Historical Society of America and the Presbyterian Historical Society of England, 1943.

HANZSCHE, WILLIAM THOMPSON, *Our Presbyterian Church*. Philadelphia: The Board of Christian Education of the Presbyterian Church in the United States of America, 1933.

MCAFEE, CLELAND, and ELIOT, PORTER, *Why a Presbyterian Church*. Philadelphia: The Board of Christian Education of the Presbyterian Church in the United States of America, 1930.

SMITH, EGBERT WATSON, *The Creed of the Presbyterians*. New York: The Baker & Taylor Co., 1902.

A Manual of Faith and Life. Philadelphia: The Board of Christian Education of the Presbyterian Church in the United States of America, 1947.

The Book of Common Worship. Philadelphia: The Board of Christian Education of the Presbyterian Church in the United States of America, 1947.

THE REFORMED CHURCH IN AMERICA (DUTCH REFORMED CHURCH)

CORWIN, E. T., *Manual of the Reformed Church in America*. New York: The Board of Publication and Bible-School Work of the Reformed Church in America, 1922.

DEMAREST, DAVID D., *History and Characteristics of the Reformed Church in America*. New York: The Board of Publication of the Reformed Protestant Dutch Church, 1858.

——— *Notes on the Constitution of the Reformed Church in America* (printed for the use of the students of the Theological Seminary, New Brunswick, N. J.). New Brunswick: Heidingfeld's Press, 1896.

The Reformed Church—What is It? The Church Press, Box 77, Grand Rapids, Mich.

What is the Reformed Church in America? Prepared by the Board of Education Publication, and obtainable from the Department of

Publication and Sales, 156 Fifth Avenue, New York City, or 652 Turner Avenue, Grand Rapids, Mich.

THE RELIGIOUS SOCIETY OF FRIENDS (THE QUAKERS)

COMFORT, WILLIAM WISTOR, *Just Among Friends: The Quaker Way of Life*. New York: The Macmillan Co., 1941.

JONES, RUFUS, *The Quakers in the American Colonies*. London: The Macmillan Co., 1911.

RUSSELL, ELBERT, *The History of Quakerism*. New York: The Macmillan Co., 1942.

THE REORGANIZED CHURCH OF LATTER DAY SAINTS

Official Statement of Belief. Issued by the Reorganized Church of Jesus Christ of Latter Day Saints, Independence, Mo.

SMITH, ELBERT A., *Differences That Persist*. Issued by the Reorganized Church of Jesus Christ of Latter Day Saints, Independence, Mo.

——— *Faith of Our Fathers Living Still*. Issued by the Reorganized Church of Jesus Christ of Latter Day Saints, Independence, Mo.

SMITH, ISRAEL A., and ELBERT A., *The Sacrament of Christian Marriage*. Issued by the Reorganized Church of Jesus Christ of Latter Day Saints, Independence, Mo.

The Book of Mormon. Published by the Church of Jesus Christ of Latter-day Saints, Salt Lake City, Utah, 1947.

THE SEVENTH-DAY ADVENTISTS

(The following publications are obtainable from the Review and Herald Publishing Association, Takoma Park, Washington, D.C.)

HAYNES, CARLYLE B., *The Seventh-day Adventists* (1940).

NICHOL, FRANCIS D., *The Midnight Cry* (1944).

——— *Why I am a Seventh-day Adventist* (1943).

SMITH, URIAH, *Daniel and the Revelation* (1944).

SPICER, W. A., *After One Hundred Years* (1944).

——— *The Spirit of Prophecy* (1937).

WHITE, ELLEN G., *The Desire of Ages.*
——— *Education.*
——— *The Great Controversy.*
——— *The Ministry of Healing.*
——— *Steps to Christ.*

THE AMERICAN UNITARIAN ASSOCIATION

BOOTH, JOHN NICHOLS, *Introducing Unitarianism.* Boston, Mass.: American Unitarian Association, 1947.
DAVIES, A. POWELL, *Unitarianism—What Is It?* (1946)